SELECTED

CHARLES LAMB was born in Lor
at Christ's Hospital, where he
with Coleridge. After school, h........u a post at the South
Sea House and was then promoted to the India House, where
he worked until his retirement in 1825. In 1796 his sister Mary
murdered their mother in a fit of insanity. Lamb was appointed
her guardian, and cared for her for the rest of his life. He is best
known for the essays he contributed to the *London Magazine*
between 1820 and 1823, under the name of 'Elia', although he
also wrote poetry, plays, literary criticism and works for
children. These include *Tales from Shakespeare* (1807), written in
collaboration with Mary, and *Specimens of English Dramatic
Poets* (1808). Lamb died in 1834.

J.E. MORPURGO had a distinguished career as a writer,
publisher, academic and critic. The author of histories,
biographies and travel books, he edited works by Leigh Hunt,
Keats, Trelawny, Cobbett and Fenimore Cooper. He died in
2001.

Fyfield*Books* aim to make available some of the great classics of British and European literature in clear, affordable formats, and to restore often neglected writers to their place in literary tradition.

Fyfield*Books* take their name from the Fyfield elm in Matthew Arnold's 'Scholar Gypsy' and 'Thyrsis'. The tree stood not far from the village where the series was originally devised in 1971.

> *Roam on! The light we sought is shining still.*
> *Dost thou ask proof? Our tree yet crowns the hill,*
> *Our Scholar travels yet the loved hill-side*

from 'Thyrsis'

CHARLES LAMB

Selected Writings

Edited with an introduction by
J.E. MORPURGO

FyfieldBooks

CARCANET

For C.N.K.M.

First published in Great Britain in 1993 by
Carcanet Press Limited
Alliance House
Cross Street
Manchester M2 7AQ

This impression 2003

In 1949 Penguin Books published *Charles Lamb and Elia*, selected, edited and with an introduction by J.E. Morpurgo. This Fyfield book is based on similar editorial principles, but the selection has been considerably changed and the introduction and notes are new.

Selection, introduction and editorial matter © the estate of J.E. Morpurgo 1993, 2003

A CIP catalogue record for this book is available from the British Library
ISBN 1 85754 721 7

The publisher acknowledges financial assistance from Arts Council England

Printed and bound in England by SRP Ltd, Exeter

Table of Contents

It is not often that it can be said of a writer that he is better known for himself than for his works. Through four centuries Shakespeare's genius has intrigued learned commentators but, such is the scarcity of irreproachable evidence about his life, and such the abundance of legend and speculation, that the writer whose fame has outstripped the fame of any other in all history is, as man, no more than an insubstantial shadow, without 'the pith and marrow of his attributes'. Of the many who have read *Paradise Lost* but a handful could tell more of Milton than that he was a Parliament man who went blind at the age of forty-two. The Greeks, most of whom cannot read his verse, still cherish the memory of Byron, but it is the earnest champion of liberty whose name is inscribed in their calendar of national saints, and the martyr of Missolonghi bears but scant resemblance to the creator of *Childe Harold* and *Mazeppa*. Dickens, next only to Shakespeare, through all succeeding generations has served as shrine for pilgrim-biographers, yet it is not Mr Charles Dickens but his wondrous galaxy of unforgettable characters – Pickwick, the Wellers, Miss Havisham, Scrooge, Sarah Gamp, Micawber, and a hundred more – which holds his name unforgotten in the memory of millions.

Two authors, Samuel Johnson and Charles Lamb, stand pre-eminent among their peers as much (and perhaps more) for what they were as for what they wrote.

Johnson had his attendant sycophant, ever ready to ensure 'reference to futurity' by recording the Doctor's mumblings and roarings, ever eager to thrust him forward as he made his ponderous way towards immortality over the mangled corpses of his victims.

Lamb, too, had his intimate chronicler, his name Elia, a mischievous memorialist much given to improving the appearance of fact by covering its face with the mask of fiction. Even more discommoding to any who would read through the gauze of the essays an autobiography of that author, when Lamb wrote from behind the cover of the pseudonym Elia even the puckish teller of half-truths was not always in charge. Often the course of his imagination was set by the tormented spirit who had dedicated his life to the care of the unstable sister who had murdered their mother.

The essays, the fruits of this unusual collaboration between jester and saint, cannot be viewed as truly preparatory sketches for an authentic self-portrait, but rather as cartoons for a canvas depicting the life of the artist as he imagined that it might have been lived had circumstances been other than they were, with, in the foreground, various portrayals of Charles Lamb as he would have liked to be known to his contemporaries and as he hoped that he would be remembered by succeeding generations.

But throughout his adult years there was always in attendance upon Lamb another and more austere biographer, C.L. the letter-writer, a monitor for the fancies and mendacities of Elia (an anagram for 'a lie'). Few authors have come even close to matching (and none to surpassing) Lamb for energy and skill as correspondent. When writing to his friends Lamb knew no cause for reticence, no reason even for genial dissembling. His passions, his sorrows, his likes and his dislikes: all he recorded without reservation in his letters; and with them his unabashed comments on books, plays, pictures and men, and his observations on the minutiae of his day-to-day existence.

(His friends knew his letters to be much more than casual social communications; many preserved them for posterity. Lamb himself was more cavalier with what came to him in return; only two of the letters he had received survived for long enough to be read by Talfourd, his biographer. And so it is that there was lost forever half of what must otherwise have been one of the most fascinating exchanges in all literary history: the forty-year-long correspondence between Coleridge and Lamb.)

Read *in tandem*, the essays interlaced with the letters, together these two elements in Lamb's autobiographical writing produce a self-portrait entire and truthful, the letters often evidently the sparks which set fire to Elia's imagination, the essays as fanciful elaboration, a stream of whimsy superimposed on the actuality of Lamb's life as recorded in the letters.

But there is more: a rich anthology of footnotes from authoritative and eloquent contemporaries which transforms Lamb's 'autobiography' into one of the most comprehensive of all biographies. He was the social – and from time to time also the intellectual – focus of a circle of genius. Almost every member of that glittering company – Coleridge, Wordsworth, Hazlitt, De Quincey, Leigh Hunt,

Crabb Robinson, Thomas Barnes, Landor, Southey, Hood, and many more – made permanent in print his affection for Lamb and his admiration for Elia, some of them several times and at considerable length.

Even the very few who disliked Lamb and despised Elia were not content to demonstrate their distaste by ignoring the man and his works but instead screeched their virulence as if determined that their dissonant voices be heard above the chorus of praise. (Carlyle, in that small hostile band the most venomous and the most vociferous, was still ranting many decades after Lamb's death.)

A reader of the *Life of Johnson*, and even more often a reader of *Rasselas*, may be tempted to question that Johnson deserved the devotion of Boswell. So close to unanimity is the affection for Charles Lamb and admiration for his works evident in the writings of his contemporaries and such the quality and diversity of those who expressed those sentiments that it is not possible to doubt that he was, for himself and for his writings, worthy of their tribute. One cannot dismiss as hyperbole, for example, Coleridge's comment, 'His genius is talent, and his talent is genius, and his heart is as whole and one as his head'; of Landor, 'He leaves behind him . . . the love of friends without a single foe'; of Southey, 'Dear . . . for rarest genius and for sterling worth'; and of Wordsworth, 'O, he was good if e'er a good man lived'.

It is, however, the lavishness and unanimity of adulation visited upon him in his lifetime and for more than a century thereafter – and above all the simple yet magniloquent phrase 'the gentle Elia' – which in the last decades have tended to diminish Lamb's reputation with a generation which mistrusts paragons, mistakes gentleness for meekness or sentimentality, is convinced that goodness is not an attribute appropriate to an artist, and which is ever eager to discuss a saint's feet of clay.

In truth Lamb was neither meek nor sentimental and his goodness was flawed, though the flaws were for the most part of a kind that made him all the more lovable.

Lamb was unique and yet – it is a paradox that he would have relished – he was also in many respects a patently ordinary, middleclass Englishman, born away from the handicap of poverty and never achieving the disgrace of riches.

As unadventurous in all things practical as he was bold in

imagining, he worked for thirty-three years at a mundane job, as a clerk in the East India House. He lived all his life in London or its suburbs, he was scarcely touched by the beauty of rural England which delighted and inspired his friends, Coleridge and Wordsworth, and he was restless when separated from city bustle – 'I could not *live* in Skiddaw . . . I must have a prospect of seeing Fleet Street.' He ventured only once to the Continent, to Paris in 1822, and so meagre was the impact upon him of this unique experience that he, customarily so quick to seize upon even the most trivial event in his life as cue for creative elaboration, never so much as mentioned his visit to Paris in any work intended for publication, though in a letter to the poet John Clare he gave to those few days abroad their full significance: 'I have been in France, and I have eaten frogs.'

His competence in foreign languages was no greater than that of most of his countrymen, his French accent so execrable that once during those few days in Paris he ordered an *eau-de-vie* the waiter brought him an egg – a misunderstanding that would not have dismayed Charles Lamb. With his sister Mary and their adopted daughter, Emma Isola, he attempted to read Dante's *Divina Commedia* in the original but soon fell back on the translation by his 'amiable acquaintance', Henry Cary. (Mary progressed beyond his capacity; she moved on to Tasso, and later gave Italian lessons to Emma.) As was well-nigh inevitable for any man reared under the rod of James Boyer, Upper Grammar Master of Christ's Hospital, he was a proficient Latinist and from his schooldays on he gathered to himself a profound knowledge of the Roman classics. He was familiar with the great works of Greece, but in English translation. He had read, and stored in memory for subsequent and apt use in conversation or in writing, almost everything in English worth reading and much that not even he thought worthy of the effort, yet, though Goethe, Schiller and Heine were his contemporaries, he scarcely noticed that they existed, and once – perhaps as a perverse response to Leigh Hunt's vaunted cosmopolitanism – he shrugged off as to him inconsequential virtually the whole of French Literature from Rabelais to Voltaire. (He did, however, borrow from France the theme for *Prince Dorus*, his fairy-tale in rhyme.)

Like many another Englishman with similar backgrounds, Lamb could not cleanse his mind of the suspicion that all foreigners were unreliable, nor rid himself of the conviction that little worthy of notice had come out of the Continent since the Fall of Rome. (In his case with the exception of *Don Quixote* and Italian painting.) But, as foreigners generally ignored him and never caused him hurt, he seldom gave voice to his xenophobia.

Lamb's opinion of the Scots was of a different order, heartfelt and varied. For the most part he expressed his disdain for a people not quite foreign yet patently not English in half-jocular gibes of a kind that have been hurled at their northern neighbours by Englishmen – among them Johnson and even Shakespeare – since the days before the two kingdoms were united, but not infrequently the hurt done to him by Scotsmen could not be salved by *bleating* (the Elian pun is Christopher North's) extravagant, and therefore not to be believed, libels against Scotland. The truth, the whole truth, would out. 'I have been trying all my life to like Scotsmen and am obliged to desist from the experiment in despair.'

He had good reason for this antipathy. Of that small but vocal and notably malignant band which despised his work, most were Edinburgh-based. The *Edinburgh Review* and *Blackwood's* excoriated not only Lamb himself but also, and with even greater ferocity, many of those whom he treasured as friends and as writers admired above all others. (At the last, it is true, persuaded so to do by Christopher North, a reluctant convert to Elia, *Blackwood's* allowed him to add his consequential ammunition to its heavy armament.) Only one of his contemporaries north of the border, Walter Scott, joined the chorus of protest for Lamb and for Elia, and he only in a whisper.

And there was Thomas Carlyle. Lamb's dislike of Scotsmen cannot be set to the score of Scotland's plenipotentiary in Cheyne Row. They met only once, in 1831, when Carlyle was within weeks of his thirty-sixth birthday and Lamb by twenty years his senior. There was evident on that occasion antipathy between the two men but Carlyle's lengthy and vindictive description of the meeting, together with his sour comments on Lamb's person, his character and his works, he entered into his diary, which was not made public for many years. Mercifully Lamb had been for thirty years in his grave before Carlyle returned to his self-appointed task of savaging the reputation, personal and professional, of Charles Lamb; this time at even greater length, with even more venom – and in print.

But Carlyle's was the loudest and most influential voice dissonant to that chorus of admiration and adulation raised in honour of Lamb, and so it is that he, the arch-priest of the tiny congregation of Lamb-haters, forces his way into any assessment of Charles Lamb and Elia.

It is not surprising that Carlyle did not enjoy Lamb's company; he despised the company that Lamb kept. No more is it cause for wonder that he could not appreciate Lamb's humour – 'It was only a thin streak of Cockney wit' – for the humourless are deaf and blind to the humour of other men. That he would fail to comprehend Elia (and also Charles Lamb) was inevitable for while he was the Apostle of Truth, Elia (and also Lamb) made prevarication into an art. It is surprising that the laureate of heroes found nothing heroic in Lamb's cheerful acceptance of a life of self-sacrifice, and it is surprising – indeed, even after more than a century, it is shocking – that on the strength of one encounter, Carlyle, a man convinced of his own probity and determined upon revealing the voices of past events, should have seized upon every hesitant slander about Lamb and given to it the quality of incontrovertibility – even in a diary which, at all events, as honour due to his worth, he hoped would not remain for all time private:

> Charles Lamb, I sincerely believe to be in some considerable degree insane. A more pitiful, rickety, gasping, staggering, stammering Tomfool I do not know.... Besides, he is now a confirmed, shameless drunkard; *asks* for gin and water in strangers' houses, tipples till he is utterly mad, and is only not thrown out of doors because he is too much despised for taking such trouble with him.

Even more disreputable is the manner in which Carlyle persisted with such calumnies long after Talfourd had published his two Lamb biographies and long after many another writer who had known Lamb for more than one evening had made public impressions of Lamb which denied the validity of almost everything Carlyle had to say about him. In his *Remembrances* (which he knew would come to print), Carlyle wrote:

> Insuperable proclivity to *gin* in poor old Lamb. His talk contemptibly small indicating wondrous ignorance and shallowness,

even when it was serious and good-mannered, which it seldom was; usually *ill*-mannered (to a degree) screwed into frosty artificialities, ghastly make-believe of wit: – in fact more like 'diluted insanity' (as I define it) than anything of real jocosity, 'humour', or geniality.

Had Lamb read every word of Carlyle's diatribe it is probable that he would have dismissed most of them, as when Carlyle found Lamb guilty of uncouth behaviour what he was really expressing was resentment for damage to his own dignity. There is on the accounts of the November 1831 meeting nothing to support this conjecture but evidence abounds of Lamb's habit of puncturing pomposity wheresoever he found it. (His treatment of the unfortunate Comptroller of Stamps at Benjamin Hayden's party was neither gentle nor genteel and has become legend.)

Had he been aware of them it is unlikely that Lamb would have been greatly disturbed by most of Carlyle's calumnies which, in all probability, he would have dismissed as no more than the excretions of acid to be expected from a sour-spirited Calvinist.

He had never attempted to hide – indeed he boasted – the fact that alcohol was one of his principal pleasures. He tested the friendship of his visitors by the measure of their eagerness to 'taste the tap of mine Host at the Horseshoe, or the Rising Sun, or Rose and Crown'. No doubt Lamb – as all of the many friends who had known him for so much longer and far more intimately than Carlyle – would have preferred to the Scotsman's scurrilous description of a gibbering drunkard the account of Lamb as drinking-man by one of their number, De Quincey:

> In regard to wine, Lamb and myself had the same habit – perhaps it rose to the dignity of a principle – viz., to take a great deal *during* dinner, none *after* it. Consequently, as Miss Lamb (who drank only water) retires almost with the dinner itself, nothing remained for men of our principles, the rigours of which we had illustrated by taking rather too much of old port before the cloth was drawn, but talking.

But neither Lamb himself nor yet any of his convivial friends could have expected that a puritan from Ecclefechan would understand that Elia's 'Confessions of a Drunkard' (see pp.79-88) must be taken with a liberal dash of scepticism.

As Lamb himself testified more than once, the potentates of the East India Company were not tender with clerks whose behaviour did not measure to the austere standards of propriety and dialogue demanded of them. Had Lamb been the habitual drunkard described by Elia (and by Carlyle) it is unthinkable that he would have been allowed to remain for thirty-three years in the Company's service or that at the last he would have been retired honourably, with a generous pension of £450 a year.

Lamb had other weaknesses, none of them heinous – unless it be heinous in a man generally so immaculate in his tastes to regard tripe and cow-heels as 'rare dainties' – and most of them, the trifling eccentricities permissible even to a man in other respects sturdily conventional, of a kind which makes him even more likeable to those who (as Lamb himself) prefer a man 'who is as he ought not to be'.

He was addicted to whist and he was addicted to tobacco. Like most heavy smokers he was forever on the brink of giving up the habit. 'This very night I am going to leave off Tobacco! Surely there must be some other world in which this unconquerable purpose shall be realised.' He never could, never did, and finally recanted even the wish to reform: 'May my last breath be drawn through a pipe and exhaled in a pun.' Such minor follies did not disturb Lamb's conscience and passed uncondemned by any of his contemporaries, even by Carlyle.

But no malicious goading was needed to make Lamb aware of the demons who threatened his mental stability. Through all his adult years he feared madness, for himself and, with even greater intensity, for his sister. To him insanity was more than a disease; it was an all-pervading symbol of calamity. Once, in early manhood, Lamb suffered dementia. In the first of his letters to Coleridge he wrote of that experience in his characteristically cheerful, self-mocking fashion:

> The six weeks that finished last year and began this, your very humble servant spent very agreeably in a madhouse at Hoxton. I am got somewhat rational, and don't bite anyone. But mad I was; and many a vagary my imagination played with me, enough to make a volume.

A few months later the hideous death of his mother at the hands of his sister made doubly terrifying the menace of mental collapse.

For ever after not only was he burdened by fear – sadly, only too often justified by events – that the sister he loved so dearly might at any time suffer a relapse, but also he was never free of the horrifying thought that if he suffered a recurrence of mental breakdown, Mary would be left without provider and cherisher – a disaster which, happily, never occurred. Immediately he was 'wedded to the future of my sister and my poor old father' and only once in the thirty-eight years that were left to him did his inclination to matrimony so far outstrip his determination to stay at Mary's side as to allow him to seek a wife.

The fear of madness became itself an obsession and the name of insanity in its many synonyms forced its way again and again into his writings. The narrative of his novel *Rosamund Gray*, which he began to write very soon after his mother's death and which he published in 1798, is interrupted by soliloquy:

> False things are told concerning thee fair planet, for I will ne'er believe that thou canst take a perverse pleasure in distorting the brains of us book-mortals. Lunatics! Moonstruck! Calumy invented, and folly took up these names.

Seeking to describe the condition of *Don Quixote* after Sancho Panza had lost faith with his master he found a phrase, 'a treatable lunatic', which tells as much about his view of his own state as it does about Cervantes' Knight. 'Madness', 'lunacy', 'imbecility', 'insanity': words such as these punctuate the overt cheerfulness of his later writing even after the first cry of pain, *Rosamund Gray*; these are the words which beat discord through the sweet symphony of Charles Lamb's mind.

Sadness, even gloom, were never far away. It is not only the plot that makes *Rosamund Gray* read like a novel by Thomas Hardy. The desperate repetition, 'All, all are gone, the old familiar faces', in the best-known of all his poems (see p.93), cuts with tragic knife the cord of his restraint, but when the original opening stanza is omitted (a practice initiated by Lamb himself and continued ever since) though the general quality of the poem is thereby enhanced, it loses its potency as explanation of the source of all Lamb's miseries:

> Where are they gone, the old familiar faces?
> I had a mother, but she has died, and left me,

Died prematurely, in a day of horrors –
All, all are gone, the old familiar faces.

Whether writing for publication or in letters intended only for the eyes of his friends, he wrote quietly and, much more often than not, in a manner which seems to deny the existence of the grim shadow which darkened his life, but this light-heartedness, like his enthusiasm for all good things – books, pictures, food, drink and, above all else, friendship – is symptomatic of his quest for momentary liberation from the shackles of misfortune. It is as if he was bent on shaming his misery, as if he was determined to force himself to be all-interested to spite the monotony of tragic routine. 'I had been,' he wrote once to Coleridge, 'in a sad quandary of spirits but a Pipe and some generous Port and *King Lear* had their effects as solaces.'

No wonder then that John Webster 'found his first recognition at the pious and fortunate hands of Charles Lamb', for few critics have had reason as profound as his for empathy with Webster's awareness of the menace of tragedy. None has paralleled that affinity with Webster which allowed Lamb to illuminate his ability 'to touch a soul to the quick, to play upon fear as much as it can bear, to wean and weary a life till it is ready to drop, and then step in with mortal instruments to take the last forfeit'.

Hovering 'as one between earth and heaven, neither hoping much nor fearing anything', Lamb had no use for the facile consolations offered by the Church. He was not anti-Christian, but he abominated bigotry and, needing something more immediate than a promissory-note on Heaven to hold his mind against bitterness, he found his surety in humour.

Humour is the best of all specifics for tears but in the writings of some of the finest humorists – as in the memorable comic characters of literature and as in the performance of great comic actors – the tears are there behind the laughter, not obvious and yet obviously imminent. It is so with Charles Lamb. He dressed himself in his jester's motley, presented himself as Edax, Pensilis, Lepus, Crito or Burton Junior, and played the part of Fool, as much to persuade himself as to convince his audience that there was in his existence nothing for melancholy. Once he purloined the costume, but not the personality, of his friend Coleridge, but even when he put on the trappings which were for all time to be identified with his name and fame, though in his imagination he could live contentedly as Elia, he could never shake off entirely the sad realities of life as Charles Lamb. Yet, in all probability, it was the vigour and vividness of that life in the imagination which saved him from the fate he feared, final and irremedial mental break-down, for in that life he found compensation for many of the solaces he longed for so fervently but which were denied to him by the restrictions he had imposed on himself. More than all else it was by imagining that he consoled himself for his lack of wife and children.

At ease with men, he was happy in the company of the children of friends but, perversely, he was never quite so contented as when surrounded by his own dream-children:

> We are not of Alice, nor of thee, nor are we children at all.... We are nothing, and less than nothing, and dreams. We are only what might have been, and must wait upon the tedious shores of Lethe millions of ages before we have existence, and a name.' (see p.122)

He liked women and women liked him but closeness to any one woman threatened a breach of the discipline he had designed for himself, and other than his sister Mary, few women held his affection: his adopted daughter, Emma Isola, Dorothy Wordsworth, and the one woman who came close to breaking his resolve to remain all his life a bachelor, the actress Fanny Kelly, to whom he proposed, unsuccessfully, at the age of forty – 'What a lass to go a-gypsing through the world with!'.

But as there were dream-children, so also were there dream-women: Hester Savary, a Quaker girl he had never met though he had seen her often walking past his home, to whom nevertheless he gave immortality in one of his finest poems (see p.120), the lament 'When maidens such as Hester die'; Anna of the sonnets, Alice W— and Ann Simmons of the essays; these were his dream-loves more real to him than reality. And they loved him, Pygmalion and Galatea moved forward together, contentedly, towards old age.

Bitterness, anger, hate, resentment: all self-destructive passions were foreign to Lamb's character. Even as a critic his purpose was to enhance and not to diminish reputations; those writers as he considered to be without merit he ignored, he never exploited his authority nor did he ever flaunt his cleverness (as have so many critics) to shatter the work of incompetents. In private life he was subject to occasional bouts of ill-temper and he was blisteringly rude to bores, but in public he answered those who attacked him not in kind but with delicious mockery. Had he been watching over his shoulder as Carlyle entered into his diary his monstrous description, because it rubbed acid into an ever-open wound, no doubt Lamb would have defended himself with nothing more virulent than a gibe against all 'Scotchmen'.

For Lamb the one unpardonable offence, the only sin which demanded immediate and vigorous retribution, was a breach of loyalty. Himself unswervingly loyal, to people, places and institutions, he could not comprehend, condone or readily forgive disloyalty and so it came about that he, who brushed off with a quip the abuse of strangers, exploded the full fury of his wrath – in manner utterly out-of-kilter with the picture of him as the 'gentle Elia' – only over the heads of those, his friends, who, even momentarily, betrayed him: over the heads of Southey and that 'great and dear spirit', Coleridge, 'the proof and touch-stone of all my cogitations', the man of whom he said, with convenient forgetfulness, in what were to prove almost the last lines he wrote: 'He was my fifty years old friend without a dissension. Never saw I his likeness, nor probably the world can see again.'

'A Christ's Hospital boy's friends at school are his friends for life.' Lamb and Coleridge had both put on bluecoat and yellow stockings for the first time in 1782. On their way up the School Coleridge outstripped Lamb, as he outstripped all others even in a school-generation remarkable for its eventual achievements, and he stayed on, to prepare for Cambridge, for two years after Lamb had left.

Cambridge could not hold Coleridge; he came down without a degree and, after a brief and for him amazing interregnum as a dragoon, took rooms at the Salutation Tavern in Newgate Street immediately opposite Christ's Hospital. The Salutation became the favourite meeting-place of a group of young men, some former schoolfellows at Christ's Hospital, some friends newly acquired by Coleridge, and almost all of them in one way or another aspirants to Literature. At the Salutation, evening after evening they drank egg-nog, smoked Oronoco, and talked about books, plays and ideas, but mostly, as was general when he was present, they listened to Coleridge.

It was in those months, when he – sometimes with Lamb as junior collaborator – was also contributing verses and occasional paragraphs to the *Morning Chronicle*, that, under his persuasive tutelage, this group of friends began to plan to put into practice the idealised but impractical plan of emigrating to America and there establishing themselves as a Pantisocratic community. Lamb's enthusiasm for Pantisocracy was cool; the thought of passing all his days in such congenial company pleased him, but not even Coleridge ardently supported by Robert Southey could convince him that if there was any prospect of 'peace on earth and Heaven to come' it was not more likely to be achieved on the banks of the Thames than on the banks of the Susquehanna. Even so Lamb – who then and ever after was one of the very few who could entice Coleridge out of monologue and into duologue – revelled in those evenings at the Salutation, and soon, in retrospect, for him they came to represent an idyll no longer attainable.

Nevertheless in the tortured months which followed upon that tragic day in September 1796 when Mary killed her mother, the friendship between Lamb and Coleridge deepened, largely by reason of Coleridge's selflessness. In a manner foreign to his nature he dedicated himself to the care of his stricken friend. He bullied, he cajoled, he encouraged Lamb to write his misery out of his system. It could not last, and it was dangerous for this was no longer a relationship between equals; Lamb had become Coleridge's dependent, and Coleridge could not sustain the responsibility.

There was the time when, as never again in all his life, Coleridge's mind was brimming over with poetry. Almost every one of his finest poems – 'The Ancient Mariner', 'Christabel', 'Frost at Midnight', 'Kubla Khan', 'This Lime-tree Bower my Prison' – was composed between 1796 and 1798, though some were not published until twenty years later. It was the time when, with Wordsworth, he was preparing for the publication of *Lyrical Ballads*. Lamb was too sensitive to poetry to fail to see that, as poet, Coleridge was close to fulfilment. He was married. He had a son. He had all that Lamb now believed he could never attain. And Coleridge had moved out of London, did not write for months on end, and when he did his letters were not of a kind that Lamb wished to read.

In June 1797, Lamb visited Coleridge at Nether Stowey and there, for the first time, he met Wordsworth. The two men took to each other, and their friendship was to grow with the years, but Lamb knew almost at once that Wordsworth was a poet better fitted to be Coleridge's peer than he could ever be, and as hour after hour he watched the two of them so obviously in personal and intellectual concord, his spirit shrivelled and he was overtaken by fear (as it turned out not well-founded) that Wordsworth would shatter the relationship which was his mainstay.

Lamb was still only twenty-one years old (Coleridge three years older). As yet he had not learnt the merit of imagination as barricade against despair, indeed as yet he had not found any of the keys cut to unlock his genius; but it is inconceivable, had he not been floundering in depression, he would have acted as he did in the months that followed upon his visit to Nether Stowey.

Immediately he was to a degree reassured by the warmth of the tribute paid to him both by the dedication and in the text of 'This Lime-tree Bower my Prison'.* But in times less fraught he would not have been greatly disturbed by the hint that Coleridge had it in mind to omit from the revised edition of a collection of his poems four sonnets by Lamb originally contributed to the earlier editions at his invitation. When the new edition appeared without the verses by Charles Lloyd, but recently Coleridge's pupil and now accounted by Lamb as more his friend than Coleridge's, before condemning it as trespass on the sanctity of friendship he might have held himself in patience for long enough to discover that it was Lloyd's arrogant refusal to be any longer associated with Coleridge's poetry that had led to the excision of his poems. Undoubtedly, had Lamb

---

* The poem was written whilst Lamb was staying at Nether Stowey and immediately was sent to two other friends, Southey and Lloyd. That Lamb had read it as soon as it was finished is clear from a letter to Coleridge written by Lamb in 1800 when the poem was printed, for the first time, in the *Annual Anthology*.

By that time the breach between Lamb and Coleridge had been healed, and Lamb had so far recovered his confidence as to rebuke his friend not only for ascribing to him the attribute of gentleness, 'which almost always means poor-spirited', but also for the quality of his poetry:

For God's sake (I never was more serious), don't make me ridiculous any more by terming me gentle-hearted in print, *or do it in better verses*. It did well enough five [three] years ago when I came to see you, and was moral coxcomb enough to feed upon such epithets; but . . . I hope my *virtues* have done *sucking*.

not mislaid his sense of humour in the gloom all around him, he would not have taken offence at the 'Higginbottom Sonnets' for these 'Sonnets Attempted in the Manner of Contemporary Writers' were frivolities of a kind which, in happier times, Lamb would have enjoyed and which he would have fashioned more craftily than Coleridge. And Coleridge had parodied himself as well as Lamb and others of the new Romantics.

But then, in private conversation, Coleridge let slip a remark which was, of course, immediately reported to Lamb. 'Poor Lamb, if he wants any knowledge, he may apply to me.' Lamb had known Coleridge for sixteen years, for much of that time intimately. He had seen him often when Coleridge was in his last years at Christ's Hospital and he must have known that this comment was not untypical of the superior air adopted by those who had achieved at Christ's Hospital the lordly status of Grecian when speaking of superannuated Deputy Grecian, but the insult exploded every raw nerve in Lamb's body and he gave back much more than he had received (See pp.138-40). Coleridge left for Germany and for two years the two did not meet or communicate. Then they were reconciled and soon they were once again the best of friends, but the burst of fury had removed from Lamb all sense of inferiority and ever after Coleridge was his 'archangel a little damaged'.

Lamb found no pleasure in his private quarrel with Coleridge but when, later, he let fly his poison arrows at public targets, his satisfaction was close to being smug, and when, two decades after the breach with Coleridge had been closed, Southey gave him cause for attack, Lamb showed no compunction. Southey had deprived himself of the privacy due to a one-time friend by allying himself to the blackest of Lamb's *bêtes noires*, the Prince of Wales, George Canning, William Gifford and his colleagues on the *Quarterly Review*.

Conservative in his love of familiar things so that 'the disappearance of the old clock from St Dunstan's Church drew tears from his eyes', Lamb was nevertheless an ardent Reformer. He shared Coleridge's mistrust of Pitt, but not its wordiness. He seldom referred to the most sensational phenomenon of the age, the Emperor Napoleon – 'I heard that he is small, even less than me, who am less than the least of the Apostles', or again, 'I should not mind standing barehead at his table to do him service in his fall. They should give him Hampton Court or Kensington' – but when he did enter into political controversy he was as sharp and as effective as any of his contemporaries.

It was Leigh Hunt who went to gaol for his uninhibited attack on the Prince Regent published by him in his paper the *Examiner* – 'a corpulent man of fifty...a violator of his vows, a libertine...' – but Lamb must have helped him on his way to prison with his no less scabrous assault, 'The Triumph of the Whale' which Hunt had printed in the previous edition of the *Examiner*.

Canning, a wit and a man of taste, was, as Leigh Hunt admitted, 'not a man to be treated with contempt'. Both Leigh Hunt and Lamb blamed his failure to take the side appropriate to his many attributes and talents, the side of Radicalism, upon his upbringing and the early 'direction of his conscience'. Lamb thought him thrice guilty: he had used his money and his influence to establish *The Anti-Jacobin* and in *The Anti-Jacobin* he had used his wit and his talents to damn both Lamb's political and his literary allegiances.

William Gifford was also smeared by association with *The Anti-Jacobin*; he had worked for Canning's paper before he took on the editorship of the *Quarterly*, but, by Lamb's reckoning, he was beneath contempt, a man without so much as a whisper of literary genius, who by his servile dedication to the Tory principles of his superiors, made John Murray's journal the plague of Lamb, his friends and many he admired through much of Lamb's literary career.

It was for such as these, Lamb's arch-villains, that, as Lamb had it, Southey abandoned his 'principle' and deserted his friends. He became a Tory, he wrote regularly for the *Quarterly*, and he accepted the tainted office of Poet Laureate. Southey's backsliding was, by Lamb's judgement, flagrant and shameful. None the less for many years the two men maintained at least a show and, it would seem, the reality of amiability.

In 1818, when Ollier published for Lamb a book with the deliberately magniloquent title, *The Works of Charles Lamb*, Lamb wrote begging Southey to notice its publication in the *Quarterly*, Southey gave back damning silence, and Lamb did not protest.

The collected *Essays of Elia* appeared early in 1823 and this time, without a nudge from its author, Southey mentioned the book, nor directly but gratuitously, in a *Quarterly* article significantly entitled

'The Progress of Infidelity' prompted by an obscure book on Deism by an obscure French writer. He was patronising about the charms of *Elia* but damned its author for being irreligious. Lamb was hurt and furious, but still determined to avoid a break with Southey. He wrote to Bernard Barton, a devout Quaker: 'Southey has attacked Elia on the score of infidelity... He might have spared an old friend such a construction of a few careless flights that meant no harm to religion.... But I love and respect Southey – and will not retort.' And then, with upper-case emphasis, 'I HATE HIS REVIEW, and his being a Reviewer.'

Despite his good intention not to reply to Southey's attack the slur rankled; he insisted that his refusal to identity himself with any organised Church did not mean that he was some sort of anti-Christ. No doubt he was also concerned with the more mundane consequence of Southey's article. As he wrote to Barton: 'The hint he has dropped will knock the sale of the book on its head.' But all possibility of practising saintly forebearance vanished as he dwelt upon the damnable fact that this libel had not only been written by a friend, but had been published in the hated *Quarterly*, the paper which had once labelled him 'a maniac' and which had asserted that the 'Confessions of a Drunkard' were verifiable and without qualification. Southey had made public – and in the *Quarterly* – sentiments private to Lamb; Lamb had his own platform from which to make public his resentment and hurt.

In October 1823 *The London Magazine* printed the 'Letter of Elia to Robert Southey, Esquire' (see pp.140-52). To his credit, immediately upon reading this severe and public reproof, Southey wrote to Lamb a placatory letter. Lamb replied, shifting all the blame for his outburst on to his own exaggerated sensitivity and on to the *Quarterly*. He invited Southey and his wife to visit him at Colebrook Cottage ('I shall be ashamed to see you... I will muster up courage...').

Southey promised not to reply in kind to Elia's *London Magazine* 'letter', and kept his promise. The most public quarrel of Lamb's life was ended and in 1830, when Lamb's *Album Verses* was received contemptuously by the *Literary Gazette* Southey wrote a poem in honour of its author and sent it, not to the *Quarterly* which, for all that Gifford was dead and the *Quarterly* had modified somewhat its Toryism, might not have welcomed even from the Poet Laureate such praise of Lamb, but to a paper which he knew would print it, to *The Times* edited by Thomas Barnes, one of Lamb's closest friends and most fervent admirers.

But Lamb was never one to waste good material. In 1833 when he published *The Last Essays of Elia* he included in the volume the 'Letter to Southey', subtly but not dramatically revised, renamed 'The Tombs in the Abbey', but still carrying the superscription 'In a Letter to R— S—, Esq'.

Though conducted in full view of the reading-public, the dispute with Southey did not bruise his conscience as had the quarrel with Coleridge twenty-six years earlier and, unlike that previous episode, it made no impact whatsoever on his career as writer. His friendship for Southey had never been as intense as his friendship for Coleridge. He had no reason to go in awe of Southey's learning and intellect as he and almost everyone else who ever came into contact with Coleridge was awed by that 'mighty mind'. Already well before 1823 public acclaim and the affection of friends had built for him confidence in himself, both as man and as writer.

The origins of that sureness can be traced back to the break with Coleridge. In a sense made substantial by his letters and by the record of his publications, the years of frosty silence between him and Coleridge were the turning-point in his life, more obviously seminal to all that he did thereafter even than the death of his mother. In those years he was forced into independence from Coleridge; indeed, as time went by and Coleridge's noble spirit and creative genius began to deteriorate, it was Lamb who anchored that friendship. And in those years he discovered himself as writer. There is irony in the fact that it was Coleridge himself who set Lamb on his way to independence and fulfilment, Coleridge who urged him to break the vows, made when Mary murdered their mother, never to write again. Lamb accepted the advice but he did not immediately discover his proper *métier*.

At the time Coleridge (and it must appear Lamb himself) considered that Lamb's destiny was a poet's, that he would remain for ever 'Steadfast and rooted in the heavenly Muse, / And wash'd and sanctified to Poesy.' Lamb never abandoned versifying. He was adept in producing vigorous and appropriately ill-tempered treasonable rhymes, but of all his poems only 'Hester' and 'The Old Familiar Faces' are worthy companions in the anthologies for the poems of his great poet-friends, Coleridge and Wordsworth. His poetic technique is facile, his versifying mannered, imitative and more often appropriate to the destination for which so much of it was written, the albums of friends and the children of friends, than to play a part in a seismic poetic-revolution.

As writer of prose Lamb was an original, without predecessor or successor, and inimitable. His style, liberated from the formalism of the eighteenth century and untouched by the good-mannered orotundity which some of his contemporaries carried forward into the Age of Victoria, was an unintended but manifest self-portrait. His prose rambles, stammers like his speech. He uses outmoded constructions and archaic words as if he had in that moment invented them. He chases an insignificant idea into significance and turns an interloping inspiration into a literary occasion. His writing is casual, his work often seemingly without design, but in achievement it stands high among the glories of English Literature.

Even when he had come to suspect that prose was the medium in which he was most likely to succeed he did not immediately hit upon the form his prose-writing should take. In common with many of his male contemporaries he regarded novel-writing with some scorn, dismissing it as literary exercise but suited to fill the idle hours of genteel ladies. (For literary historians, who would dearly like to know his opinion of a writer who by all appearances would have been of all his contemporaries the one whose books must have appealed to his taste, Lamb, who read so much and so widely, does not seem to have noticed Jane Austen, born as he was in 1775 and the greatest 'lady novelist' of that – or any other? – age.) Even so, Lamb tried his hand at a novel but without success, either financial or literary. *Rosamund Gray* has little to commend it except for the hints that it gives to Lamb's state of mind in 1797 and 1798 and for the fact that years later it caught Shelley's fancy.

Lamb tried play-writing. His first effort, *John Woodvil*, is a dubious pastiche of Elizabethan and Jacobean drama (but, significantly, not in verse). The proprietors of Drury Lane considered it for staging, not surprisingly they turned it down, and Lamb was reduced to vanity publishing, the last resort of the hopeful but unsuccessful author. In 1800 he paid to have it printed, and circulated copies to all his friends.

Six years later, and still Lamb had not given up all hope of proving himself as a playwright. *Mr. H*, a farce, was put on at Drury Lane and was comprehensively damned by the audience, by critics, by Lamb's dearest friends, by his sister, and by Lamb himself. (Comprehensively but not quite conclusively: in the United States it was staged, and staged successfully, many times. But *Mr. H* had a glorious future.)

Five years later he contributed to Leigh Hunt's *Reflector* the essay 'On the Custom of Hissing at the Theatre, with Some Account of a Club of Damned Authors' (see pp.224-30). The essay, written over the signature of Semel-Damnatus, nine years before its author adopted the pseudonym which became, at once and for all time, as famous as his given name, has in it so many Elian qualities, and particularly the quality of self-mocking humour, that, almost, it can be called the first of the essays of Elia.

Occasionally in his neophyte days Lamb wrote specifically for children but not all the credit (or discredit) for the *Tales from Shakespear* can be set to his account. William Godwin suggested the book and proposed that it be written by Mary Lamb. Charles Lamb supported the idea enthusiastically, in part because he saw it as therapy for his sister, in part for reason more mundane – 'Besides money. It is to bring in 60 guineas' – and though, when the book was published at the end of 1806, and presumably to satisfy the publisher's commercial instinct, it appeared as 'By Charles Lamb', in fact Charles wrote only six of the twenty tales (all of them tragedies).

(As is true of many another of the acknowledged classics of literature for the young Lamb's most resplendent gift to young readers was not conceived with them in mind. The young person – or indeed the adult – who has not read 'A Dissertation upon Roast Pig' (see pp.197-204) might well have spared himself the effort of learning to read.)

Measured one by one in the distant perspective of latter-day commentators all those early ventures – the plays and the children's books – may be dismissed as failures, follies, a misuse of genius, but these were Lamb's apprentice exercises in a craft of which very soon he became a master with very few rivals.

Years later, when he wrote 'An Autobiographical Sketch' (see p.89), he boasted that he was the first to draw the public's attention to the old English dramatists. Previously he had challenged Coleridge to take up this task. In June 1796 he wrote to his friend:

I wish you would try and do something to bring our elder bards into more general fare. I writhe with indignation when in books of Criticism...I find no mention of such as Massinger or B[eaumont] and F[letcher], men with whom succeeding Dramatic Writers (Otway alone excepted) can bear no manner of comparison.

Coleridge was not tempted, and even when, in 1808, the year in which he was helping his sister to prepare *Tales from Shakespear*, Lamb produced the book to which he refers with pride in 'An Autobiographical Sketch', his critical precepts were not yet fully developed.

The preparation of *Specimens* was the kind of task that many a young writer takes on in the hope of acquiring prestige and 'Besides money'. Lamb made of it more than a hack job by the originality of his selection and there is in the Preface evidence to the way his mind was turning, but it was not until three years later when, at the instigation of Leigh Hunt, the Editor-in-Chief to the Romantic Movement, he wrote for *The Reflector* the essay 'On the Tragedies of Shakespeare considered with Reference to their Fitness for Stage Representation' (see pp.241-59) that he emerged freed from his prentice indentures.

Even in a generation remarkable for the profusion and authority of its writings on dramatic literature and the theatre, Lamb was *sui generis*. His knowledge of the literature was prodigious: it is notable that at the moment when he begged Coleridge to 'do something to bring our elder bards into more general fame' he was still only twenty years old; with the years his learning became encyclopaedic. In this he was superior even to his paragon, Coleridge. But Lamb's criticism was not all study-bred; he had practised play-writing and for him theatre-going was an addiction. In this he had qualifications more apposite to dramatic criticism even than Hazlitt's. Lamb restored to readers many of the mislaid glories of the English Renaissance. He convicted such as Nahum Tate and David Garrick of impertinent editorial trespass on the plays of Shakespeare. He helped to cure the public of its obsession with the 'artificial' (his word) drama of the eighteenth century. These, his writings on dramatic literature, more than anything else he wrote justify a place for Lamb amongst the leaders of the revolutionary Romantic Movement, but he stands almost alone among his great contemporaries for his pioneering contributions to the editors of dramatic criticism.

He wrote of plays and players; the presentation, even the atmosphere induced in the theatre by performance and the capacity of an audience to absorb and to comprehend what came to them from the stage as they sat in pit or gallery: all were live in his mind as he considered the stillness of printed text.

'And I do not know, my boy, that you have written about Shakespeare, and Shakespeare's own Lear, finer than any one ever did in the world, and won't I let the world know it.' Thus, 'his fists clenched, his eyes flashing', the most powerful journalist in London, Thomas Barnes, a man not ordinarily given to hyperbole except when damning those who offended against the principles espoused by *The Times*. The source for Barnes's over-flowing enthusiasm may be traced to that day, some twenty years earlier, when he, a small boy in his first term at Christ's Hospital, had first met Charles Lamb, but recently out of the School and, though Leigh Hunt (another of that intensely loyal fraternity) said of Barnes that 'no man (if he had cared for it) could have been more certain of attaining celebrity for wit and literature', his praise for Lamb's writings on Shakespeare is open to challenge. 'Finer', perhaps it was but it is difficult to accept his opinion that, although they were the noblest ever written, Shakespeare's plays are 'less calculated for performance on a stage than those of almost any other dramatist', and his statement (supported a century later by Thomas Hardy) that the character King Lear 'cannot be acted' has been confounded by the performances of several actors, though certainly not by all who have dared the part.

With such reservations conceded, it remains that for his rare contribution to the literature of the theatre alone still Lamb would command a prominent place in the pantheon of English letters. That place is his, beyond challenge, for the combined and interwoven achievement of his essays on drama and the theatre, his Elia essays, and his letters – a letter so often father to an idea which grew under his sensitive but seemingly casual care to full, independent and vibrant manhood as an essay.

But there is something more, and even more to be cherished. Take all together – the published prose, a few verses, and the letters – and the amalgam is the unforgettable double singularity, Charles Lamb and Elia.

I

MR CHARLES LAMB

His faculties were extraordinary. The wit that he brought with
him from school continued to flow uniformly and to increase
through the whole course of his life. It was almost as natural with
him to say witty things as to breathe; he could not enter a room
without a joke, and he may be said to have almost conversed in
extemporaneous humour. Nor did his discourse consist of merely
sportive pleasantries; they had often the force of eloquence,
joined with the solidity of argument, enlivened and softened by
a humanity and benevolence which invariably beamed in his
countenance.

George Dyer, *Gentleman's Magazine*, 1835

Charles Lamb was born, the younger surviving child of John and Elizabeth Lamb, at 2 Crown Office Row in the Temple where his family occupied one of two sets of chambers of Samuel Salt, Bencher of the Inner Temple and the employer of both his parents. His birthplace made him from the beginning what he was to remain for the rest of his life, quintessentially a Londoner.

At the time of his birth his sister Mary was eleven years old and his brother John, by eighteen months Mary's senior, had been already for five years at school at Christ's Hospital, in Newgate Street, a few hundred yards from the family home.

Lamb's mother (Aunt Hetty in the *Elia* essay 'My Relations') served Salt as housekeeper. His father (Lionel of the *Elia* essay 'The Old Benchers of the Inner Temple') was by profession a scrivenor. He acted as Salt's clerk, manservant and factotum, dabbled in verse-writing and had strong opinions on many subjects, including (a foretaste of what was to come from his son) dramatic performance. All the Lamb family were devoted to Samuel Salt and he repaid their devotion with many kindnesses (see p.8).

Lamb's early childhood passed contentedly. Closeted in the elegance of the Temple and making occasional trips out into rural Hertfordshire, he was protected from awareness of the harsher evidence of life in a great city by a loving family and warm-hearted friends. His eager eye recorded the characteristics and idiosyncrasies of all he met, and in later years his adult genius made unforgettable for generations of readers many of those actors on the stage of his early years who he himself had never forgotten.

There was his father:

> ...a merrier man,
> A man more apt to frame matter for mirth,
> Mad jokes, and antics for a Christmas eve,
> Making life social, and the laggard time
> To move on nimbly, never yet did cheer
> The little circle of domestic friends.

There was Samuel Salt: 'who never dressed for dinner but he forgot his sword'. There was Betsy Chambers, his first teacher and later one of his two pensioners:

> ...prim Betsy Chambers
> Decayed in her members
> No longer remembers
> Things she once did.

3

and William Bird, 'in the main a humane and judicious master'. But of all the influences on his early life none, save only his companionship with his sister, was more potent than his visits to his Hertfordshire relatives, to his grandmother, Mary Field, housekeeper to the Plumers at Blakesware (Blakesmoor in the *Elia* essay) – 'She knew all the Psalms by heart, ay, and a great part of the Testament' – and to his great-aunt Ann Gladman at Mackery End.

The Old Benchers of the Inner Temple

I was born, and passed the first seven years of my life, in the Temple. Its church, its halls, its gardens, its fountain, its river, I had almost said – for in those young years, what was this king of rivers to me but a stream that watered our pleasant places? – these are of my oldest recollections. I repeat, to this day, no verses to myself more frequently, or with kindlier emotion, than those of Spenser, where he speaks of this spot.

> There when they came, whereas those bricky towers,
> The which on Themmes brode aged back doth ride,
> Where now the studious lawyers have their bowers,
> There whylome wont the Templer knights to bide,
> Till they decayed through pride.

Indeed, it is the most elegant spot in the metropolis. What a transition for a countryman visiting London for the first time – the passing from the crowded Strand or Fleet-street, by unexpected avenues, into its magnificent ample squares, its classic green recesses! What a cheerful, liberal look hath that portion of it, which, from three sides, overlooks the greater garden: that goodly pile

> Of building strong, albeit of Paper hight,

confronting, with massy contrast, the lighter, older, more fantastically shrouded one, named of Harcourt, with the cheerful Crown-office Row (place of my kindly engendure), right opposite the stately stream, which washes the garden-foot with her yet scarcely trade-polluted waters, and seems but just weaned from

4

her Twickenham Naiades! a man would give something to have been born in such places. What a collegiate aspect has that fine Elizabethan hall, where the fountain plays, which I have made to rise and fall, how many times! to the astoundment of the young urchins, my contemporaries, who, not being able to guess at its recondite machinery, were almost tempted to hail the wondrous work as magic! What an antique air had the now almost effaced sun-dials, with their moral inscriptions, seeming coevals with that Time which they measured, and to take their revelations of its flight immediately from heaven, holding correspondence with the fountain of light! How would the dark line steal imperceptibly on, watched by the eye of childhood, eager to detect its movement, never catched, nice as an evanescent cloud, or the first arrests of sleep!

> Ah! yet doth beauty like a dial-hand
> Steal from his figure, and no pace perceived!

What a dead thing is a clock, with its ponderous embowelments of lead and brass, its pert or solemn dulness of communication, compared with the simple altar-like structure, and silent heart-language of the old dial! It stood as the garden god of Christian gardens. Why is it almost every where vanished? If its business-use be superseded by more elaborate inventions, its moral uses, its beauty, might have pleaded for its continuance. It spoke of moderate labours, of pleasures not protracted after sun-set, of temperance, and good-hours. It was the primitive clock, the horologe of the first world. Adam could scarce have missed it in Paradise. It was the measure appropriate for sweet plants and flowers, to spring by, for the birds to apportion their silver warblings by, for flocks to pasture and be led to fold by. The shepherd 'carved it out quaintly in the sun'; and, turning philosopher by the very occupation, provided it with mottos more touching than tombstones. It was a pretty device of the gardener, recorded by Marvell, who, in the days of artificial gardening, made a dial out of herbs and flowers. I must quote his verses a little higher up, for they are full, as all his serious poetry was, of a witty delicacy. They will not come in awkwardly, I hope, in a talk of fountains and sun-dials. He is speaking of sweet garden scenes:

What wondrous life in this I lead!
Ripe apples drop about my head.
The luscious clusters of the vine
Upon my mouth do crush their wine.
The nectarine, and curious peach,
Into my hands themselves do reach.
Stumbling on melons, as I pass,
Insnared with flowers, I fall on grass.
Meanwhile the mind from pleasure less
Withdraws into its happiness.
The mind, that ocean, where each kind
Does straight its own resemblance find;
Yet it creates, transcending these,
Far other worlds, and other seas;
Annihilating all that's made
To a green thought in a green shade.
Here at the fountain's sliding foot,
Or at some fruit-tree's mossy root,
Casting the body's vest aside,
My soul into the boughs does glide:
There, like a bird, it sits and sings,
Then whets and claps its silver wings;
And, till prepared for longer flight,
Waves in its plumes the various light.
How well the skilful gardener drew,
Of flowers and herbs, this dial new!
Where, from above, the milder sun
Does through a fragrant zodiac run:
And, as it works, the industrious bee
Computes its time as well as we.
How could such sweet and wholesome hours
Be reckon'd, but with herbs and flowers?

The artificial fountains of the metropolis are, in like manner, fast vanishing. Most of them are dried up, or bricked over. Yet, where one is left, as in that little green nook behind the South-Sea House, what a freshness it gives to the dreary pile! Four little winged marble boys used to play their virgin fancies, spouting out ever fresh streams from their innocent-wanton lips, in the square of Lincoln's-inn, when I was no bigger than they were figured. They are gone, and the spring choked up. The fashion, they tell me, is gone by, and these things are esteemed childish. Why not then gratify children, by letting them stand? Lawyers, I suppose, were children once. They are awakening images to them at least. Why must every thing smack of man, and mannish? Is the world all grown up? Is childhood dead? Or is there not in the bosoms of the wisest and the best some of the child's heart left, to respond to its earliest enchantments? The figures were grotesque. Are the stiff-wigged living figures, that still flitter and chatter about that area, less gothic in appearance? or is the splutter of their hot rhetoric one half so refreshing and innocent as the little cool playful streams those exploded cherubs uttered?

They have lately gothicised the entrance to the Inner Temple-hall, and the library front, to assimilate them, I suppose, to the body of the hall, which they do not at all resemble. What is become of the winged horse that stood over the former? a stately arms! and who has removed those frescoes of the Virtues, which Italianized the end of the Paper-buildings? – my first hint of allegory! They must account to me for these things, which I miss so greatly.

The terrace is, indeed, left, which we used to call the parade; but the traces are passed away of the footsteps which made its pavement awful! It is become common and profane. The old benchers had it almost sacred to themselves, in the forepart of the day at least. They might not be sided or jostled. Their air and dress asserted the parade. You left wide spaces betwixt you, when you passed them. We walk on even terms with their successors. The roguish eye of J[eky]ll, ever ready to be delivered of a jest, almost invites a stranger to vie a repartee with it. But what insolent familiar durst have mated Thomas Coventry? – whose person was a quadrate, his step massy and elephantine, his face square as the lion's, his gait peremptory and path-keeping, indivertible from his way as a moving column, the scarecrow of his inferiors, the brow-beater of equals and superiors, who made a solitude of children wherever he came, for they fled his insufferable presence, as they would have shunned an Elisha bear.

His growl was as thunder in their ears, whether he spake to them in mirth or in rebuke, his invitatory notes being, indeed, of all, the most repulsive and horrid. Clouds of snuff, aggravating the natural terrors of his speech, broke from each majestic nostril, darkening the air. He took it, not by pinches, but a palmful at once, diving for it under the mighty flaps of his old-fashioned waistcoat pocket; his waistcoat red and angry, his coat dark rappee, tinctured by dye original, and by adjuncts, with buttons of obsolete gold. And so he paced the terrace.

By his side a milder form was sometimes to be seen; the pensive gentility of Samuel Salt. They were coevals, and had nothing but that and their benchership in common. In politics Salt was a whig, and Coventry a staunch tory. Many a sarcastic growl did the latter cast out – for Coventry had a rough spinous humour – at the political confederates of his associate, which rebounded from the gentle bosom of the latter like cannon-balls from wool. You could not ruffle Samuel Salt.

S. had the reputation of being a very clever man, and of excellent discernment in the chamber practice of the law. I suspect his knowledge did not amount to much. When a case of difficult disposition of money, testamentary or otherwise, came before him, he ordinarily handed it over with a few instructions to his man Lovel, who was a quick little fellow, and would despatch it out of hand by the light of natural understanding, of which he had an uncommon share. It was incredible what repute for talents S. enjoyed by the mere trick of gravity. He was a shy man; a child might pose him in a minute – indolent and procrastinating to the last degree. Yet men would give him credit for vast application in spite of himself. He was not to be trusted with himself with impunity. He never dressed for a dinner party but he forgot his sword – they wore swords then – or some other necessary part of his equipage. Lovel had his eye upon him on all these occasions, and ordinarily gave him his cue. If there was any thing which he could speak unseasonably, he was sure to do it. – He was to dine at a relative's of the unfortunate Miss Blandy on the day of her execution; – and L. who had a wary foresight of his probable hallucinations, before he set out, schooled him with great anxiety not in any possible manner to allude to her story

8

that day. S. promised faithfully to observe the injunction. He had not been seated in the parlour, where the company was expecting the dinner summons, four minutes, when, a pause in the conversation ensuing, he got up, looked out of window, and pulling down his ruffles – an ordinary motion with him – observed, 'it was a gloomy day,' and added, 'Miss Blandy must be hanged by this time, I suppose.' Instances of this sort were perpetual. Yet S. was thought by some of the greatest men of his time a fit person to be consulted, not alone in matters pertaining to the law, but in the ordinary niceties and embarrassments of conduct – from force of manner entirely. He never laughed. He had the same good fortune among the female world, – was a known toast with the ladies, and one or two are said to have died for love of him – I suppose, because he never trifled or talked gallantry with them, or paid them, indeed, hardly common attentions. He had a fine face and person, but wanted, methought, the spirit that should have shown them off with advantage to the women. His eye lacked lustre. – Not so, thought Susan P[eirson]; who, at the advanced age of sixty, was seen, in the cold evening time, unaccompanied, wetting the pavement of B[edfor]d Row, with tears that fell in drops which might be heard, because her friend had died that day – he, whom she had pursued with a hopeless passion for the last forty years – a passion, which years could not extinguish or abate; nor the long resolved, yet gently enforced, puttings off of unrelenting bachelorhood dissuade from its cherished purpose. Mild Susan P[eirson], thou hast now thy friend in heaven!

Thomas Coventry was a cadet of the noble family of that name. He passed his youth in contracted circumstances, which gave him early those parsimonious habits which in after-life never forsook him; so that, with one windfall or another, about the time I knew him he was master of four or five hundred thousand pounds; nor did he look, or walk, worth a moidore less. He lived in a gloomy house opposite the pump in Serjeant's-inn, Fleet-street. J., the counsel, is doing self-imposed penance in it, for what reason I divine not, at this day. C. had an agreeable seat at North Cray, where he seldom spent above a day or two at a time in the summer; but preferred, during the hot months, standing at his window in this damp, close, well-like mansion, to watch, as he said, 'the maids drawing water all day long.' I suspect he had his within-door reasons for the preference. *Hic currus et arma fuêre.* He might think his treasures more safe. His house had the aspect of a strong box. C. was a close hunks – a hoarder rather than a miser – or, if a miser, none of the mad Elwes breed, who have brought discredit upon a character, which cannot exist without certain admirable points of steadiness and unity of purpose. One may hate a true miser, but cannot, I suspect, so easily despise him. By taking care of the pence, he is often enabled to part with the pounds, upon a scale that leaves us careless generous fellows halting at an immeasurable distance behind. C. gave away 30,000*l.* at once in his life-time to a blind charity. His house-keeping was severely looked after, but he kept the table of a gentleman. He would know who came in and who went out of his house, but his kitchen chimney was never suffered to freeze.

Salt was his opposite in this, as in all – never knew what he was worth in the world; and having but a competency for his rank, which his indolent habits were little calculated to improve, might have suffered severely if he had not had honest people about him. Lovel took care of every thing. He was at once his clerk, his good servant, his dresser, his friend, his 'flapper,' his guide, stop-watch, auditor, treasurer. He did nothing without consulting Lovel, or failed in any thing without expecting and fearing his admonishing. He put himself almost too much in his hands, had they not been the purest in the world. He resigned his title almost to respect as a master, if L. could ever have forgotten for a moment that he was a servant.

I knew this Lovel. He was a man of an incorrigible and losing honesty. A good fellow withal, and 'would strike.' In the cause of the oppressed he never considered inequalities, or calculated the number of his opponents. He once wrested a sword out of the hand of a man of quality that had drawn upon him; and pommelled him severely with the hilt of it. The swordsman had offered insult to a female – an occasion upon which no odds against him could have prevented the interference of Lovel. He would stand next day bare-headed to the same person, modestly to excuse his interference – for L. never forgot rank, where something better was not concerned. L. was the liveliest little fellow breathing, had a face as gay as Garrick's, whom he was said greatly to resemble (I have a portrait of him which confirms it), possessed a fine turn for humorous poetry – next to Swift and Prior – moulded heads in clay or plaster of Paris to admiration, by the dint of natural genius merely; turned cribbage boards, and such small cabinet toys, to perfection; took a hand at quadrille or bowls with equal facility; made punch better than any man of his degree in England; had the merriest quips and conceits, and was altogether as brimful of rogueries and inventions as you could desire. He was a brother of the angle, moreover, and just such a free, hearty, honest companion as Mr Isaac Walton would have chosen to go a fishing with. I saw him in his old age and the decay of his faculties, palsy-smitten, in the last sad stage of human weakness – 'a remnant most forlorn of what he was,' – yet even then his eye would light up upon the mention of his favourite Garrick. He was the greatest, he would say, in Bayes – 'was upon the stage nearly throughout the whole performance, and as busy as a bee.' At intervals, too, he would speak of his former life, and how he came up a little boy from Lincoln to go to service, and how his mother cried at parting with him, and how he returned, after some few years' absence, in his smart new livery to see her, and she blessed herself at the change, and could hardly be brought to believe that it was 'her own bairn.' And then, the excitement subsiding, he would weep, till I have wished that sad second-childhood might have a mother still to lay its head upon her lap. But the common mother of us all in no long time after received him gently into hers.

With Coventry, and with Salt, in their walks upon the terrace, most commonly Peter Pierson would join, to make up a third. They did not walk linked arm in arm in those days – 'as now our stout triumvirs sweep the streets,' – but generally with both hands folded behind them for state, or with one at least behind, the other carrying a cane. P. was a benevolent, but not a prepossessing man. He had that in his face which you could not term unhappiness; it rather implied an incapacity of being happy. His cheeks were colourless, even to whiteness. His look was uninviting, resembling (but without his sourness) that of our great philanthropist. I know that he *did* good acts, but I could never make out what he *was*. Contemporary with these, but subordinate, was Daines Barrington – another oddity – he walked burly and square – in imitation, I think, of Coventry – howbeit he attained not to the dignity of his prototype. Nevertheless, he did pretty well, upon the strength of being a tolerable antiquarian, and having a brother a bishop. When the account of his year's treasurership came to be audited, the following singular charge was unanimously disallowed by the bench: 'Item, disbursed Mr Allen, the gardener, twenty shillings, for stuff to poison the sparrows, by my orders.' Next to him was old Barton – a jolly negation, who took upon him the ordering of the bills of fare for the parliament chamber, where the benchers dine – answering to the combination rooms at college – much to the easement of his less epicurean brethren. I known nothing more of him. – Then Read, and Twopenny – Read, good-humoured and personable – Twopenny, good-humoured, but thin, and felicitous in jests upon his own figure. If T. was thin, Wharry was attenuated and fleeting. Many must remember him (for he was rather of later date) and his singular gait, which was performed by three steps and a jump regularly succeeding. The steps were little efforts, like that of a child beginning to walk; the jump comparatively vigorous, as a foot to an inch. Where he learned this figure, or what occasioned it, I could never discover. It was neither graceful in itself, nor seemed to answer the purpose any better than common walking. The extreme tenuity of his frame, I suspect, set him upon it. It was a trial of poising. Twopenny would often rally him upon his leanness, and hail him as Brother Lusty; but W. had no relish of a joke. His features were spiteful. I have heard that he would pinch his cat's ears extremely, when any thing had offended him. Jackson – the omniscient Jackson he was called – was of this period. He had the reputation of possessing more multifarious knowledge than any man of his time. He was the Friar Bacon of the less literate portion of the Temple. I remember a pleasant passage, of the cook applying to him, with much formality of apology, for instructions how to write down *edge* bone of beef in his bill of commons. He was supposed to know, if any man in the world did. He decided the orthography to be – as I have given it – fortifying his authority with such anatomical reasons as dismissed the manciple (for the time) learned and happy. Some do spell it yet perversely, *aitch* bone, from a fanciful resemblance between its shape, and that of the aspirate so denominated. I had almost forgotten Mingay with the iron hand – but he was somewhat later. He had lost his right hand by some accident, and supplied it with a grappling hook, which he wielded with a tolerable adroitness. I detected the substitute, before I was old enough to reason whether it were artificial or not. I remember the astonishment it raised in me. He was a blustering, loud-talking person; and I reconciled the phenomenon to my ideas as an emblem of power – somewhat like the horns in the forehead of Michael Angelo's Moses. Baron Maseres, who walks (or did till very lately) in the costume of the reign of George the Second, closes my imperfect recollections of the old benchers of the Inner Temple.

Fantastic forms, whither are ye fled? Or, if the like of you exist, why exist they no more for me? Ye inexplicable, half-understood appearances, why comes in reason to tear away the preternatural mist, bright or gloomy, that enshrouded you? Why make ye so sorry a figure in my relation, who made up to me – to my childish eyes – the mythology of the Temple? In those days I saw Gods, as 'old men covered with a mantle,' walking upon the earth. Let the dreams of classic idolatry perish, – extinct be the fairies and fairy trumpery of legendary fabling, – in the heart of childhood, there will, for ever, spring up a well of innocent or wholesome superstition – the seeds of exaggeration will be busy there, and vital – from every-day forms educing the unknown and the uncommon. In that little Goshen there will be light, when the grown world flounders about in the darkness of sense and materiality. While childhood, and while dreams, reducing childhood, shall be left, imagination shall not have spread her holy wings totally to fly the earth.

P.S. – I have done injustice to the soft shade of Samuel Salt.

13

See what it is to trust to imperfect memory, and the erring notices of childhood! Yet I protest I always thought that he had been a bachelor! This gentleman, R.N. informs me, married young, and losing his lady in child-bed, within the first year of their union, fell into a deep melancholy, from the effects of which, probably, he never thoroughly recovered. In what a new light does this place his rejection (O call it by a gentler name!) of mild Susan P[ierson], unravelling into beauty certain peculiarities of this very shy and retiring character! – Henceforth let no one receive the narratives of Elia for true records! They are, in truth, but shadows of fact – verisimilitudes, not verities – or sitting but upon the remote edges and outskirts of history. He is no such honest chronicler as R.N., and would have done better perhaps to have consulted that gentleman, before he sent these incondite reminiscences to press. But the worthy sub-treasurer – who respects his old and his new masters – would but have been puzzled at the indecorous liberties of Elia. The good man wots not, peradventure, of the license which *Magazines* have arrived at in this plain-speaking age, or hardly dreams of their existence beyond the *Gentleman's* – his furthest monthly excursions in this nature having been long confined to the holy ground of honest *Urban's* obituary. May it be long before his own name shall help to swell those columns of unenvied flattery! – Meantime, O ye New Benchers of the Inner Temple, cherish him kindly, for he is himself the kindliest of human creatures. Should infirmities over-take him – he is yet in green and vigorous senility – make allowances for them, remembering that 'ye yourselves are old'. So may the Winged Horse, your ancient badge and cognisance, still flourish! so may future Hookers and Seldens illustrate your church and chambers! so may the sparrows, in default of more melodious quiristers, unpoisoned hop about your walks! so may the fresh-coloured and cleanly nursery maid, who, by leave, airs her playful charge in your stately gardens, drop her prettiest blushing curtsy as ye pass, reductive of juvenescent emotion! so may the younkers of this generation eye you, pacing your stately terrace, with the same superstitious veneration, with which the child Elia gazed on the Old Worthies that solemnised the parade before ye!

The London Magazine, 1821

Blakesmoor in H—shire

I do not know a pleasure more affecting than to range at will over the deserted apartments of some fine old family mansion. The traces of extinct grandeur admit of a better passion than envy: and contemplations on the great and good, whom we fancy in succession to have been its inhabitants, weave for us illusions, incompatible with the bustle of modern occupancy, and vanities of foolish present aristocracy. The same difference of feeling, I think, attends us between entering an empty and a crowded church. In the latter it is chance but some present human frailty – an act of inattention on the part of some of the auditory – or a trait of affectation, or worse, vain-glory, on that of the preacher – puts us by our best thoughts, disharmonising the place and the occasion. But would'st thou know the beauty of holiness? – go alone on some week-day, borrowing the keys of good Master Sexton, traverse the cool aisles of some country church: think of the piety that has kneeled there – the congregations, old and young, that have found consolation there – the meek pastor – the docile parishioner. With no disturbing emotions, no cross conflicting comparisons, drink in the tranquillity of the place, till thou thyself become as fixed and motionless as the marble effigies that kneel and weep around thee.

Journeying northward lately, I could not resist going some few miles out of my road to look upon the remains of an old great house with which I had been impressed in this way in infancy. I was apprised that the owner of it had lately pulled it down; still I had a vague notion that it could not all have perished, that so much solidity with magnificence could not have been crushed all at once into the mere dust and rubbish which I found it.

The work of ruin had proceeded with a swift hand indeed, and the demolition of a few weeks had reduced it to – an antiquity.

I was astonished at the indistinction of everything. Where had stood the great gates? What bounded the court-yard? Whereabout did the out-houses commence? a few bricks only lay as representatives of that which was so stately and so spacious.

Death does not shrink up his human victim at this rate. The burnt ashes of a man weigh more in their proportion.

Had I seen these brick-and-mortar knaves at their process of destruction, at the plucking of every pannel I should have felt the varlets at my heart. I should have cried out to them to spare a plank at least out of the cheerful store-room, in whose hot window-seat I used to sit and read Cowley, with the grass-plat before, and the hum and flappings of that one solitary wasp that ever haunted it about me – it is in mine ears now, as oft as summer returns; or a pannel of the yellow room.

Why, every plank and pannel of that house for me had magic in it. The tapestried bed-rooms – tapestry so much better than painting – not adorning merely, but peopling the wainscots – at which childhood ever and anon would steal a look, shifting its coverlid (replaced as quickly) to exercise its tender courage in a momentary eye-encounter with those stern bright visages, staring reciprocally – all Ovid on the walls, in colours vivider than his descriptions. Actæon in mid sprout, with the unappeasable prudery of Diana; and the still more provoking, and almost culinary coolness of Dan Phœbus, eel-fashion, deliberately divesting of Marsyas.

Then, that haunted room – in which old Mrs Battle died – whereinto I have crept, but always in the day-time, with a passion of fear; and a sneaking curiosity, terror-tainted, to hold communication with the past. – *How shall they build it up again?*

It was an old deserted place, yet not so long deserted but that traces of the splendour of past inmates were everywhere apparent. Its furniture was still standing – even to the tarnished gilt leather battledores, and crumbling feathers of shuttlecocks in the nursery, which told that children had once played there. But I was a lonely child, and had the range at will of every apartment, knew every nook and corner, wondered and worshipped everywhere.

The solitude of childhood is not so much the mother of thought, as it is the feeder of love, and silence, and admiration. So strange a passion for the place possessed me in those years, that, though there lay – I shame to say how few roods distant from the mansion – half hid by trees, what I judged some romantic lake, such was

16

the spell which bound me to the house, and such my carefulness not to pass its strict and proper precincts, that the idle waters lay unexplored for me; and not till late in life, curiosity prevailing over elder devotion, I found, to my astonishment, a pretty brawling brook had been the Lacus Incognitus of my infancy. Variegated views, extensive prospects – and those at no great distance from the house – I was told of such – what were they to me, being out of the boundaries of my Eden? – So far from a wish to roam, I would have drawn, methought, still closer the fences of my chosen prison; and have been hemmed in by a yet securer cincture of those excluding garden walls. I could have exclaimed with that garden-loving poet –

> Bind me, ye woodbines, in your 'twines,
> Curl me about, ye gadding vines;
> And oh so close your circles lace,
> That I may never leave this place;
> But, lest your fetters prove too weak,
> Ere I your silken bondage break,
> Do you, O brambles, chain me too,
> And, courteous briars, nail me through!

I was here as in a lonely temple. Snug firesides – the low-built roof – parlours ten feet by ten – frugal boards, and all the homeliness of home – these were the condition of my birth – the wholesome soil I was planted in. Yet, without impeachment to their tenderest lessons, I am not sorry to have had glances of something beyond; and to have taken, if but a peep, in childhood, at the contrasting accidents of a great fortune.

To have the feeling of gentility, it is not necessary to have been born gentle. The pride of ancestry may be had on cheaper terms than to be obliged to an importunate race of ancestors; and the coatless antiquary in his inemblazoned cell, revolving the long line of a Mowbray's or De Clifford's pedigree, at those sounding names may warm himself into as gay a vanity as those who do inherit them. The claims of birth are ideal merely, and what herald shall go about to strip me of an idea? Is it trenchant to their swords? can it be hacked off as a spur can? or torn away like a tarnished garter?

17

What, else, were the families of the great to us? what pleasure should we take in their tedious genealogies, or their capitulatory brass monuments? What to us the uninterrupted current of their bloods, if our own did not answer within us to a cognate and correspondent elevation?

Or wherefore, else, O tattered and diminished 'Scutcheon that hung upon the time-worn walls of thy princely stairs, BLAKES-MOOR! have I in childhood so oft stood poring upon thy mystic characters – thy emblematic supporters, with their prophetic 'Resurgam' – till, every dreg of peasantry purging off, I received into myself Very Gentility? Thou wert first in my morning eyes; and of nights, hast detained my steps from bedward, till it was but a step from gazing at thee to dreaming on thee.

This is the only true gentry by adoption; the veritable change of blood, and not, as empirics have fabled, by transfusion.

Who it was by dying that had earned the splendid trophy, I know not, I inquired not; but its fading rags, and colours cobweb-stained, told that its subject was of two centuries back.

And what if my ancestor at that date was some Damœtas – feeding flocks, not his own, upon the hills of Lincoln – did I in less earnest vindicate to myself the family trappings of this once proud Ægon? – repaying by a backward triumph the insults he might possibly have heaped in his life-time upon my poor pastoral progenitor.

If it were presumption so to speculate, the present owners of the mansion had least reason to complain. They had long forsaken the old house of their fathers for a newer trifle; and I was left to appropriate to myself what images I could pick up, to raise my fancy, or to soothe my vanity.

I was the true descendant of those old W—s; and not the present family of that name, who had fled the old waste places.

Mine was that gallery of good old family portraits, which as I have gone over, giving them in fancy my own family name, one – and then another – would seem to smile, reaching forward from the canvas, to recognise the new relationship; while the rest looked grave, as it seemed, at the vacancy in their dwelling, and thoughts of fled posterity.

That Beauty with the cool blue pastoral drapery, and a lamb –

18

that hung next the great bay window – with the bright yellow H[ertford]shire hair, and eye of watchet hue – so like my Alice! – I am persuaded she was a true Elia – Mildred Elia, I take it.

Mine too, BLAKESMOOR, was thy noble Marble Hall, with its mosaic pavements, and its Twelve Cæsars – stately busts in marble – ranged round: of whose countenances, young reader of faces as I was, the frowning beauty of Nero, I remember, had most of my wonder; but the mild Galba had my love. There they stood in the coldness of death, yet freshness of immortality.

Mine too, thy lofty Justice Hall, with its one chair of authority, high-backed and wickered, once the terror of luckless poacher, or self-forgetful maiden – so common since, that bats have roosted in it.

Mine too – whose else? – thy costly fruit-garden, with its sun-baked southern wall; the ampler pleasure-garden, rising backwards from the house in triple terraces, with flower-pots now of palest lead, save that a speck here and there, saved from the elements, bespeak their pristine state to have been gilt and glittering; the verdant quarters backwarder still; and, stretching still beyond, in old formality, thy firry wilderness, the haunt of the squirrel, and the day-long murmuring woodpigeon, with that antique image in the centre, God or Goddess I wist not; but child of Athens or old Rome paid never a sincerer worship to Pan or to Sylvanus in their native groves, than I to that fragmental mystery.

Was it for this, that I kissed my childish hands too fervently in your idol worship, walks and windings of BLAKESMOOR! for this, or what sin of mine, has the plough passed over your pleasant places? I sometimes think that as men, when they die, do not die all, so of their extinguished habitations there may be a hope – a germ to be revivified.

The London Magazine, 1824

AND IN MY JOYFUL SCHOOLDAYS

Charles Lamb was entered into Christ's Hospital on 9 October 1782 on the Presentation of Timothy Yeats, a friend of Samuel Salt, and it was Salt, not as was usual his presenting Governor, who deposited with the School authorities a bond for the seven-year old child – as previously he had done for Lamb's brother John.

On that same day Samuel Taylor Coleridge from Ottery St Mary in Devon also put on bluecoat and yellow stockings for the first time. He was twenty-seven months older than Lamb.

Much is known about the School as it was in Lamb's day. It is described in rich detail in three of the greatest autobiographical works in English, the composite autobiography drawn from Lamb's own essays and letters, the *Autobiography of Leigh Hunt* and Coleridge's *Biographia Literaria*, but of Lamb himself as a schoolboy the most vivid description was given by Valentine Le Grice to Lamb's biographer, Thomas Talfourd:

> Lamb was an amiable, gentle boy, very sensitive and keenly observing, indulged by his schoolfellows and by his master on account of his infirmity of speech. His countenance was mild, his complexion clear brown, with an expression which might lead you to think that he was of Jewish descent. His eyes were not each of the same colour, one was hazel, the other had specks of grey in the iris, mingled as we see red spots in the blood stone. His step was plantigrade, which made his walk slow and peculiar, adding to the staid appearance of his figure. I never heard his name mentioned without the addition of Charles, although as there was no other boy of the name of Lamb the addition was unnecessary, but there was an implied kindness in it, and it was proof that his gentle manners excited that kindness.

By his own frequently expressed testimony, Lamb's schooldays were indeed 'joyful'. Discipline was harsh; no eighteenth century schoolboy expected gentleness; the food was appalling; so has been the food in all boarding-schools in all eras – at least by the reports of its recipients; but the teaching was sound. More than all else conducive to his boyhood happiness and more than all else compelling upon his enduring loyalty, then, as in all its 440 years, there was within the Christ's Hospital community a sense of fraternity and an awareness of the uniqueness of the Foundation, whose 'charitable benevolence' had raised all from being 'children in need' to the privilege of an education scarce equalled by that of any of the other great schools of the age, and which had opened to them

20

the eventual advantages of the Hospital's wide and substantial influence.

Not only the boys but also their seniors were conscious of the uniqueness of their school. The Upper Grammar Master and most of the teaching staff were themselves Blues, so were a number of those who had responsibility for the boys outside the classroom, and so also were many of the Governors. All worked conscientiously for the well-being of 'the children of Christ's Hospital'. All were diligent to ensure that Blues were well-prepared to enter upon the promising careers to which, more often than not, the Hospital or its friends arranged their entry.

In the last quarter of the eighteenth century, life at Christ's Hospital was dominated by the awesome personality of the Upper Grammar Master, James Boyer. The adult achievements of his pupils not only justify his well-nigh unique standing in the School's legend and history but also merit for him a high place in the pantheon of English education. A Governor-General of Upper Canada (John Colborne), the first Bishop of Calcutta (Thomas Middleton), an Ambassador (Edward Thornton) and his own successor (A.N. Trollope): all these were among Boyer's boys who achieved eminence, and none of them had started life with any advantage from family money or family influence, but his greatest glory lies in the resplendence of the contribution to English letters made by his products, Lamb, Coleridge, Leigh Hunt, Thomas Barnes of *The Times* and a remarkable number of lesser-writers – novelists, versifiers, translators, theologians – came from the School in the Boyer years.

It cannot be alleged that this outpouring of literary energy was a coincidence. Many of Boyer's pupils who turned to writing paid tribute to the vital role that Boyer had played in their apprenticeship, among their number the three who profited from it most, Lamb, Leigh Hunt and, most vividly, Coleridge:

> ...he showed no mercy to phrase, metaphor, or image, unsupported by a sound sense, or where the same sense might have been conveyed with equal force and dignity in plainer words. *Lute, harp,* and *lyre, Muse, Muses,* and *inspirations, Pegasus, Parnassus,* and *Hippocrene* were all abominations to him. In fancy I can almost hear him now, exploding 'Harp? Harp? Lyre? Pen and ink, boy, you mean! Muse, boy, Muse? Your nurse's daughter, you mean! Pierian spring? Oh aye! the cloister-pump, I suppose!'

Boyer's only literary efforts were dismissed as 'grating as a scrannel pipe' but he cared for the English language, he loved English literature, and he taught his boys to use the language scrupulously and to cherish the great works which they had inherited. Even more

21

to his credit, he appreciated the value of verse-writing as exercise in the use of language. (Of the sixty-five contributions to the *Liber Aureus* into which he allowed scholars to enter work of more than ordinary merit, forty-six are in verse – more by Coleridge than by any other boy.)

As handed down in the writings of his three greatest pupils, the verdict on Boyer as teacher and mentor to his literary genius is unanimous. Each in his turn affirms that his strength was by no means all in his right arm, that he was a knowledgeable and effective tutor, unfailingly capable of holding the interest of those he taught, and that his judgements were invariably shrewd.

The Christ's Hospital boy's friends at school are commonly his intimates throughout life, and thus it was for Lamb. His 'dearest friend', Coleridge, Allen, White, the two Le Grices and Favell: all were his contemporaries at School and all were close to him for many years after they had left Christ's Hospital. As so many of them aspired to the careers in letters which some of them achieved magnificently, instinctively they formed themselves into an inner coterie within the larger but still intimate society of literary London. They met others, they wrote to each other frequently, sometimes they collaborated and, when they were in a position so to do, they used such patronage as was available to them to the advantage of their former school-fellows. But the Christ's Hospital solidarity was not then, nor has it ever been, limited by contemporaneity at school. George Dyer had left Christ's Hospital in the year before Lamb entered the School, Thomas Barnes and Leigh Hunt became Bluecoat boys a few years after he had left. All three were members of the coterie and had Lamb's friendship. When, in 1812, Christ's Hospital came under public attack for allowing what was said to be a breach of the principle that its benefits be reserved for 'children in need', the four most influential literary Old Blues – Coleridge, Leigh Hunt, Thomas Barnes and Lamb – all hurried into print in defence of their alma mater. Lamb's contribution to the cause was the essay 'Recollections of Christ's Hospital'.

Seven years later he wrote and published in *The London Magazine* his second Christ's Hospital essay. The title Lamb chose carried faint implications that he intended something more judicious than the patent advocacy of 'Recollections' and at the outset he promised to be objective, to 'put the other side' to [Mr Lamb's] 'magnificent eulogy of my old school'. Even, as if to make detachment easier for himself, he hid the person of Mr Lamb behind not just one but two *personnae*. The first person singular according to the signature, is Elia, but the character he adopts – at least for the first part of the essay – is Coleridge.

This double duplicity confused even its author. At one point he

writes of 'Mr Coleridge's *Literary Life*' and at another he describes
Coleridge as one of 'the Grecians of my time', but this confusion
only serves to justify the impression that, despite the protestations
of dispassion, this is the more personal, the more intimate, of the
two Christ's Hospital essays, and once Lamb calls back to memory
the personalities of Christ's Hospital in his day, masters and boys,
the innocent and always penetrable deceits become irrelevant.

This is, for all its protestations of objectivity, a eulogy to Christ's
Hospital, a public demonstration of indebtedness to the School and
a warm-hearted tribute to the friends discovered at school with
whom he was intimate still 'at the age of forty' (Lamb was in fact
forty-five and Coleridge, the purported author, forty-eight). And,
though Coleridge must have recognised as stolen, as it were, from
his own memoires of occasional unhappiness in his early school-
days, his tribute to Christ's Hospital was even more fervent than
Lamb. 'I say solemnly and on my conscience, that we can hardly
imagine a larger sum of goodness struck off at once from the ledger
of useful benevolence.'

Christ's Hospital

Five-and-Thirty Years Ago

In Mr Lamb's 'Works', published a year or two since, I find a
magnificent eulogy on my old school, such as it was, or now
appears to him to have been, between the years 1782 and 1789.
It happens, very oddly, that my own standing at Christ's was
nearly corresponding with his; and, with all gratitude to him for
his enthusiasm for the cloisters, I think he has contrived to bring
together whatever can be said in praise of them, dropping all the
other side of the argument most ingeniously.

I remember L. at school; and can well recollect that he had
some peculiar advantages, which I and other of his schoolfellows
had not. His friends lived in town, and were near at hand; and
he had the privilege of going to see them, almost as often as he
wished, through some invidious distinction, which was denied
to us. The present worthy sub-treasurer to the Inner Temple can
explain how that happened. He had his tea and hot rolls in a
morning, while we were battening upon our quarter of a penny

loaf – our *crug* – moistened with attenuated small beer, in wooden piggins, smacking of the pitched leathern jack it was poured from. Our Monday's milk porritch, blue and tasteless, and the peas soup of Saturday, coarse and choking, were enriched for him with a slice of 'extra-ordinary bread and butter', from the hot-loaf of the Temple. The Wednesday's mess of millet, somewhat less repugnant (we had three banyan to four meat days in the week) – was endeared to his palate with a lump of double-refined, and a smack of ginger (to make it go down the more glibly) or the fragrant cinnamon. In lieu of our *half-pickled* Sundays, or *quite fresh* boiled beef on Thursdays (strong as *caro equina*), with detestable marigolds floating in the pail to poison the broth – our scanty mutton crags on Fridays – and rather more savoury, but grudging, portions of the same flesh, rotten-roasted or rare, on the Tuesdays (the only dish which excited our appetites, and disappointed our stomachs, in almost equal proportion) – he had his hot plate of roast veal, or the more tempting griskin (exotics unknown to our palates), cooked in the paternal kitchen (a great thing), and brought him daily by his maid or aunt! I remember the good old relative (in whom love forbade pride) squatting down upon some odd stone in a by-nook of the cloisters, disclosing the viands (of higher regale than those cates which the ravens ministered to the Tishbite); and the contending passions of L. at the unfolding. There was love for the bringer; shame for the thing brought, and the manner of its bringing; sympathy for those who were too many to share in it; and, at top of all, hunger (eldest, strongest of the passions!) predominant, breaking down the stony fences of shame and awkwardness, and a troubling over-consciousness.

I was a poor friendless boy. My parents, and those who should care for me, were far away. Those few acquaintances of theirs, which they could reckon upon being kind to me in the great city, after a little forced notice, which they had the grace to take of me on my first arrival in town, soon grew tired of my holiday visits. They seemed to them to recur too often, though I thought them few enough; and, one after another, they all failed me, and I felt myself alone among six hundred playmates.

O the cruelty of separating a poor lad from his early homestead!

The yearnings which I used to have towards it in those unfledged years! How, in my dreams, would my native town (far in the west) come back, with its church, and trees, and faces! How I would wake weeping, and in the anguish of my heart exclaim upon sweet Calne in Wiltshire!

To this late hour of my life, I trace impressions left by the recollection of those friendless holidays. The long warm days of summer never return but they bring with them a gloom from the haunting memory of those *whole-day leaves*, when, by some strange arrangement, we were turned out, for the live-long day, upon our own hands, whether we had friends to go to, or none. I remember those bathing-excursions to the New River, which L. recalls with such relish, better, I think, than he can – for he was a home-seeking lad, and did not much care for such water-pastimes: – How merrily we would sally forth into the fields; and strip under the first warmth of the sun; and wanton like young dace in the streams; getting us appetites for noon, which those of us that were penniless (our scanty morning crust long since exhausted) had not the means of allaying – while the cattle, and the birds, and the fishes, were at feed about us, and we had nothing to satisfy our cravings – the very beauty of the day, and the exercise of the pastime, and the sense of liberty, setting a keener edge upon them! – How faint and languid, finally, we would return, towards night-fall, to our desired morsel, half-rejoicing, half-reluctant, that the hours of our uneasy liberty had expired!

It was worse in the days of the winter, to go prowling about the streets objectless – shivering at cold windows of print shops, to extract a little amusement; or haply, as a last resort, in the hopes of a little novelty, to pay a fifty-times repeated visit (where our individual faces should be as well-known to the warden as those of his own charges) to the Lions in the Tower, to whose *levee*, by courtesy immemorial, we had a prescriptive title to admission.

L.'s governor (so we called the patron who presented us to the foundation) lived in a manner under his paternal roof. Any complaint which he had to make was sure of being attended to. This was understood at Christ's, and was an effectual screen to him against the severity of masters, or worse tyranny of the monitors. The oppressions of these young brutes are heart-sickening to call to recollection. I have been called out of my bed, and *waked for the purpose*, in the coldest winter nights – and this not once, but night after night – in my shirt, to receive the discipline of a leathern thong, with eleven other sufferers, because it pleased my callow overseer, when there has been any talking heard after we were gone to bed, to make the six last beds in the dormitory, where the youngest children of us slept, answerable for an offence they neither dared to commit, nor had the power to hinder. The same execrable tyranny drove the younger part of us from the fires, when our feet were perishing with snow; and, under the cruellest penalties, forbade the indulgence of a drink of water, when we lay in sleepless summer nights, fevered with the season and the day's sports.

There was one H[odges], who, I learned in after-days, was seen expiating some maturer offence in the hulks. (Do I flatter myself in fancying that this might be the planter of that name, who suffered – at Nevis, I think, or St Kitts, – some few years since? My friend Tobin was the benevolent instrument of bringing him to the gallows.) This petty Nero actually branded a boy who had offended him with a red-hot iron; and nearly starved forty of us with exacting contributions, to the one-half of our bread, to pamper a young ass, which, incredible as it may seem, with the connivance of the nurse's daughter (a young flame of his) he had contrived to smuggle in, and keep upon the leads of the *ward*, as they called our dormitories. This game went on for better than a week, till the foolish beast, not able to fare well but he must cry roast meat – happier than Caligula's minion, could he have kept his own counsel, but, foolisher alas! than any of his species in the fables – waxing fat, and kicking, in the fulness of bread, one unlucky minute would needs proclaim his good fortune to the world below; and, laying out his simple throat, blew such a ram's horn blast, as (toppling down the walls of his own Jericho) set concealment any longer at defiance. The client was dismissed, with certain attentions, to Smithfield; but I never understood that the patron underwent any censure on the occasion. This was in the stewardship of L.'s admired Perry.

Under the same *facile* administration, can L. have forgotten the cool impunity with which the nurses used to carry away openly, in open platters, for their own tables, one out of two of every hot joint, which the careful matron had been seeing scrupulously weighed out for our dinners? These things were daily practised in that magnificent apartment, which L. (grown connoisseur since, we presume) praises so highly for the grand paintings 'by Verrio and others', with which it is 'hung round and adorned'. But the sight of sleek well-fed blue-coat boys in pictures was, at that time, I believe, little consolatory to him, or us, the living ones, who saw the better part of our provisions carried away before our faces by harpies; and ourselves reduced (with the Trojan in the hall of Dido)

To feed our mind with idle portraiture.

L. has recorded the repugnance of the school to *gags* or the fat of fresh beef boiled; and sets it down to some superstition. But these unctuous morsels are never grateful to young palates (children are universally fat-haters), and in strong, coarse, boiled meats, *unsalted*, are detestable. A *gag-eater* in our time was equivalent to a *goul*, and held in equal detestation. — suffered under the imputation.

– 'Twas said
He ate strange flesh.

He was observed, after dinner, carefully to gather up the remnants left at his table (not many, nor very choice fragments, you may credit me) – and, in an especial manner, these disreputable morsels, which he would convey away, and secretly stow in the settle that stood at his bedside. None saw when he ate them. It was rumoured that he privately devoured them in the night. He was watched, but no traces of such midnight practices were discoverable. Some reported, that, on leave-days, he had been seen to carry out of the bounds a large blue check handkerchief, full of something. This then must be the accursed thing. Conjecture next was at work to imagine how he could dispose of it. Some said he sold it to the beggars. This belief generally prevailed. He went about moping. None spake to him. No one would play with him. He was excommunicated; put out of the pale of the school. He was too powerful a boy to be beaten, but he underwent every mode of that negative punishment which is more grievous than many stripes. Still he persevered. At length he was observed by two of his schoolfellows, who were determined to get at the secret, and had traced him one leave-day for that purpose, to enter a large worn-out building, such as there exist specimens of in Chancery Lane, which are let out to various scales of pauperism, with open door, and a common staircase. After him they silently slunk in, and followed by stealth up four flights, and saw him tap at a poor wicket, which was opened by an aged woman, meanly clad. Suspicion was now ripened into certainty. The informers had secured their victim. They had him in their toils. Accusation was formally preferred, and retribution most signal was looked for. Mr Hathaway, the then steward (for this happened a little after my time), with that patient sagacity which tempered all his conduct, determined to investigate the matter, before he proceeded to sentence. The result was, that the supposed mendicants, the receivers or purchasers of the mysterious scraps, turned out to be the parents of —, an honest couple come to decay, – whom this seasonably supply had, in all probability, saved from mendicancy; and that this young stork, at the expense of his own good name, had all this while been only feeding the old birds! – The governors on this occasion, much to their honour, voted a present relief to the family of —, and presented him with a silver medal. The lesson which the steward read upon RASH JUDGMENT, on the occasion of publicly delivering the medal to —, I believe, would not be lost upon his auditory. – I had left school then, but I well remember —. He was a tall, shambling youth, with a cast in his eye, not at all calculated to conciliate hostile prejudices. I have since seen him carrying a baker's basket. I think I heard he did not do quite so well by himself as he had done by the old folks.

I was a hypochondriac lad; and the sight of a boy in fetters, upon the day of my first putting on the blue clothes, was not exactly fitted to assuage the natural terrors of initiation. I was of tender years, barely turned of seven; and had only read of such things in books, or seen them but in dreams. I was told he had *run away*. This was the punishment for the first offence. – As a novice I was soon after taken to see the dungeons. These were little, square, Bedlam cells, where a boy could just lie at his length upon straw and a blanket – a mattress, I think, was afterwards substituted – with a peep of light, let in askance, from a prison-orifice at top, barely enough to read by. Here the poor boy was locked in by himself all day, without sight of any but the porter who brought him his bread and water – who *might not speak to him;* – or of the beadle, who came twice a week to call him out to receive his periodical chastisement, which was almost welcome, because it separated him for a brief interval from solitude: – and here he was shut up by himself *of nights*, out of the reach of any sound, to suffer whatever horrors the weak nerves, and superstition incident to his time of life, might subject him to. This was the penalty for the second offence. Wouldst thou like, Reader, to see what became of him in the next degree?

The culprit, who had been a third time an offender, and whose expulsion was at this time deemed irreversible, was brought forth, as at some solemn *auto da fé*, arrayed in uncouth and most appalling attire, all trace of his late 'watchet-weeds' carefully effaced, he was exposed in a jacket, resembling those which London lamplighters formerly delighted in, with a cap of the same. The effect of this divestiture was such as the ingenious devisers of it could have anticipated. With his pale and frighted features, it was as if some of those disfigurements in Dante had seized upon him. In this disguisement he was brought into the hall (*L.'s favourite state-room*), where awaited him the whole number of his schoolfellows, whose joint lessons and sports he was thenceforth to share no more; the awful presence of the steward, to be seen for the last time; of the executioner beadle, clad in his state robe for the occasion; and of two faces more, of direr import, because never but in these extremities visible. These were governors; two of whom, by choice, or charter, were always accustomed to officiate at these *Ultima Supplicia*; not to mitigate (so at least we understood it) but to enforce the uttermost stripe. Old Bamber Gascoigne, and Peter Aubert, I remember, were colleagues on one occasion, when, the beadle turning rather pale, a glass of brandy was ordered to prepare him for the mysteries. The scourging was, after the old Roman fashion, long and stately. The lictor accompanied the criminal quite round the hall. We were generally too faint with attending to the previous disgusting circumstances to make accurate report with our eyes of the degree of corporal suffering inflicted. Report, of course, gave out the back knotty and livid. After scourging, he was made over, in his *San Benito*, to his friends, if he had any (but commonly such poor runagates were friendless), or to his parish officer, who, to enhance the effect of the scene, had his station allotted to him on the outside of the hall gate.

These solemn pageantries were not played off so often as to spoil the general mirth of the community. We had plenty of exercise and recreation *after* school hours; and, for myself, I must confess, that I was never happier than *in* them. The Upper and the Lower Grammar Schools were held in the same room; and an imaginary line only divided their bounds. Their character was as different as that of the inhabitants on the two sides of the Pyrenees. The Rev James Boyer was the Upper Master, but the Rev Matthew Field presided over that portion of the apartment of which I had the good fortune to be a member. We lived a life as careless as birds. We talked and did just what we pleased, and nobody molested us. We carried an accidence, or a grammar, for form; but, for any trouble it gave us, we might take two years in getting through the verbs deponent, and another two in forgetting all that we had learned about them. There was now and then the formality of saying a lesson, but if you had not learned it, a brush across the shoulders (just enough to disturb a fly) was the sole remonstrance. Field never used the rod; and in truth he wielded the cane with no great good will – holding it 'like a dancer'. It looked in his hands rather like an emblem than an instrument of authority; and an emblem, too, he was ashamed of. He was a good easy man, that did not care to ruffle his own peace, nor perhaps set any great consideration upon the value of juvenile time. He came among us, now and then, but often stayed away whole days from us; and when he came, it made no difference to us – he had his private room to retire to, the short time he stayed, to be out of the sound of our noise. Our mirth and uproar went on. We had classics of our own, without being beholden to 'insolent Greece or haughty Rome', that passed current among us – Peter Wilkins, the Adventures of the Hon Captain Robert Boyle, the Fortunate Bluecoat Boy, and the like. Or we cultivated a turn for mechanic or scientific operations; making little sun-dials of paper; or weaving those ingenious parentheses, called *cat's-cradles*; or making dry peas to dance upon the end of a tin pipe; or studying the art military over that laudable game 'French and English', and a hundred other such devices to pass away the time – mixing the useful with the agreeable – as would have made the souls of Rousseau and John Locke chuckle to have seen us.

Matthew Field belonged to that class of modest divines who affect to mix in equal proportion the *gentleman*, the *scholar*, and the *Christian*; but, I know not how, the first ingredient is generally found to be the predominating dose in the composition. He was engaged in gay parties, or with his courtly bow at some episcopal *levée*, when he should have been attending upon us. He had for many years the classical charge of a hundred children, during the four or five first years of their education; and his very highest form seldom proceeded further than two or three of the introductory fables of Phædrus. How things were suffered to go on thus, I cannot guess. Boyer, who was the proper person to have remedied these abuses, always affected, perhaps felt, a delicacy in interfering in a province not strictly his own. I have not been without my suspicions, that he was not altogether displeased at the contrast we presented to his end of the school. We were a sort of Helots to his young Spartans. He would sometimes, with ironic deference, send to borrow a rod of the Under Master, and then, with Sardonic grin, observe to one of his upper boys, 'how neat and fresh the twigs looked'. While his pale students were battering their brains over Xenophon and Plato, with a silence as deep as that enjoined by the Samite, we were enjoying ourselves at our ease in our little Goshen. We saw a little into the secrets of his discipline, and the prospect did but the more reconcile us to our lot. His thunders rolled innocuous for us; his storms came near, but never touched us; contrary to Gideon's miracle, while all around were drenched, our fleece was dry. His boys turned out the better scholars; we, I suspect, have the advantage in temper. His pupils cannot speak of him without something of terror allaying their gratitude; the remembrance of Field comes back with all the soothing images of indolence, and summer slumbers, and work like play, and innocent idleness, and Elysian exemptions, and life itself a 'playing holiday'.

Though sufficiently removed from the jurisdiction of Boyer, we were near enough (as I have said) to understand a little of his system. We occasionally heard sounds of the *Ululantes*, and caught glances of Tartarus. B. was a rabid pedant. His English style was crampt to barbarism. His Easter anthems (for his duty obliged him to those periodical flights) were grating as scrannel pipes. He would laugh – ay, and heartily – but then it must be at Flaccus's quibble about *Rex*— or at the *tristis severitas in vultu*, or *inspicere in patinas*, of Terence – thin jests, which at their first broaching could hardly have had *vis* enough to move a Roman muscle. – He had two wigs, both pedantic, but of different omen. The one serene, smiling, fresh powdered, betokening a mild day. The other, an old, discoloured, unkempt, angry caxon, denoting frequent and bloody execution. Woe to the school, when he made his morning appearance in his *passy*, or *passionate wig*. No comet expounded surer. – J.B. had a heavy hand. I have known him double his knotty fist at a poor trembling child (the maternal milk hardly dry upon its lips) with a 'Sirrah, do you presume to set your wits at me?' – Nothing was more common than to see him make a headlong entry into the school-room, from his inner recess, or library, and, with turbulent eye, singling out a lad, roar out, 'Od's my life, Sirrah' (his favourite adjuration), 'I have a great mind to whip you' – then, with as sudden a retracting impulse, fling back into his lair – and, after a cooling lapse of some minutes (during which all but the culprit had totally forgotten the context) drive headlong out again, piecing out his imperfect sense, as if it had been some Devil's Litany, with the expletory yell – '*and I* WILL *too*.' In his gentler moods, when the *rabidus furor* was assuaged, he had resort to an ingenious method, peculiar, for what I have heard, to himself, of whipping the boy, and reading the Debates, at the same time; a paragraph and a lash between; which in those times when parliamentary oratory was most at a height and flourishing in these realms, was not calculated

32

to impress the patient with a veneration for the diffuser graces of rhetoric.

Once, and but once, the uplifted rod was known to fall ineffectual from his hand – when droll squinting W— having been caught putting the inside of the master's desk to a use for which the architect had clearly not designed it, to justify himself, with great simplicity averred, that *he did not know that the thing had been forewarned*. This exquisite irrecognition of any law antecedent to the *oral* or *declaratory*, struck so irresistibly upon the fancy of all who heard it (the pedagogue himself not excepted) that remission was unavoidable.

L. has given credit to B.'s great merits as an instructor. Coleridge, in his literary life, has pronounced a more intelligible and ample encomium on them. The author of the Country Spectator doubts not to compare him with the ablest teachers of antiquity. Perhaps we cannot dismiss him better than with the pious ejaculation of C. – when he heard than his old master was on his death-bed: 'Poor J.B.! – may all his faults be forgiven; and may he be wafted to bliss by little cherub boys, all head and wings, with no *bottoms* to reproach his sublunary infirmities.'

Under him were many good and sound scholars bred. – First Grecian of my time was Lancelot Pepys Stevens, kindest of boys and men, since Co-grammar-master (and inseparable companion) with Dr T[rollop]e. What an edifying spectacle did this brace of friends present to those who remembered the anti-socialities of their predecessors! – You never met the one by chance in the street without a wonder, which was quickly dissipated by the almost immediate subappearance of the other. Generally arm-in-arm, these kindly coadjutors lightened for each other the toilsome duties of their profession, and when, in advanced age, one found it convenient to retire, the other was not long in discovering that it suited him to lay down the fasces also. Oh, it is pleasant, as it is rare, to find the same arm linked in yours at forty, which at thirteen helped it to turn over the *Cicero De Amicitia*, or some tale of Antique Friendship, which the young heart even then was burning to anticipate! Co-Grecian with S. was [Edward] Th[ornton] who has since executed with ability various diplomatic functions at the Northern courts. Th[ornton] was a tall, dark, saturnine youth, sparing of speech, with raven locks. Thomas Fanshaw Middleton followed him (now Bishop of Calcutta), a scholar and a gentleman in his teens. He has the reputation of an excellent critic; and is author (besides the Country Spectator) of a Treatise on the Greek Article, against Sharpe. – M. is said to bear his mitre high in India, where the *regni novitas* (I dare say) sufficiently justifies the bearing. A humility quite as primitive as that of Jewel or Hooker might not be exactly fitted to impress the minds of those Anglo-Asiatic diocesans with a reverence for home institutions, and the church which those fathers watered. The manners of M. at school, though firm, were mild and unassuming. – Next to M. (if not senior to him) was Richards, author of the Aboriginal Britons, the most spirited of the Oxford Prize Poems; a pale, studious Grecian. – Then followed poor S[cott], ill-fated M[aunde]! of these the Muse is silent.

Finding some of Edward's race
Unhappy, pass their annals by.

Come back into memory, like as thou wert in the dayspring of thy fancies, with hope like a fiery column before thee – the dark pillar not yet turned – Samuel Taylor Coleridge, – Logician, Metaphysician, Bard! – How have I seen the casual passer through the Cloisters stand still, intranced with admiration (while he weighed the disproportion between the *speech* and the *garb* of the young Mirandula) to hear thee unfold, in thy deep and sweet intonations, the mysteries of Jamblichus, or Plotinus (for even in those years thou waxedst not pale at such philosophic draughts), or reciting Homer in his Greek, or Pindar – while the walls of the old Grey Friars re-echoed to the accents of the *inspired charity-boy!* – Many were the 'wit-combats' (to dally awhile with the words of old Fuller), between him and C.V. Le G[rice], 'which two I behold like a Spanish great galleon, and an English man-of-war: Master Coleridge, like the former, was built far higher in learning, solid, but slow in his performances. C.V.L., with the English man-of-war, lesser in bulk, but lighter in sailing, could turn with all times, tack about, and take advantage of all winds, by the quickness of his wit and invention.'

Nor shalt thou, their compeer, be quickly forgotten, Allen,

34

with the cordial smile, and still more cordial laugh, with which thou wert wont to make the old Cloisters shake, in thy cognition of some poignant jest of theirs; or the anticipation of some more material, and peradventure practical one, of thine own. Extinct are those smiles, with that beautiful countenance, with which (for thou wert the *Nireus formosus* of the school), in the days of thy maturer waggery, thou didst disarm the wrath of infuriated town-damsel, who, incensed by provoking pinch, turning tigress-round, suddenly converted by thy angel-look, exchanged the half-formed terrible '*bl*—,' for a gentler greeting – '*bless thy hand-some face!*'

Next follow two, who ought to be now alive, and the friends of Elia – the junior Le G[rice] and F[avell]; who impelled, the former by a roving temper, the latter by too quick a sense of neglect – ill capable of enduring the slights poor Sizars are some-times subject to in our seats of learning – exchanged their Alma Mater for the camp; perishing, one by climate, and one on the plains of Salamanca: – Le G[rice], sanguine, volatile, sweet-natured; F[avell], dogged, faithful, anticipative of insult, warm-hearted, with something of the old Roman height about him.

Fine, frank-hearted Fr[anklin], the present master of Hertford, with Marmaduke T[hompson], mildest of Missionaries – and both my good friends still – close the catalogue of Grecians in my time.

The London Magazine, 1820

After leaving school, Lamb worked for a brief period in the office of Joseph Paice 'of Bread Hill ... the only pattern of consistent gallantry I have met with', and then moved to the Examiner's Office of the South-Sea Company, his salary half-a-guinea a week.

He was with the Company for only five months but thirty years later, when he was invited to contribute to the *London Magazine*, it was those five months which gave him the subject for his first essay over the signature Elia. From the South-Sea House he passed on to the East India Company in whose service he spent all the rest of his daytime career.

Such little evidence as there is suggests that as man of business Mr Lamb was more effective than Elia made him out to be, but whether or no 'living accounts and accountants' puzzled him, there was at the South-Sea House and at the East India House much that delighted him. He enjoyed the bustle and the panoply, the throng of clerks, beadles, doorkeepers, the 'directors seated in solemn form on solemn days to proclaim dead dividends'.

And, in those early years, if in the daytime he felt himself condemned to drudgery at an office-desk, the evenings brought ample compensation. He was 'drinking late, sitting late' with 'boon companions' at the Salutation, he was writing poetry and he was in love – with Ann Simmons.

Then, in the last weeks of 1795, for the first time he glimpsed the 'strange face of calamity'. He suffered what in all probability would now be described as a temporary loss of mental stability but was then diagnosed as lunacy. There is no substantial evidence as to the manner of this breakdown beyond Lamb's own letter to Coleridge (27 May 1796, the earliest of his letters still extant) and it could be no more than a coincidence and a romanticism that it followed hard upon the enforced ending of his courtship of Ann but, whatever the cause and whatever the symptoms, this one brief but unforgettable experience haunted him for the rest of his life, and all the more so because of the hideous events of September 1796.

Previously Mary Lamb had suffered occasional episodes of instability. Through all the years of her adolescence and early womanhood she had also been much irritated by her mother. During the evening of 21 September Charles noticed in Mary signs of returning mania. Next morning he sent for the family doctor but failed to get him. He went off to work, troubled in his mind but not unduly so; Mary's earlier bouts had always responded to care and medication. That afternoon, for reasons that would not have excited an entirely sane person, Mary exploded into a frenetic torrent of abuse over the

Lamb's servant-girl. Elizabeth Lamb, it seems, protested. Mary seized a knife and stabbed her mother in the heart.

The consequences for Charles Lamb were, both immediately and in the long term, seismic.

Immediately, he determined to break with his past. Henceforth he would keep nothing that reminded him of the happy days before Mary's act of matricide. (It is, however, significant of the uniqueness of the friendship between him and Coleridge that when, as symbolic gesture, he burnt the correspondence he had received, he rescued from the flames Coleridge's letter of sympathy and, lest it be sacrificed to some future outburst, gave it to a friend for safe-keeping.) As if to demonstrate that his muse had been shattered by the events of that September day, he also pledged himself never again to write verse; a vow which, principally through Coleridge's persuasion, he did not honour for very long. And, for all the thirty-eight years that were still allowed to him, that one awful day held him away from much in life which hitherto he had good reason to expect and which, as all the evidence shows, he had previously intended. He determined never to marry (and made but one unsuccessful attempt to break with this determination). He would dedicate himself to the care of his sister.

To S.T. Coleridge

27th September, 1796

MY DEAREST FRIEND,

White or some of my friends or the public papers by this time may have informed you of the terrible calamities that have fallen on our family. I will only give you the outlines. My poor dear dearest sister in a fit of insanity has been the death of her own mother. I was at hand only time enough to snatch the knife out of her grasp. She is at present in a madhouse, from whence I fear she must be moved to an hospital. God has preserved to me my senses – I eat and drink and sleep, and have my judgment I believe very sound. My poor father was slightly wounded, and I am left to take care of him and my aunt. Mr Norris of the Bluecoat School has been very kind to us, and we have no other friend, but thank God I am very calm and composed, and able to do the best that remains to do. Write, as religious a letter as possible but no mention of what is gone and done with – with me the former things are passed away, and I have something more to do than to feel –

God Almighty have us all in his keeping.

C. LAMB.

To S.T. Coleridge

Monday, May 12th, 1800

My dear Coleridge,

I don't know why I write, except from the propensity misery has to tell her griefs. Hetty died on Friday night, about eleven o'clock, after eight days' illness; Mary, in consequence of fatigue and anxiety, is fallen ill again, and I was obliged to remove her yesterday. I am left alone in a house with nothing but Hetty's dead body to keep me company. Tomorrow I bury her, and then I shall be quite alone, with nothing but a cat to remind me that the house has been full of living beings like myself. My heart is quite sunk, and I don't know where to look for relief. Mary will get better again; but her constantly being liable to such relapses is dreadful, nor is it the least of our evils that her case and all our story is so well known around us. We are in a manner *marked*. Excuse my troubling you; but I have nobody by me to speak to me. I slept out last night, not being able to endure the change and the stillness. But I did not sleep well, and I must come back to my own bed. I am going to try and get a friend to come and be with me tomorrow. I am completely shipwrecked. My head is quite bad. I almost wish that Mary were dead. – God bless you! Love to Sara and Hartley.

C. LAMB.

Already in his school-days Lamb was convinced that he was deter-mined to be a writer and in the years which followed immediately upon his leaving Christ's Hospital his determination to fulfil his destiny was bolstered by association with many other young men who shared his literary aspirations, but he did not immediately discover his proper *métier* and his first efforts added little to his fame and almost nothing to his fortune.

Some of his verses appeared with Coleridge's in collections pub-lished in 1796 and 1797 and his novel, *Rosamund Grey*, in the summer of 1798. Later Shelley wrote 'What a lovely thing is his *Rosamund Grey*. How much knowledge of the sweetest and deepest parts of our nature in it!', but immediately the notices were few and, such as there were, most of them cool or even dismissive.

Lamb needed an audience and even more he needed money so he turned to journalism, the trade which is so often the refuge of impecunious and unrecognised aspirants to literature. There was in Lamb the debutant paragraph-spinner and lampooner none of that mildness of spirit already recognised by his schoolfellows and his more-intimate acquaintances. Gentleness, the quality which above all others was to be attributed to him not only in his lifetime but throughout succeeding centuries, was seldom evident in his early contributions to newspapers and journals. His opinions were unqualified, his prejudices many and he wrote with a pen dipped in vitriol. This was no way to ease himself towards a successful journalistic career; much of what he wrote was meat too strong for the editors of the popular prints and he was rewarded with more rejection than acceptance.

One editor, John Fenwick of *The Albion* (Bigod of the *Elia* essay, 'The Two Races of Men'), was bolder than his peers. He printed the earliest of Lamb's most scabrous epigrams, the last, in August 1801, an assault on James Mackintosh:

> When he had gotten his ill-purchased pelf,
> He went away, and wisely hanged himself:
> This thou may'st do at last; yet much I doubt,
> If thou hast any bowels to gush out!

In that same month, August 1801, perhaps not surprisingly, Fen-wick was forced to close down *The Albion*. Lamb turned his attention to *The Morning Chronicle* where, according to Southey, 'more than two-thirds of his materials are superciliously rejected', and then to *The Morning Post*, a paper which found a place for contributions from Coleridge.

Lamb's association with the *Post* was at first little happier than the association with the *Chronicle*. One essay, 'The Londoner', was accepted for publication in February 1802, and the Editor, Daniel Stuart, somewhat grudgingly allowed Lamb to contribute occasional dramatic criticism and a few 'fillers' at 'sixpence a joke'. But Stuart and Lamb were constitutionally antipathetic (after Lamb's death Stuart wrote 'As for poor Charles Lamb, I never could make anything of him'). Stuart was not interested in Lamb's literary criticism and he would have none of a significant development in Lamb's writing, rejecting all those contributions 'that are personal, where my forte lies'.

For some time Lamb had been prospecting a different field of literary endeavour. In 1798 he had begun work on the play which was eventually called *John Woodvil* and when it was finished he had it read by several friends and was justified in this hope that through Kemble's influence it would be staged at Drury Lane. Half-promises were not made whole and when the managers of *The Morning Post* refused to give any support to its publication, Lamb severed his tenuous connection with the paper, and himself paid to have the book printed. But when, in September 1803, the *Post* changed hands and Stuart ceased to be Editor, Lamb renewed the connection with the paper as 'its chief jester' and as such continued to contribute regularly for a year.

Even at the time, Lamb had no high opinion of his contributions to *The Morning Chronicle* and *The Morning Post*. Many were no more than vehicles for contrived puns. His epigrams were clever but, as most of them were political and directed at ephemeral targets whose offences, like their names, were soon forgotten, added little to his reputation. One only, his four-line assault on Canning and Frere, the pillars of the *Anti-Jacobin*, has retained some currency among students of early nineteenth-century politics:

> At Eton School brought up with dull boys,
> We shone like men among the school-boys;
> But since we in the world have been,
> We are but school-boys among men.

When Lamb came to tell the story of his years as a hack as was his habit he was free with chronology and fact; it was in truth thirty and not thirty-five years since he had been, tenuously, a newspaperman and he had not moved from *The Morning Post* to *The Albion*; but Lamb never troubled himself with such trifles. His rare genius as chronicler was revealed by his capacity to represent the atmosphere of a period, and by his ability to re-present himself as he had been at the time of which he was writing. The mores of the Press in the first years of the century are more evident in 'Newspapers Thirty-Five Years Ago' than they are in any scholarly history.

More vivid than all else is the self-portrait drawn from memory of a young writer who had not yet discovered an outlet appropriate to his literary skills and who could not gather in the money he needed even by demeaning his talents, the portrait of a frustrated genius.

In 1804 when, as it then seemed for all time, Lamb's career as a free-lance journalist came to an end, his sister Mary wrote perspicaciously: 'What we dreaded as an evil has proved a great blessing, for we have both strangely recovered our health and spirits since this has happened'.

Newspapers Thirty-Five Years Ago

Dan Stuart once told us, that he did not remember that he ever deliberately walked into the Exhibition at Somerset House in his life. He might occasionally have escorted a party of ladies across the way that were going in; but he never went in of his own head. Yet the office of the *Morning Post* newspaper stood then just where it does now – we are carrying you back, Reader, some thirty years or more – with its gilt-globe-topt front facing that emporium of our artists' grand Annual Exposure. We sometimes wish, that we had observed the same abstinence with Daniel.

A word or two of D.S. He ever appeared to us one of the finest tempered of Editors. Perry, of the *Morning Chronicle*, was equally pleasant, with a dash, no slight one either, of the courtier. S. was frank, plain, and English all over. We have worked for both these gentlemen.

It is soothing to contemplate the head of the Ganges; to trace the first little bubblings of a mighty river;

> With holy reverence to approach the rocks,
> Whence glide the streams renowned in ancient song.

Fired with a perusal of the Abyssinian Pilgrim's exploratory ramblings after the cradle of the infant Nilus, we well remember on one fine summer holyday (a 'whole day's leave' we called it at Christ's Hospital) sallying forth at rise of sun, not very well provisioned either for such an undertaking, to trace the current of the New River – Middletonian stream! – to its scaturient source, as we had read, in meadows by fair Amwell. Gallantly did we commence our solitary quest – for it was essential to the dignity of a DISCOVERY, that no eye of schoolboy, save our own, should beam on the detection. By flowery spots, and verdant lanes, skirting Hornsey, Hope trained us on in many a baffling turn; endless, hopeless meanders, as it seemed; or as if the jealous waters had *dodged* us, reluctant to have the humble spot of their nativity revealed; till spent, and nigh famished, before set of the same sun, we sate down somewhere by Bowes Farm, near Tottenham, with a tithe of our proposed labours only yet accomplished; sorely convinced in spirit, that the Brucian enterprise was as yet too arduous for our young shoulders.

Not more refreshing to the thirsty curiosity of the traveller is the tracing of some mighty waters up to their shallow fontlet, than it is to a pleased and candid reader to go back to the inexperienced essays, the first callow flights in authorship, of some established name in literature; from the Gnat which preluded to the *Æneid*, to the Duck which Samuel Johnson trod on.

In those days every Morning Paper, as an essential retainer to its establishment, kept an author, who was bound to furnish daily a quantum of witty paragraphs. Sixpence a joke – and it was thought pretty high too – was Dan Stuart's settled remuneration in these cases. The chat of the day, scandal, but, above all, *dress*, furnished the material. The length of no paragraph was to exceed seven lines. Shorter they might be, but they must be poignant.

A fashion of *flesh*, or rather *pink*-coloured hose for the ladies, luckily coming up at the juncture, when we were on our probation for the place of Chief Jester to S.'s Paper, established our reputation in that line. We were pronounced a 'capital hand'. O the conceits which we varied upon *red* in all its prismatic differences! from the trite and obvious flower of Cytherea, to the flaming costume of the lady that has her sitting upon 'many waters'. Then there was the collateral topic of ankles. What an occasion to a truly chaste writer, like ourself, of touching that nice brink, and yet never tumbling over it, of a seemingly ever approximating something 'not quite proper'; while, like a skilful posture-master, balancing betwixt decorums and their opposites, he keeps the line, from which a hair's-breadth deviation is destruction; hovering in the confines of light and darkness, or where 'both seem either'; a hazy uncertain delicacy; Autolycus-like in the Play, still putting off his expectant auditory with 'Whoop, do me no harm, good man!' But, above all, that conceit arrided us most at that time, and still tickles our midriff to remember, where, allusively to the flight of Astræa – *ultima Cœlestûm terras reliquit* – we pronounced – in reference to the stockings still – that MODESTY TAKING HER FINAL LEAVE OF MORTALS, HER LAST BLUSH WAS VISIBLE IN HER ASCENT TO THE HEAVENS BY THE TRACT OF THE GLOWING INSTEP. This might be called the crowning conceit; and was esteemed tolerable writing in those days.

But the fashion of jokes, with all other things, passes away; as did the transient mode which had so favoured us. The ankles of our fair friends in a few weeks began to re-assume their whiteness, and left us scarce a leg to stand upon. Other female whims followed, but none, methought, so pregnant, so invitatory of shrewd conceits, and more than single meanings.

Somebody has said, that to swallow six cross-buns daily consecutively for a fortnight would surfeit the stoutest digestion. But to have to furnish as many jokes daily, and that not for a fortnight, but for a long twelvemonth, as we were constrained to do, was a little harder execution. 'Man goeth forth to his work until the evening' – from a reasonable hour in the morning, we presume it was meant. Now as our main occupation took us up from eight till five every day in the City; and as our evening hours, at that time of life, had generally to do with any thing rather than business, it follows, that the only time we could spare for this manufactory of jokes – our supplementary livelihood, that supplied us in every want beyond mere bread and cheese – was exactly that part of the day which (as we have heard of No Man's Land) may be fitly denominated No Man's Time; that is, no time in which a man ought to be up, and awake, in. To speak more plainly, it is that time, of an hour, or an hour and a half's duration, in which a man, whose occasions call him up so preposterously, has to wait for his breakfast.

O those headaches at dawn of day, when at five, or half-past-five in summer, and not much later in the dark seasons, we were compelled to rise, having been perhaps not above four hours in bed – (for we were no go-to-beds with the lamb, though we anticipated the lark ofttimes in her rising – we liked a parting cup at midnight, as all young men did before these effeminate times, and to have our friends about us – we were not constellated under Aquarius, that watery sign, and therefore incapable of Bacchus, cold, washy, bloodless – we were none of your Basilian water-sponges, nor had taken our degrees at Mount Ague – we were right toping Capulets, jolly companions, we and they) – but to have to get up, as we said before, curtailed of half our fair sleep, fasting, with only a dim vista of refreshing Bohea in the distance – to be necessitated to rouse ourselves at the detestable rap of an old hag of a domestic, who seemed to take a diabolical pleasure in her announcement that it was 'time to rise'; and whose chappy knuckles we have often yearned to amputate, and string them up at our chamber door, to be a terror to all such unseasonable rest-breakers in future –

'Facil' and sweet, as Virgil sings, had been the 'descending' of the over-night, balmy the first sinking of the heavy head upon the pillow; but to get up, as he goes on to say,

– revocare gradus, superasque evadere ad auras –

and to get up moreover to make jokes with malice prepended – there was the 'labour', there the 'work'.

No Egyptian taskmaster ever devised a slavery like to that, our slavery. No fractious operants ever turned out for half the tyranny, which this necessity exercised upon us. Half a dozen jests in a day (bating Sundays too), why, it seems nothing! We make twice the number every day in our lives as a matter of course, and claim no Sabbatical exemptions. But then they come into our head. But when the head has to go out to them – when the mountain must go to Mahomet –

Reader, try it for once, only for one short twelvemonth.

It was not every week that a fashion of pink stockings came up; but mostly, instead of it, some rugged, untractable subject; some topic impossible to be contorted into the risible; some feature, upon which no smile could play; some flint, from which no process

44

of ingenuity could procure a distillation. There they lay; there your appointed tale of brick-making was set before you, which you must finish, with or without straw, as it happened. The craving Dragon – *the Public* – like him in Bel's temple – must be fed; it expected its daily rations; and Daniel, and ourselves, to do us justice, did the best we could on this side bursting him.

While we were wringing our coy sprightlinesses for the Post, and writhing under the toil of what is called 'easy writing', Bob Allen, our *quondam* schoolfellow, was tapping his impracticable brains in a like service for the 'Oracle'. Not that Robert troubled himself much about wit. If his paragraphs had a sprightly air about them, it was sufficient. He carried this nonchalance so far at last, that a matter of intelligence, and that no very important one, was not seldom palmed upon his employers for a good jest; for example sake – *'Walking yesterday morning casually down Snow Hill, and who should we meet but Mr Deputy Humphreys! we rejoice to add, that the worthy Deputy appeared to enjoy a good state of health. We do not remember ever to have seen him look better.'* This gentleman, so surprisingly met upon Snow Hill, from some peculiarities in gait or gesture, was a constant butt for mirth to the small paragraph-mongers of the day; and our friend thought that he might have his fling at him with the rest. We met A. in Holborn shortly after this extraordinary rencounter, which he told with tears of satisfaction in his eyes, and chuckling at the anticipated effects of its announcement where the wit of it lay at the time; nor was it easy to be detected, when the thing came out, advantaged by type and letter-press. He had better have met any thing that morning than a Common Council Man. His services were shortly after dispensed with, on the plea that his paragraphs of late had been deficient in point. The one in question, it must be owned, had an air, in the opening especially, proper to awaken curiosity; and the sentiment, or moral, wears the aspect of humanity, and good neighbourly feeling. But somehow the conclusion was not judged altogether to answer to the magnificent promise of the premises. We traced our friend's pen afterwards in the 'True Briton', the 'Star', the 'Traveller', – from all which he was successively dismissed, the Proprietors having 'no further occasion for his services'. Nothing was easier than to detect him. When wit failed, or topics

ran low, there constantly appeared the following – '*It is not generally known that the three Blue Balls at the Pawnbrokers' shops are the
ancient arms of Lombardy. The Lombards were the first money-brokers
in Europe.*' Bob has done more to set the public right on this
important point of blazonry, than the whole College of Heralds.

The appointment of a regular wit has long ceased to be a part
of the economy of a Morning Paper. Editors find their own jokes,
or do as well without them. Parson Este, and Topham, brought
up the set custom of 'witty paragraphs', first in the 'World'.
Boaden was a reigning paragraphist in his day, and succeeded
poor Allen in the Oracle. But, as we said, the fashion of jokes
passes away; and it would be difficult to discover in the Biographer of Mrs Siddons, any traces of that vivacity and fancy
which charmed the whole town at the commencement of the
present century. Even the prelusive delicacies of the present writer – the curt 'Astræan allusion' – would be thought pedantic,
and out of date, in these days.

From the office of the *Morning Post* (for we may as well exhaust
our Newspaper Reminiscences at once) by change of property in
the paper, we were transferred, mortifying exchange! to the office
of the *Albion* Newspaper, late Rackstrow's Museum, in Fleet-
street. What a transition – from a handsome apartment, from
rose-wood desks, and silver-inkstands, to an office – no office,
but a *den* rather, but just redeemed from the occupation of dead
monsters, of which it seemed redolent – from the centre of loyalty
and fashion, to a focus of vulgarity and sedition! Here in murky
closet, inadequate from its square contents to the receipt of the
two bodies of Editor, and humble paragraph-maker, together at
one time, sat in the discharge of his new Editorial functions (the
'Bigod' of Elia) the redoubted John Fenwick.

F., without a guinea in his pocket, and having left not many in
the pockets of his friends whom he might command, had purchased
(on tick doubtless) the whole and sole Editorship, Proprietorship,
with all the rights and titles (such as they were worth) of the *Albion*,
from one Lovell; of whom we know nothing, save that he had
stood in the pillory for a libel on the Prince of Wales. With this
hopeless concern – for it had been sinking ever since its commencement, and could now reckon upon not more than a hundred

subscribers – F. resolutely determined upon pulling down the Government in the first instance, and making both our fortunes by way of corollary. For seven weeks and more did this infatuated Democrat go about borrowing seven shilling pieces, and lesser coin, to meet the daily demands of the Stamp Office, which allowed no credit to publications of that side in politics. An outcast from politer bread, we attached our small talents to the forlorn fortunes of our friend. Our occupation now was to write treason.

Recollections of feelings – which were all that now remained from our first boyish heats kindled by the French Revolution, when if we were misled, we erred in the company of some, who are accounted very good men now – rather than any tendency at this time to Republican doctrines – assisted us in assuming a style of writing, while the paper lasted, consonant in no very under-tone to the right earnest fanaticism of F. Our cue was now to insinuate, rather than recommend, possible abdications. Blocks, axes, Whitehall tribunals, were covered with flowers of so cunning a periphrasis – as Mr Bayes says, never naming the *thing* directly – that the keen eye of an Attorney General was insufficient to detect the lurking snake among them. There were times, indeed, when we sighed for our more gentlemanlike occupation under Stuart. But with change of masters it is ever change of service. Already one paragraph, and another, as we learned afterwards from a gentleman at the Treasury, had begun to be marked at that office, with a view of its being submitted at least to the attention of the proper Law Officers – when an unlucky, or rather lucky epigram from our pen, aimed at Sir J[ame]s M[ackintos]h, who was on the eve of departing for India to reap the fruits of his apostacy, as F. pronounced it, (it is hardly worth particularising), happening to offend the nice sense of Lord, or, as he then delighted to be called, Citizen Stanhope, deprived F. at once of the last hopes of a guinea from the last patron that had stuck by us; and breaking up our establishment, left us to the safe, but somewhat mortifying, neglect of the Crown Lawyers. – It was about this time, or a little earlier, that Dan. Stuart made that curious confession to us, that he had 'never deliberately walked into an Exhibition at Somerset House in his life.'

The Englishman's Magazine, 1831

Still in the years that followed immediately upon the end of his association with *The Morning Post* Lamb was groping for a way to his literary destiny. *John Woodvil* had not been staged and in book form had lost him more money than he had spare, yet again he tried his hand as dramatist.

Mr H, his too-clever farce, was accepted for Drury Lane in 1806, shown for one night to a well-papered house and then died ignominiously, its author dancing in its funeral procession. (See the *Elia* essay 'On the Custom of Hissing at the Theatres', p.224.) The damning of *Mr H* spelt the waste of two years' work, a year of hope, and three hundred pounds.

In that same year, 1806, Mary Lamb began work on *Tales from Shakespear*. The book was intended by Mary as her supplement to the small addition she made to their undoubtedly meagre family budget by her work as needlewoman, and was envisaged by Charles as a means of turning her away from the horrors which so often filled her mind. Charles admitted that he was responsible for six of the Tales (all tragedies), 'for occasional tail-pieces or correcting of grammar, for none of the cuts and all the spelling', but it was not in the fullest sense a collaborative effort and though he must have been delighted could he have known that his forecast that 'it will be popular among the little people' was to prove amply justified; *Tales from Shakespear* retained its status as a children's classic for more than a century; he might have been less gratified had he known that long after both he and his sister died this one book, slight and some would say insignificant in its achievement, would hold his fame more securely than anything else he had written, except perhaps the *Elia* essays.

The immediate, if modest, success of *Tales from Shakespear* encouraged Mary to attempt another book for young readers. (*Mrs Leicester's School* was even more truly her book than its predecessor; Charles wrote only three of its ten stories.) It also spurred the two of them to write the verses which when collected were published as *Poetry for Children*, and it persuaded Charles to prepare – this time by himself – what was in essence a sequel to the *Tales*.

The Adventures of Ulysses was published early in 1808. It did not enjoy then, nor has it ever achieved, popularity equivalent to that of *Tales from Shakespear* and such interest as can still spring from the work springs not from its intrinsic quality, but from what it reveals of the direction that Lamb's mind was taking at the time when it was written. He did not base his re-telling of the story on the translation by Pope, though that was the version most popular with his contemporaries. Instead, he went back to a much older translation, the work of a dramatist contemporary of Shakespeare, George Chapman. And, later in that same year, 1805, Longman began to publish (in parts) *Specimens of English Dramatic Poets Who Lived About the Time of Shakespeare*, the book which, knowingly or unknowingly, he had been preparing himself to produce since his school-days.

His knowledge was vast of the dramatic literature of the late sixteenth and early seventeenth centuries – 'within which time nearly all that we have of excellence in serious dramatic composition was produced'. His selection was shrewd; he fulfilled his purpose, to represent those plays 'which treat of human life and manners, rather than masques and Arcadian pastorals', to illustrate 'that which is more nearly allied to poetry than to wit, and to tragic rather than to comic poetry'. But *Specimens* was much more than a cunning and, by the conventional standards of the age, an original anthology. Preface and Notes proved Lamb to be a subtle and original critic. Preface, Notes and selection together made one persuasive and intellectually unified argument. The *Specimens* pioneered a seismic amendment to what had for long been the popular perception of Britain's heritage in dramatic literature.

Lamb did not challenge the supremacy of Shakespeare in the affections of his countrymen. Indeed for him Shakespeare was superhuman – 'how much Shakespeare shines in the great men his contemporaries, and how far in his divine mind and manners he surpasses them and all mankind' – but the novelty in Lamb's thesis was that he recognised and elucidated the greatness of those others, Shakespeare's coevals, and not just 'Fletcher and Massinger, in the estimation of the world the only dramatic poets of that age who are entitled to be considered after Shakespeare', but also 'old Marlow, Heywood, Webster, Ford and others'.

It would be hyperbolic to pretend that *Specimens* made Lamb famous; literary criticism, however original, however influential and however elegant does not excite public acclaim; but the book did establish his reputation with the *cognoscenti*. Hitherto even his closest friends had looked upon Lamb as a writer whose promise far outstripped his achievement, and, outside his own circle, sophisticated observers regarded him as, at best, a competent occasional versifier who had also produced one or two interesting essays. Most of his contributions to *The Albion*, *The Mercury Chronicle* and *The Morning Post* had been either anonymous or pseudonymous and so if he was known at all to the reading-public at large it was as the author of books for children. Henceforth his was a name of consequence in the literary world.

With *Specimens* as his justification he had the right to claim (as he did twenty years after the book's publication) that he 'was the first to draw the Public's attention to the old English Dramatists'.

But still Lamb was shackled to his desk at the East India House, his most compelling need not public fame or literary reputation but financial security, for himself and for Mary. He was a journeyman and never too proud to take on any task that might help him to 'rattle his pocket at the foul fiend', even he agreed to write puffs for the London Lottery, an institution which he had known well in his school-days for Christ's Hospital boys drew the winning-numbers.

Lamb was seldom free of the fear that some calamity – the most likely a recurrence of his sister's illness even more serious than those to which he was accustomed – would so strain his financial resources as to make it impossible for him to find the money with which to pay the bills for Mary's care, for their household, and for the luxuries which he regarded as essentials: tobacco, drink, books and conviviality. But in 1810 at last Lamb found an editor capable of appreciating writings of the kind that *The Morning Chronicle* and *The Morning Post* had consistently rejected. By accepting for publication in his short-lived *Reflector* several intensely personal essays by Lamb, Leigh Hunt allowed to their author a substantial measure of literary confidence and by so doing he heralded the birth of Elia.

Leigh Hunt, like Lamb, was one of that remarkable group whose talents had been fostered in James Boyer's Christ's Hospital. He had entered Christ's Hospital after Lamb had left but he had known him since the days when Lamb was in the habit of visiting his old school on his way to the neighbouring Salutation Inn. Though they were friendly one with the other, they were never so close as Lamb to Coleridge, or Leigh Hunt himself to his school-contemporary Thomas Barnes, but Leigh Hunt merits a place of honour in the chronicle of Lamb's advance towards immortality – as in the stories of Keats and Shelley – not by virtue of the amity between them but is his by reason of his rare editorial percipience and editorial courage.

None of Leigh Hunt's journals survived for very long but he never allowed disappointment, frustration, or even persecution to still his determination to produce a periodical which would serve as vehicle for liberal ideas and for writing not inhibited by the conventions of the time. Whether in the *Reflector, The Examiner* or *The Indicator* he always found space for contributions from Lamb – personal or critical essays, epigrams, verses – and through the long and often unhappy years that were left to him after all his true contemporaries – Lamb, Shelley, Keats, Wordsworth, Byron – had died, still Leigh Hunt remained steadfast and vocal in his advocacy of Lamb's genius.

In 1818 Lamb demonstrated to the world his confidence – or, as some of his contemporaries suggested, his arrogance – by collecting his previously-published writings into two volumes grandiloquently if accurately entitled *The Works of Charles Lamb*. Two years later the publishing-house Baldwin and Cradock established *The London Magazine* to combat the conservatism of *Blackwood's*. A home was ready for Elia.

John Scott, the first Editor of *The London Magazine*, demonstrated his good taste and editorial shrewdness by immediately looking for contributions to Hazlitt and to Lamb (now wearing Elia's transparent mask) but Scott's temper was fiery and his resentment so intense at the gibes by their Edinburgh rivals that he allowed himself to be dragged into a quarrel with the *Blackwood's* entourage. The consequence was more sinister than an exchange of verbal insults: he achieved the dubious and tragic distinction of dying from wounds suffered in a duel.

The magazine was transferred to Taylor and Hessey, Keats's publisher, and was edited by John Taylor himself. Taylor was an indecisive editor and he favoured pedantic contributions that were not likely to win for the journal a wide circulation. Even so, he persevered with some of those enlisted by Scott, among them both Hazlitt and Lamb, and so it was that in the five years of its existence *The London Magazine* contrived a roll-call of distinction rarely, if ever, surpassed in literary history: Hazlitt, Hood, Lamb, De Quincey, Cary, Clare, Miss Mitford and even, with some posthumously published poems, Keats. In his five years with the *London Magazine* Lamb produced many of his best-known and most-loved essays.

Lamb wrote a great deal about himself but very little about his work as essayist. But at the end of 1822, being perhaps temporarily bored with his creation but more likely because to that moment Elia had earned only £170 for Charles Lamb, he put him to death, and wrote for him an obituary-notice ('A Character of the Late Elia') which was printed in *The London Magazine* in January 1823.

But Elia would not stay quietly in his grave. Within months of his death at the hands of Lamb his Ghost was active in the pages of the *London Magazine* and so he continued until Taylor and Hessey sold the journal in 1825, and then at last Elia was silenced.

A Character of the Late Elia

By a Friend

This gentleman, who for some months past had been in a declining way, hath at length paid his final tribute to Nature. He just lived long enough (it was what he wished) to see his papers collected into a volume. The pages of the *London Magazine* will henceforth know him no more.

Exactly at twelve last night his queer spirit departed, and the bells of Saint Bride's rang him out with the old year. The mournful vibrations were caught in the dining-room of his friends, T[aylor] and H[essey], and the company, assembled there to welcome in another first of January, checked their carousals in mid-mirth and were silent. Janus wept. The gentle P[ratt], in a whisper, signified his intention of devoting an elegy; and Allan C[unnngham], nobly forgetful of his countrymen's wrongs, vowed a memoir to his manes full and friendly as a 'Tale of Lyddalcross'.

To say truth, it is time he were gone. The humour of the thing, if there was ever much in it, was pretty well exhausted; and a two years and a half's existence has been a tolerable duration for a phantom.

I am now at liberty to confess that much which I have heard objected to my late friend's writings was well founded. Crude they are, I grant you, a sort of unlicked, incondite things, villainously pranked in an affected array of antique modes and phrases. They had not been *his* if they had been other than such, and better it is that a writer should be natural in a self-pleasing quaintness than to affect a naturalness (so called) that should be strange to him. Egotistical they have been pronounced by some who did not know that what he tells us of himself was often true only (historically) of another, as in his third essay (to save many instances), where, under the *first person* (his favourite figure), he shadows forth the forlorn estate of a country boy placed at a London school, far from his friends and connections, in direct opposition to his own early history. If it be egotism to imply and twine with his own identity the griefs and affections of another, making himself many, or reducing, many unto himself, then is the skilful novelist, who all along brings his hero or heroine speaking of themselves, the greatest egoist of all, who yet has never, therefore been accused of that narrowness. And how shall the intenser dramatist escape being faulty, who doubtless, under cover of passion uttered by another, oftentimes gives blameless vent to his most inward feelings, and expresses his own story modestly?

My late friend was in many respects a singular character. Those who did not like him hated him, and some, who once liked him, afterwards became his bitterest haters. The truth is, he gave himself too little concern about what he uttered, and in whose presence. He observed neither time nor place, and would ever out with what came uppermost. With the severe religionist he would pass for a free-thinker, while the other faction set him down for a bigot, or persuaded themselves that he belied his sentiments. Few understood him, and I am not certain that at all times he quite understood himself. He too much affected that dangerous figure – irony. He sowed doubtful speeches and reaped plain, unequivocal hatred. He would interrupt the gravest discussion with some light jest, and yet, perhaps, not quite irrelevant in ears that could understand it. Your long and much talkers hated him. The informal habits of his mind, joined to an inveterate impediment of speech, forbade him to be an orator, and he seemed determined that no one else should play that part when he was present. He was *petit* and ordinary in his person and appearance. I have seen him sometimes in what is called good company, but where he has been a stranger, sit silent, and be suspected for an odd fellow, till, some unlucky occasion provoking it, he would stutter out some senseless pun (not altogether senseless, perhaps, if rightly taken), which has stamped his character for the evening. It was hit or miss with him, but, nine times out of ten, he contrived by his device to send away a whole company of his enemies. His conceptions rose kindlier than his utterance, and his happiest impromptus had the appearance of effort. He has been accused of trying to be witty, when in truth he was but struggling to give his poor thoughts articulation. He chose his companions for some individuality of character which they manifested. Hence not many persons of science, and few

53

professed *literati*, were of his counsels. They were, for the most part, persons of an uncertain fortune, and as to such people commonly nothing is more obnoxious than a gentleman of settled (though moderate) income, he passed with most of them for a great miser. To my knowledge this was a mistake. His *intimados*, to confess a truth, were, in the world's eye, a ragged regiment. He found them floating on the surface of society, and the colour, or something else in the weed, pleased him. The burrs stuck to him, but they were good and loving burrs for all that. He never greatly cared for the society of what are called good people. If any of these were scandalised (and offences were sure to arise), he could not help it. When he had been remonstrated with for not making more concessions to the feelings of good people, he would retort by asking, what one point did these good people ever concede to him? He was temperate in his meals and diversions, but always kept a little on this side of abstemiousness. Only in the use of the Indian weed he might be thought a little excessive. He took it, he would say, as a solvent of speech. Marry! as the friendly vapour ascended, how his prattle would curl up sometimes with it! The ligaments which tongue-tied him were loosened, and the stammerer proceeded a statist!

I do not know whether I ought to bemoan or rejoice that my old friend is departed. His jests were beginning to grow obsolete and his stories to be found out. He felt the approach of age, and, while he pretended to cling to life, you saw how slender were the ties left to bind him. Discoursing with him latterly on this subject, he expressed himself with a pettishness which I thought unworthy of him. In our walks about his suburban retreat (as he called it) at Shacklewell, some children belonging to a school of industry had met us, and bowed and courtesied, as he thought, in an especial manner to *him*. 'They take me for a visiting governor,' he muttered earnestly. He had a horror, which he carried to a foible, of looking like anything important and parochial. He thought that he approached nearer to that stamp daily. He had a general aversion from being treated like a grave or respectable character, and kept a wary eye upon the advances of age that should so entitle him. He herded always, while it was possible, with people younger than himself. He did not conform to the march of time, but was dragged along in the procession. His manners lagged behind his years. He was too much of the boy-man. The *toga virilis* never sat gracefully on his shoulders. The impressions of infancy had burnt into him, and he resented the impertinence of manhood. These were weaknesses; but, such as they were, they are a key to explicate some of his writings.

He left little property behind him. Of course, the little that is left (chiefly in India bonds) devolves upon his cousin Bridget. A few critical dissertations were found in his *escritoire*, which have been handed over to the editor of this magazine, in which it is to be hoped they will shortly appear, retaining his accustomed signature.

He has himself not obscurely hinted that his employment lay in a public office. The gentlemen in the export department of the East India House will forgive me if I acknowledge the readiness with which they assisted me in the retrieval of his few manuscripts. They pointed out in the most obliging manner the desk at which he had been planted for forty years, showed me ponderous tomes of figures, in his own remarkably neat hand, which, more properly than his few printed tracts, might be called his 'Works'. They seemed affectionate to his memory, and universally commended his expertness in book-keeping. It seemed he was the inventor of some ledger which should combine the precision and certainty of the Italian double entry (I think they called it) with the brevity and facility of some newer German system; but I am not able to appreciate the worth of the discovery. I have often heard him express a warm regard for his associates in office, and how fortunate he considered himself in having his lot thrown in amongst them. There is more sense, more discourse, more shrewdness, and even talent, among these clerks (he would say), than in twice the number of authors by profession that I have conversed with. He would brighten up sometimes upon the 'old days of the India House', when he consorted with Woodroffe, and Wissett, and Peter Corbet (a descendant and worthy representative, bating the point of sanctity of old facetious Bishop Corbet); and Hoole, who translated Tasso; and Bartlemy Brown, whose father (God assoil him therefore!) modernised Walton; and sly, warm-hearted old Jack Cole (King Cole they called him in those days), and Campe and Fombelle, and a world of choice spirits, more than I can remember to name, who associated in those days with Jack Burrell, (the *bon vivant* of the South Sea House), and little Eyton (said to be a *facsimile* of Pope – he was a miniature of a gentleman), that was cashier under him, and Dan Voight of the Custom House, that left the famous library.

Well, Elia is gone, for aught I know, to be reunited with them, and these poor traces of his pen are all we have to show for it. How little survives of the wordiest authors! Of all they said or did in their lifetime, a few glittering words only! His essays found some favourers as they appeared separately. They shuffled their way in the crowd well enough singly: how they will *read* now they are brought together, is a question for the publishers, who have thus ventured to draw out into one piece his 'weaved-up follies'.

PHIL-ELIA.

The London Magazine, 1823. (Reprinted with considerable omissions as *Preface* to *The Last Essays of Elia*, 1833.)

BY DUTY CHAINED

In the days when Britain still ruled India, the India Office in Whitehall celebrated the history of British hegemony by flaunting from its walls the portraits of the men who had conquered, defended and administered the Sub-Continent. Eccentric to that glittering assembly of past, and even vanished, glory, surrounded by a guard of honour of viceroys, governors, generals and nabobs, and its presence there appropriate to an Elian fantasy, there was one portrait of a man who had never come nearer to Bombay, Karachi or Peshawar than he did on the one and only occasion in all his life when he walked the rue de Rivoli, a man who in all his working days had never achieved the dignity of an office to himself: 'Charles Lamb, Clerk in the India House, 1792-1825'.

Throughout his most active years as a writer Lamb served in the Accountants Department of the East India Company. Despite his frequent complaint that he was over-worked, the Company seems to have been an indulgent task-master. In the long intervals between entering up accounts and drafting official letters, Lamb busied himself with his private correspondence (most of it written on East India House notepaper), talked to his colleagues and received visitors. Never responsive to discipline, at least one of his responses to an office superior who dared to rebuke him for his consistent unpunctuality merits a place in his works as perhaps the most outrageous example of impertinence in the history of bureaucratic organizations. 'I notice, Mr Lamb, that you come late every morning.' 'Yes, but see how early I go.'

Nevertheless he was looked upon with affection and pride by his colleagues and even by his superiors, and he must have been more efficient than he pretended in such work as he did perform, for he was regularly promoted and his salary raised from £40 a year after his three unpaid years as a probationer to £730 in the year when he retired – no mean sum in 1825.

His love of companionship was some compensation for the dreariness of his office routine, and it was separation from the company of his East India House colleagues which he missed most in his retirement. But for many years before he became a superannuated man he looked towards retirement as to the gateway to happiness. Early in 1825, when he was approaching his fiftieth birthday, he offered his resignation. After several weeks delay, on 29 March it was accepted. He scribbled a note to Crabb Robinson that is the shortest in all his correspondence, and yet full of feeling: 'I leave the d—d India House Forever! Give me great joy.'

Work

Who first invented work, and bound the free
And holyday-rejoicing spirit down
To the ever-haunting importunity
Of business in the green fields, and the town –
To plough, loom, anvil, spade – and oh! most sad,
To that dry drudgery at the desk's dead wood?
Who but the Being unblest, alien from good,
Sabbathless Satan! he who his unglad
Task ever plies 'mid rotatory burnings,
That round and round incalculably reel –
For wrath divine hath made him like a wheel –
In that red realm from which are no returnings;
Where toiling, and turmoiling, ever and aye
He, and his thoughts, keep pensive working-day.

The Examiner, 1819.

To William Wordsworth

April 7th, 1815.

Dear Wordsworth,
– You have made me very proud with your successive book
presents. I have been carefully through the two volumes, to see
that nothing was omitted which used to be there. I think I miss
nothing but a character in the antithetic manner, which I do not
know why you left out, – the moral to the boys building the giant,
the omission whereof leaves it, in my mind, less complete – and
one admirable line gone (or something come instead of it), 'the
stone-chat, and the glancing sand-piper', which was a line quite
alive. I demand these at your hand. I am glad that you have not
sacrificed a verse to those scoundrels. I would not have had you
offer up the poorest rag that lingered upon the stript shoulders

58

of little Alice Fell, to have atones all their malice; I would not
have given 'em a red cloak to save their souls. I am afraid lest
that substitution of a shell (a flat falsification of the history) for
the household implement, as it stood at first, was a kind of tub
thrown out to the beast, or rather thrown out for him. The tub
was a good honest tub in its place, and nothing could fairly be
said against it. You say you made the alteration for the 'friendly
reader', but the 'malicious' will take it to himself. Damn 'em, if
you give 'em an inch, &c. The Preface is noble, and such as you
should write. I wish I could set my name to it, *Imprimatur*, – but
you have set it there yourself, and I thank you. I would rather
be a door-keeper in your margin, than have their proudest text
swelling with my eulogies. The poems in the volumes which are
new to me are so much in the old tone that I hardly received
them as novelties. Of those of which I had no previous knowledge, the 'Four Yew Trees', and the mysterious company which
you have assembled there, most struck me – 'Death the Skeleton
and Time the Shadow'. It is a sight not for every youthful poet
to dream of, it is one of the last results he must have gone thinking
on for years for. 'Laodamia' is a very original poem; I mean original with reference to your own manner. You have nothing like
it. I should have seen it in a strange place, and greatly admired
it, but not suspected its derivation.

Let me in this place, for I have writ you several letters naming
it, mention that my brother, who is a picture-collector, has picked
up an undoubtable picture of Milton. He gave a few shillings for
it, and could get no history with it, but that some old lady had
had it for a great many years. Its age is ascertainable from the
state of the canvas, and you need only see it to be sure that it is
the original of the heads in the Tonson editions, with which we
are all so familiar. Since I saw you I have had a treat in the reading
way, which comes not every day, the Latin Poems of V. Bourne,
which were quite new to me. What a heart that man had! all laid
out upon town schemes, a proper counterpoise to *some people's*
rural extravaganzas. Why I mention him is, that your 'Power of
Music' reminded me of his poem of 'The Ballad Singer in the
Seven Dials'. Do you remember his epigram on the old woman
who taught Newton the A B C? which, after all, he says, he

hesitates not to call Newton's 'Principia'. I was lately fatiguing myself with going through a volume of fine words by Lord Thurlow, excellent words, and if the heart could live by words alone, it could desire no better regales; but what an aching vacuum of matter! I don't stick at the madness of it, for that is only a consequence of shutting his eyes and thinking he is in the age of the old Elizabeth poets. From thence I turned to Bourne. What a sweet, unpretending, pretty-mannered, *matter-ful* creature! sucking from every flower, making a flower of every thing, his diction all Latin, and his thoughts all English. Bless him! Latin wasn't good enough for him. Why wasn't he content with the language which Bay and Prior wrote in?

I am almost sorry that you printed extracts from those first poems,[1] or that you did not print them at length. They do not read to me as they do altogether. Besides, they have diminished the value of the original, which I possess as a curiosity. I have hitherto kept them distinct in my mind as referring to a particular period of your life. All the rest of your poems are so much of a piece, they might have been written in the same week, these decidedly speak of an earlier period. They tell more of what you had been reading. We were glad to see the poems 'by a female friend'.[2] The one of the Wind is masterly, but not new to us. Being only three, perhaps you might have clapt a D. at the corner, and let it have past as a printer's mark to the uninitiated, as a delightful hint to the better instructed. As it is, expect a formal criticism on the poems of your female friend, and she must expect it. I should have written before, but I am cruelly engaged, and like to be. On Friday I was at office from ten in the morning (two hours dinner except) to eleven at night; last night till nine. My business and office business in general have increased so; I don't mean I am there every night, but I must expect a great deal of it. I never leave till four, and do not keep a holiday now once in ten times, where I used to keep all red-letter days, and some five days besides, which I used to dub Nature's holidays. I have had

---

[1] The 'Evening Walk', and 'Descriptive Sketches among the Alps' – Wordsworth's earliest poems.
[2] Dorothy Wordsworth.

my day. I had formerly little to do. So of the little that is left of life, I may reckon two-thirds as dead, for time that a man may call his own is his life; and hard work and thinking about it taints even the leisure hours, – stains Sunday with work-day contemplation. This is Sunday: and the headache I have is part late hours at work the two preceding nights, and part later hours over a consoling pipe afterwards. But I find stupid acquiescence coming over me. I bend to the yoke, and it is almost with me and my household as with the man and his consort –

> 'To them each evening had its glittering star,
> And every Sabbath Day its golden sun' –

to such straits am I driven for the life of life, Time! O that from that superfluity of holiday leisure my youth wasted, 'Age might but take some hours youth wanted not!' N.B. – I have left off spirituous liquors for four or more months, with a moral certainty of its lasting. Farewell, dear Wordsworth!

O happy Paris, seat of idleness and pleasure! from some returned English I hear that not such a thing as a counting-house is to be seen in her streets, – scarce a desk. Earth-quakes swallow up this mercantile city and its 'gripple merchants', as Drayton hath it – 'born to be the curse of this brave isle!' I invoke this, not on account of any parsimonious habits the mercantile interest may have, but, to confess truth, because I am not fit for office.

Farewell, in haste, from a head that is too ill to methodise, a stomach too weak to digest, and all out of tune. Better harmonies await you!

C. LAMB.

Excuse this maddish letter: I am too tired to write *in formâ*.

To William Wordsworth

6th April, 1825

Dear Wordsworth,

I have been several times meditating a letter to you concerning the good thing which has befallen me, but the thought of poor Monkhouse came across me. He was one that I had exulted in the prospect of congratulating me. He and you were to have been the first participators, for indeed it has been ten weeks since the first motion of it.

Here am I then, after 33 years slavery, sitting in my own room at 11 o'clock this finest of all April mornings a freed man, with £441 a year for the remainder of my life, live as I as long as John Dennis, who outlived his annuity and starved at 90. £441, *i.e.* £450, with a deduction of £9 for a provision secured to my sister, she being survivor, and pension guaranteed by Act Georgii Tertii, &c.

I came home FOR EVER on Tuesday in last week. The incomprehensibleness of my condition overwhelmed me. It was like passing from life into eternity. Every year to be as long as three, *i.e.* to have three times as much real time, time that is my own, in it! I wandered about thinking I was happy, but feeling I was not. But that tumultuousness is passing off, and I begin to understand the nature of the gift. Holydays, even the annual month, were always uneasy joys: their conscious fugitiveness – the craving after making the most of them. Now, when all is holyday, there are no holydays. I can sit at home, in rain or shine, without a restless impulse for walkings. I am daily steadying, and shall soon find it as natural to me to be my own master, as it has been irksome to have had a master. Mary wakes every morning with an obscure feeling that some good has happened to us.

Leigh Hunt and Montgomery after their releasements describe the shock of their emancipation much as I feel mine. But it hurt their frames. I eat, drink, and sleep as sound as ever. I lay no anxious scheme for going hither and thither, but take things as they occur. Yesterday I excursioned twenty miles, today I write a few letters. Pleasuring was for fugitive play-days, mine are

62

fugitive only in the sense that life is fugitive. Freedom and life co-existent.

At the foot of such a call upon you for congratulation, I am ashamed to advert to that melancholy event. Monkhouse was a character I learned to love slowly, but it grew upon me, yearly, monthly, daily. What a chasm has it made in our pleasant parties! His noble friendly face was always coming before me, till this hurrying event in my life came, and for the time has absorbed all interest. In fact it has shaken me a little. My old desk companions with whom I have had such merry hours seem to reproach me for removing my lot from among them. They were pleasant creatures, but to the anxieties of business, and a weight of possible worse ever impending, I was not equal. Tuthill and Gilman give me my certificates. I laughed at the friendly lie implied in them, but my sister shook her head, and said it was all true. Indeed, this last Winter I was jaded out, Winters were always worse than other parts of the year, because the spirits are worse, and I had no day-light. In Summer I had day-light evenings. The relief was hinted to me from a superior Power, when I poor slave had not a hope but that I must wait another 7 years with Jacob and lo! the Rachel which I coveted is brought to me. –

Have you read the noble dedication of Irving's *Missionary Orations* to S.T.C.? Who shall call this man a Quack hereafter? What the Kirk will think of it neither I nor Irving care. When somebody suggested to him that it would not be likely to do him good, videlicet, among his own people, 'That is a reason for doing it,' was his noble answer. That Irving thinks he has profited mainly by S.T.C., I have no doubt. The very style of the Ded. shows it.

Communicate my news to Southey, and beg his pardon for my being so long acknowledging his kind present of the 'Church,' which circumstances I do not wish to explain, but having no reference to himself, prevented at the time. Assure him of my deep respect and friendliest feelings.

Divide the same, or rather each take the whole to you, I mean you and all yours. To Miss Hutchinson I must write separate. What's her address?

Farewell! and end at last, long selfish letter.

C. LAMB.

63

The Superannuated Man

Sera tamen respexit
Libertas.   VIRGIL.

A Clerk I was in London gay.
                            O'KEEFE.

If peradventure, Reader, it has been thy lot to waste the golden years of thy life – thy shining youth – in the irksome confinement of an office; to have thy prison days prolonged through middle age down to decrepitude and silver hairs, without hope of release or respite; to have lived to forget that there are such things as holidays, or to remember them but as the prerogatives of childhood; then, and then only, will you be able to appreciate my deliverance.

It is now six and thirty years since I took my seat at the desk in Mincing-lane. Melancholy was the transition at fourteen from the abundant play-time, and the frequently-intervening vacations of school days, to the eight, nine, and sometimes ten hours' a-day attendance at a counting-house. But time partially reconciles us to anything. I gradually became content – doggedly contented, as wild animals in cages.

It is true I had my Sundays to myself; but Sundays, admirable as the institution of them is for purposes of worship, are for that very reason the very worst adapted for days of unbending and recreation. In particular, there is a gloom for me attendant upon a city Sunday, a weight in the air. I miss the cheerful cries of London, the music, and the ballad-singers – the buzz and stirring murmur of the streets. Those eternal bells depress me. The closed shops repel me. Prints, pictures, all the glittering and endless succession of knacks and geegaws, and ostentatiously displayed wares of tradesmen, which make a week-day saunter through the less busy parts of the metropolis so delightful – are shut out. No book-stalls deliciously to idle over – No busy faces to recreate the idle man who contemplates them ever passing by – the very face of business a charm by contrast to his temporary relaxation from it. Nothing to be seen but unhappy countenances – or half-

64

happy at best – of emancipated 'prentices and little trades-folk, with here and there a servant maid that has got leave to go out, who, slaving all the week, with the habit has lost almost the capacity of enjoying a free hour; and livelily expressing the hollowness of a day's pleasuring. The very strollers in the fields on that day look anything but comfortable.

But besides Sundays I had a day at Easter, and a day at Christmas, with a full week in the summer to go and air myself in my native fields of Hertfordshire. This last was a great indulgence; and the prospect of its recurrence, I believe, alone kept me up through the year, and made my durance tolerable. But when the week came round, did the glittering phantom of the distance keep touch with me? or rather was it not a series of seven uneasy days, spent in restless pursuit of pleasure, and a wearisome anxiety to find out how to make the most of them? Where was the quiet, where the promised rest? Before I had a taste of it, it was vanished. I was at the desk again, counting upon the fifty-one tedious weeks that must intervene before such another snatch would come. Still the prospect of its coming threw something of an illumination upon the darker side of my captivity. Without it, as I have said, I could scarcely have sustained my thraldom.

Independently of the rigours of attendance, I have ever been haunted with a sense (perhaps a mere caprice) of incapacity for business. This, during my latter years, had increased to such a degree, that it was visible in all the lines of my countenance. My health and my good spirits flagged. I had perpetually a dread of some crisis, to which I should be found unequal. Besides my daylight servitude, I served over again all night in my sleep, and would awake with terrors of imaginary false entries, errors in my accounts, and the like. I was fifty years of age, and no prospect of emancipation presented itself. I had grown to my desk, as it were; and the wood had entered into my soul.

My fellows in the office would sometimes rally me upon the trouble legible in my countenance; but I did not know that it had raised the suspicions of any of my employers, when, on the 5th of last month, a day ever to be remembered by me, L—, the junior partner in the firm, calling me on one side, directly taxed me with my bad looks, and frankly inquired the cause of them.

So taxed, I honestly made confession of my infirmity, and added that I was afraid I should eventually be obliged to resign his service. He spoke some words of course to hearten me, and there the matter rested. A whole week I remained labouring under the impression that I had acted imprudently in my disclosure; that I had foolishly given a handle against myself, and had been anticipating my own dismissal. A week passed in this manner, the most anxious one, I verily believe, in my whole life, when on the evening of the 12th of April, just as I was about quitting my desk to go home (it might be about eight o'clock) I received an awful summons to attend the presence of the whole assembled firm in the formidable back parlour. I thought, now my time is surely come, I have done for myself, I am going to be told that they have no longer occasion for me. L——, I could see, smiled at the terror I was in, which was a little relief to me, – when to my utter astonishment B——, the eldest partner, began a formal harangue to me on the length of my services, my very meritorious conduct during the whole of the time (the deuce, thought I, how did he find out that? I protest I never had the confidence to think as much). He went on to descant on the expediency of retiring at a certain time of life (how my heart panted!) and asking me a few questions as to the amount of my own property, of which I have a little, ended with a proposal, to which his three partners nodded a grave assent, that I should accept from the house, which I had served so well, a pension for life to the amount of two-thirds of my accustomed salary – a magnificent offer! I do not know what I answered between surprise and gratitude, but it was understood that I accepted their proposal, and I was told that I was free from that hour to leave their service. I stammered out a bow, and at just ten minutes after eight I went home – for ever. This noble benefit – gratitude forbids me to conceal their names – I owe to the kindness of the most munificent firm in the world – the house of Boldero, Merryweather, Bosanquet, and Lacy.

Esto perpetua!

For the first day or two I felt stunned, overwhelmed. I could only apprehend my felicity; I was too confused to taste it sincerely. I wandered about, thinking I was happy, and knowing that I was not. I was in the condition of a prisoner in the old Bastile, suddenly let loose after a forty years' confinement. I could scarce trust myself with myself. It was like passing out of Time into Eternity – for it is a sort of Eternity for a man to have his Time all to himself. It seemed to me that I had more time on my hands than I could ever manage. From a poor man, poor in Time, I was suddenly lifted up into a vast revenue; I could see no end of my possessions; I wanted some steward, or judicious bailiff, to manage my estates in Time for me. And here let me caution persons grown old in active business, not lightly, nor without weighing their own resources, to forego their customary employment all at once, for there may be danger in it. I feel it by myself, but I know that my resources are sufficient; and now that those first giddy raptures have subsided, I have a quiet home-feeling of the blessedness of my condition. I am in no hurry. Having all holidays, I am as though I had none. If Time hung heavy upon me, I could walk it away; but I do *not* walk all day long, as I used to do in those old transient holidays, thirty miles a day, to make the most of them. If Time were troublesome, I could read it away, but I do *not* read in that violent measure, with which, having no Time my own but candlelight Time, I used to weary out my head and eyesight in by-gone winters. I walk, read or scribble (as now) just when the fit seizes me. I no longer hunt after pleasure; I let it come to me. I am like the man

>   – That's born, and has his years come to him,
>   In some green desart.

'Years,' you will say! 'what is this superannuated simpleton calculating upon? He has already told us, he is past fifty.'

I have indeed lived nominally fifty years, but deduct out of them the hours which I have lived to other people, and not to myself, and you will find me still a young fellow. For *that* is the only true Time, which a man can properly call his own, that which he has all to himself; the rest, though in some sense he may be said to live it, is other people's time, not his. The remnant of my poor days, long or short, is at least multiplied for me three-fold. My ten next years, if I stretch so far, will be as long as any preceding thirty. 'Tis a fair rule-of-three sum.

Among the strange fantasies which beset me at the commencement of my freedom, and of which all traces are not yet gone, one was, that a vast tract of time had intervened since I quitted the Counting House. I could not conceive of it as an affair of yesterday. The partners, and the clerks, with whom I had for so many years, and for so many hours in each day of the year, been closely associated – being suddenly removed from them – they seemed as dead to me. There is a fine passage, which may serve to illustrate this fancy, in a Tragedy by Sir Robert Howard, speaking of a friend's death:

> – 'Twas but just now he went away;
> I have not since had time to shed a tear;
> And yet the distance does the same appear
> As if he had been a thousand years from me.
> Time takes no measure in Eternity.

To dissipate this awkward feeling, I have been fain to go among them once or twice since; to visit my old desk-fellows – my co-brethren of the quill – that I had left below in the state militant. Not all the kindness with which they received me could quite restore to me that pleasant familiarity, which I had heretofore enjoyed among them. We cracked some of our old jokes, but methought they went off but faintly. My old desk; the peg where I hung my hat, were appropriated to another. I knew it must be, but I could not take it kindly. D—l take me, if I did not feel some remorse – beast, if I had not, at quitting my old compeers, the faithful partners of my toils for six and thirty years, that smoothed for me with their jokes and conundrums the ruggedness of my professional road. Had it been so rugged then after all? or was I a coward simply? Well, it is too late to repent; and I also know, that these suggestions are a common fallacy of the mind on such occasions. But my heart smote me. I had violently broken the bands betwixt us. It was at least not courteous. I shall be some time before I get quite reconciled to the separation. Farewell, old cronies, yet not for long, for again and again I will come among ye, if I shall have your leave. Farewell Ch[ambers], dry, sarcastic, and friendly! Do[dwell], mild, slow to move, and gentlemanly! Pl[umley], officious to do, and to volunteer, good services! – and thou, thou dreary pile, fit mansion for a Gresham or a Whittington of old, stately House of Merchants; with thy labyrinthine passages, and light-excluding, pent-up offices, where candles for one half the year supplied the place of the sun's light; unhealthy contributor to my weal, stern fosterer of my living, farewell! In thee remain, and not in the obscure collection of some wandering bookseller, my 'works'! There let them rest, as I do from my labours, piled on thy massy shelves, more MSS. in folio than ever Aquinas left, and full as useful! My mantle I bequeath among ye.

A fortnight has passed since the date of my first communication. At that period I was approaching to tranquillity, but had not reached it. I boasted of a calm indeed, but it was comparative only. Something of the first flutter was left; an unsettling sense of novelty; the dazzle to weak eyes of unaccustomed light. I missed my old chains, forsooth, as if they had been some necessary part of my apparel. I was a poor Carthusian, from strict cellular discipline suddenly by some revolution returned upon the world. I am now as if I had never been other than my own master. It is natural to me to go where I please, to do what I please. I find myself at eleven o'clock in the day in Bond-street, and it seems to me that I have been sauntering there at that very hour for years past. I digress into Soho, to explore a book-stall. Methinks I have been thirty years a collector. There is nothing strange nor new in it. I find myself before a fine picture in a morning. Was it ever otherwise? What is become of Fish-street Hill? Where is Fenchurch-street? Stones of old Mincing-lane, which I have worn with my daily pilgrimage for six and thirty years, to the footsteps of what toil-worn clerk are your everlasting flints now vocal? I indent the gayer flags of Pall Mall. It is Change time, and I am strangely among the Elgin marbles. It was no hyperbole when I ventured to compare the change in my condition to a passing into another world. Time stands still in a manner to me. I have lost all distinction of season. I do not know the day of the week, or of the month. Each day used to be individually felt by me in its reference to the foreign post days; in its distance from, or propinquity to, the next Sunday. I had my Wednesday feelings, my Saturday nights' sensations. The genius of each day was upon me distinctly during the whole of it, affecting my appetite, spirits, &c. The phantom of the next day, with the dreary five to follow, sate as a load upon my poor Sabbath recreations. What charm has washed that Ethiop white? What is gone of Black Monday? All days are the same. Sunday itself – that unfortunate failure of a holyday as it too often proved, what with my sense of its fugitiveness, and over-care to get the greatest quantity of pleasure out of it – is melted down into a week day. I can spare to go to church now, without grudging the huge cantle which it used to seem to cut out of the holyday. I have Time for everything. I can visit a sick friend. I can interrupt the man of much occupation when he is busiest. I can insult over him with an invitation to take a day's pleasure with me to Windsor this fine May-morning. It is Lucretian pleasure to behold the poor drudges, whom I have left behind in the world, carking and caring; like horses in a mill, drudging on in the same eternal round – and what is it all for? A man can never have too much Time to himself, nor too little to do. Had I a little son, I would christen him NOTHING-TO-DO; he should do nothing. Man, I verily believe, is out of his element as long as he is operative. I am altogether for the life contemplative. Will no kindly earthquake come and swallow up those accursed cotton mills? Take me that lumber of a desk there, and bowl it down

As low as to the fiends.

I am no longer ******, clerk to the Firm of &c. I am Retired Leisure. I am to be met with in trim gardens. I am already come to be known by my vacant face and careless gesture, perambulating at no fixed pace, nor with any settled purpose. I walk about; not to and from. They tell me, a certain *cum dignitate* air, that has been buried so long with my other good parts, has begun to shoot forth in my person. I grow into gentility perceptibly. When I take up a newspaper, it is to read the state of the opera. *Opus operatum est*. I have done all that I came into this world to do. I have worked task work, and have the rest of the day to myself.

The London Magazine, 1825

Popular Fallacies

That We Should Rise With the Lark

At what precise minute that little airy musician doffs his night gear, and prepares to tune up his unseasonable matins, we are not naturalists enough to determine. But for a mere human gentleman – that has no orchestra business to call him from his warm bed to such preposterous exercises – we take ten, or half after ten (eleven, of course, during this Christmas solstice), to be the very earliest hour, at which he can begin to think of abandoning his pillow. To think of it, we say; for to do it in earnest, requires another half hour's good consideration. Not but there are pretty sun-risings, as we are told, and such like gawds, abroad in the world, in summer time especially, some hours before what we have assigned; which a gentleman may see, as they say, only for getting up. But, having been tempted once or twice, in earlier life, to assist at those ceremonies, we confess our curiosity abated. We are no longer ambitious of being the sun's courtiers, to attend at his morning levees. We hold the good hours of the dawn too sacred to waste them upon such observances; which have in them, besides, something Pagan and Persic. To say truth, we never anticipated our usual hour, or got up with the sun (as 'tis called), to go a journey, or upon a foolish whole day's pleasuring, but we suffered for it all the long hours after in listlessness and headachs; Nature herself sufficiently declaring her sense of our presumption, in aspiring to regulate our frail waking courses by the measures of that celestial and sleepless traveller. We deny not that there is something sprightly and vigorous, at the outset especially, in these break-of-day excursions. It is flattering to get the start of a lazy world; to conquer death by proxy in his image. But the seeds of sleep and mortality are in us; and we pay usually in strange qualms, before night falls, the penalty of the unnatural inversion. Therefore, while the busy part of mankind are fast huddling on their clothes, are already up and about their occupations, content to have swallowed their sleep by wholesale; we chose to linger a-bed, and digest our dreams. It is the very time to recombine the wandering images, which night in a confused

71

mass presented; to snatch them from forgetfulness; to shape, and mould them. Some people have no good of their dreams. Like fast feeders, they gulp them too grossly, to taste them curiously. We love to chew the cud of a foregone vision; to collect the scattered rays of a brighter phantasm, or act over again, with firmer nerves, the sadder nocturnal tragedies; to drag into day-light a struggling and half-vanishing night-mare; to handle and examine the terrors, or the airy solaces. We have too much respect for these spiritual communications, to let them go so lightly. We are not so stupid, or so careless, as that Imperial forgetter of his dreams, that we should need a seer to remind us of the form of them. They seem to us to have as much significance as our waking concerns; or rather to import us more nearly, as more nearly we approach by years to the shadowy world, whither we are hastening. We have shaken hands with the world's business; we have done with it; we have discharged ourself of it. Why should we get up? we have neither suit to solicit, nor affairs to manage. The drama has shut in upon us at the fourth act. We have nothing here to expect, but in a short time a sick bed, and a dismissal. We delight to anticipate death by such shadows as night affords. We are already half acquainted with ghosts. We were never much in the world. Disappointment early struck a dark veil between us and its dazzling illusions. Our spirits showed grey before our hairs. The mighty changes of the world already appear as but the vain stuff out of which dramas are composed. We have asked no more of life than what the mimic images in play-houses present us with. Even those types have waxed fainter. Our clock appears to have struck. We are SUPERANNUATED. In this dearth of mundane satisfaction, we contract politic alliances with shadows. It is good to have friends at court. The abstracted media of dreams seem no ill introduction to that spiritual presence, upon which, in no long time, we expect to be thrown. We are trying to know a little of the usages of that colony; to learn the language, and the faces we shall meet with there, that we may be the less awkward at our first coming among them. We willingly call a phantom our fellow, as knowing we shall soon be of their dark companionship. Therefore, we cherish dreams. We try to spell in them the alphabet of the invisible world; and think we know already, how it shall be with us. Those uncouth shapes, which, while we clung to flesh and blood, affrighted us, have become familiar. We feel attenuated into their meagre essences, and have given the hand of half-way approach to incorporeal being. We once thought life to be something; but it has unaccountably fallen from us before its time. Therefore we choose to dally with visions. The sun has no purposes of ours to light us to. Why should we get up?

New Monthly Magazine, 1826

Another Popular Fallacy:

That We Should Lie Down With the Lamb

We could never quite understand the philosophy of this arrangement, or the wisdom of our ancestors in sending us for instruction to these woolly bedfellows. A sheep, when it is dark, has nothing to do but to shut his silly eyes, and sleep if he can. Man found out long sixes. – Hail candle-light! without disparagement to sun or moon, the kindliest luminary of the three – if we may not rather style thee their radiant deputy, mild viceroy of the moon! – We love to read, talk, sit silent, eat, drink, sleep, by candle-light. They are every body's sun and moon. This is our peculiar and household planet. Wanting it, what savage unsocial nights must our ancestors have spent, wintering in caves and unillumined fastnesses! They must have lain about and grumbled at one another in the dark. What repartees could have passed, when you must have felt about for a smile, and handled a neighbour's cheek to be sure that he understood it? This accounts for the seriousness of the elder poetry. It has a sombre cast (try Hesiod or Ossian), derived from the tradition of those unlantern'd nights. Jokes came in with candles. We wonder how they saw to pick up a pin, if they had any. How did they sup? what a melange of chance carving they must have made of it! – here one had got a leg of a goat, when he wanted a horse's shoulder – there another

73

had dipt his scooped palm in a kid-skin of wild honey, when he meditated right mare's milk. There is neither good eating nor drinking in fresco. Who, even in these civilised times, has never experienced this, when at some economic table he has commenced dining after dusk, and waited for the flavour till the lights came? The senses absolutely give and take reciprocally. Can you tell pork from veal in the dark? or distinguish Sherris from pure Malaga? Take away the candle from the smoking man; by the glimmering of the left ashes, he knows that he is still smoking, but he knows it only by an inference; till the restored light, coming in aid of the olfactories, reveals to both senses the full aroma. Then how he redoubles his puffs! how he burnishes! – There is absolutely no such thing as reading, but by a candle. We have tried the affectation of a book at noon-day in gardens, and in sultry arbours; but it was labour thrown away. Those gay motes in the beam come about you, hovering and teazing, like so many coquets, that will have you all to their self, and are jealous of your abstractions. By the midnight taper, the writer digests his meditations. By the same light, we must approach to their perusal, if we would catch the flame, the odour. It is a mockery, all that is reported of the influential Phœbus. No true poem ever owed its birth to the sun's light. They are abstracted works –

Things that were born, when none but the still night,
And his dumb candle, saw his pinching throes.

Marry, daylight – daylight might furnish the images, the crude material; but for the fine shapings, the true turning and filing (as mine author hath it), they must be content to hold their inspiration of the candle. The mild internal light, that reveals them, like fires on the domestic hearth, goes out in the sunshine. Night and silence call out the starry fancies. Milton's Morning Hymn on Paradise, we would hold a good wager, was penned at midnight; and Taylor's richer description of a sun-rise smells decidedly of the taper. Even ourself, in these our humbler lucubrations, tune our best measured cadences (Prose has her cadences) not unfrequently to the charm of the drowsier watchman, 'blessing the doors'; or the wild sweep of winds at midnight. Even now a loftier speculation than we have yet attempted, courts our endeavours. We would indite something about the Solar System. – *Betty, bring the candles.*

New Monthly Magazine, 1826

To Bernard Barton

Enfield Chase Side
Saturday 25 July A.D. 1829. – 11 A.M.
There – a fuller plumper juiceier date never dropt from Idumean palm. Am I in the dateive case now? if not, a fig for dates, which is more than a date is worth. I never stood much affected by these limitary specialties. Least of all since the date of my superannuation.

> 'What have I with time to do?
> Slaves of desks, 'twas meant for you.'

Dear B.B., – Your handwriting has conveyed much pleasure to me in report of Lucy's restoration. Would I could send you as good news of my poor Lucy. But some wearisome weeks I must remain lonely yet. I have had the loneliest time near 10 weeks, broken by a short apparition of Emma for her holydays, whose departure only deepend the returning solitude, and by 10 days I have past in Town. But Town, with all my native hankering after it, is not what it was. The streets, the shops are left, but all old friends are gone. And in London I was frightfully convinced of this as I past houses and places – empty caskets now. I have ceased to care almost about any body. The bodies I cared for are in graves, or dispersed. My old Clubs, that lived so long and flourish'd so steadily, are crumbled away. When I took leave of our adopted young friend at Charing Cross, 'twas heavy unfeeling rain, and I had no where to go. Home have I none – and not a sympathising house to turn to in the great city. Never did the waters of the heaven pour down on a forlorner head. Yet I tried

75

10 days at a sort of friend's house, but it was large and straggling
– one of the individuals of my old long knot of friends, card
players, pleasant companions – that have tumbled to pieces into
dust and other things – and I got home on Thursday, convinced
that I was better to get home to my hole at Enfield, and hide like
a sick cat in my corner. Less than a month I hope will bring home
Mary. She is at Fulham, looking better in her health than ever,
but sadly rambling, and scarce showing any pleasure in seeing
me, or curiosity when I should come again. But the old feelings
will come back again, and we shall drown all sorrows over a
game at Picquet again. But 'tis a tedious cut out of a life of sixty
four, to lose twelve or thirteen weeks every year or two. And to
make me more alone, our illtempered maid is gone, who with
all her airs, was yet a home piece of furniture, a record of better
days; the young thing that has succeeded her is good and attentive, but she is nothing – and I have no one here to talk over old
matters with. Scolding and quarreling have something of familiarity and a community of interest – they imply acquaintance –
they are of resentment, which is of the family of dearness. I can
neither scold nor quarrel at this insignificant implement of household services; she is less than a cat, and just better than a deal
Dresser. What I can do, and do overdo, is to walk, but deadly
long are the days – these summer all-day days, with but a half
hour's candle-light and no firelight. I do not write, tell your kind
inquisitive Eliza, and can hardly read. In the ensuing Blackwood
will be an old rejected farce of mine, which may be new to you,
if you see that same dull Medley. What things are all the Magazines now! I contrive studiously not to see them. The popular
New Monthly is perfect trash. Poor Hessey, I suppose you see,
has failed. Hunt and Clarke too. Your 'Vulgar Truths' will be a
good name – and I think your prose must please – me at least –
but 'tis useless to write poetry with no purchasers. 'Tis cold work
Authorship without something to puff one into fashion. Could
you not write something on Quakerism – for Quakers to read –
but nominally addrest to Non Quakers? explaining your dogmas
– waiting on the Spirit – by the analogy of human calmness and
patient waiting on the judgment? I scarcely know what I mean, but
to make Non Quakers reconciled to your doctrines, by shewing

something like them in mere human operations – but I hardly understand myself, so let it pass for nothing. I pity you for over-work, but I assure you no-work is worse. The mind preys on itself, the most unwholesome food. I brag'd formerly that I could not have too much time. I have a surfeit. With few years to come, the days are wearisome. But weariness is not eternal. Something will shine out to take the load off, that flags me, which is at present intolerable. I have killed an hour or two in this poor scrawl. I am a sanguinary murderer of time, and would kill him inchmeal just now. But the snake is vital. Well, I shall write merrier anon. – 'Tis the present copy of my countenance I send – and to complain is a little to alleviate. – May you enjoy yourself as far as the wicked wood will let you – and think that you are not quite alone, as I am. Health to Lucia and to Anna and kind remembrance.

Yours forlorn.

C.L.

To Henry F. Cary

October, 1834

I protest I know not in what words to invest my sense of the shameful violation of hospitality which I was guilty of on that fatal Wednesday. Let it be blotted from the calendar. Had it been committed at a layman's house, say a merchant's or manufacturer's, a cheesemonger's or greengrocer's, or, to go higher, a barrister's, a member of Parliament's, a rich banker's, I should have felt alleviation, a drop of self-pity. But to be seen deliberately to go out of the house of a clergyman drunk! a clergyman of the Church of England too! not that alone, but of an expounder of that dark Italian Hierophant, an exposition little short of *his* who dared unfold the Apocalypse: divine riddles both and (without supernal grace vouchsafed). Arks not to be fingered without present blasting to the touchers. And then, from what house! Not a common glebe or vicarage, (which yet had been shameful), but from a kingly repository of sciences, human and divine, with the primate of England for its guardian, arrayed in public majesty, from which the profane vulgar are bid fly. Could all those volumes have taught me nothing better!

With feverish eyes on the succeeding dawn I opened upon the faint light, enough to distinguish, in a strange chamber, not immediately to be recognised, garters, hose, waistcoat, neckerchief, arranged in dreadful order and proportion, which I knew was not mine own. 'Tis the common sympton, on awaking, I judge my last night's condition from. A tolerable scattering on the floor I hail as being too probably my own, and if the candlestick be not removed, I assoil myself. But this finical arrangement, this finding every thing in the morning in exact diametrical rectitude, torments me. By whom was I divested? Burning blushes! not by the fair hands of nymphs, the Buffam Graces? Remote whispers suggested that I *coached* it home in triumph – far be that from working pride in me, for I was unconscious of

78

the locomotion; that a young Mentor accompanied a reprobate old Telemachus; that, the Trojan like, he bore his charge upon his shoulders, while the wretched incubus, in glimmering sense, hiccuped drunken snatches of flying on the bats' wings after sunset. An aged servitor was also hinted at, to make disgrace more complete: one, to whom my ignominy may offer further occasions of revolt (to which he was before too fondly inclining) from the true faith; for, at a sight of my helplessness, what more was needed to drive him to the advocacy of independency?

Occasion led me through Great Russell Street yesterday. I gazed at the great knocker. My feeble hands in vain essayed to lift it. I dreaded that Argus Poritor, who doubtless lanterned me out on that prodigious night. I called the Elginian marbles. They were cold to my suit. I shall never again, I said, on the wide gates unfolding, say, without fear of thrusting back, in a light but peremptory air, 'I am going to Mr Cary's.' I passed by the walls of Balclutha. I had imagined to myself a zodiac of third Wednesdays irradiating by glimpses the Edmonton dullness. I dreamed of Highmore! I am de-vited to come on Wednesdays.

Villainous old age, that, with second childhood, brings linked hand in hand her inseparable twin, new inexperience, which knows not effects of liquor. Where I was to have sate for a sober, middle-aged-and-a-half gentleman, literary too, the neat fingered artist can educe no notions but of a dissolute Silenus, lecturing natural philosophy to a jeering Chromius or a Mnasilus. Pudet. From the context gather the lost name of

Confessions of a Drunkard

Dehortations from the use of strong liquors have been the favourite topic of sober declaimers in all ages, and have been received with abundance of applause by water-drinking critics. But with the patient himself, the man that is to be cured, unfortunately their sound has seldom prevailed. Yet the evil is acknowledged, the remedy simple. Abstain. No force can oblige a man to raise the glass to his head against his will. 'Tis as easy as not to steal, not to tell lies.

Alas! the hand to pilfer, and the tongue to bear false witness, have no constitutional tendency. These are actions indifferent to them. At the first instance of the reformed will, they can be brought off without a murmur. The itching finger is but a figure in speech, and the tongue of the liar can with the same natural delight give forth useful truths, with which it has been accustomed to scatter their pernicious contraries. But when a man has commenced sot—

O pause, thou sturdy moralist, thou person of stout nerves and a strong head, whose liver is happily untouched, and ere thy gorge riseth at the *name* which I have written, first learn what the *thing* is; how much of compassion, how much of human allowance, thou may'st virtuously mingle with thy disapprobation. Trample not on the ruins of a man. Exact not, under so terrible a penalty as infamy, a resuscitation from a state of death almost as real as that from which Lazarus rose not but by a miracle.

Begin a reformation, and custom will make it easy. But what if the beginning be dreadful, the first steps not like climbing a mountain but going through fire? what if the whole system must undergo a change violent as that which we conceive of the mutation of form in some insects? what if a process comparable to flaying alive be to be gone through? is the weakness that sinks under such struggles to be confounded with the pertinacity which clings to other vices, which have induced no constitutional necessity, no engagement of the whole victim, body and soul?

I have known one in that state, when he has tried to abstain but for one evening, – though the poisonous potion had long ceased to bring back its first enchantments, though he was sure it would rather deepen his gloom than brighten it, – in the violence of the struggle, and the necessity he has felt of getting rid of the present sensation at any rate, I have known him to scream out, to cry aloud, for the anguish and pain of the strife within him.

Why should I hesitate to declare, that the man of whom I speak is myself? I have no puling apology to make to mankind. I see them all in one way or another deviating from the pure reason.

It is to my own nature alone I am accountable for the woe that I have brought upon it.

I believe that there are constitutions, robust heads and iron insides, whom scarce any excesses can hurt; whom brandy (I have seen them drink it like wine), at all events whom wine, taken in ever so plentiful measure, can do no worse injury to than just to muddle their faculties, perhaps never very pellucid. On them this discourse is wasted. They would but laugh at a weak brother, who, trying his strength with them, and coming off foiled from the contest, would fain persuade them that such agonistic exercises are dangerous. It is to a very different description of persons I speak. It is to the weak, the nervous; to those who feel the want of some artificial aid to raise their spirits in society to what is no more than the ordinary pitch of all around them without it. This is the secret of our drinking. Such must fly the convivial board in the first instance, if they do not mean to sell themselves for term of life.

Twelve years ago I had completed my six and twentieth year. I had lived from the period of leaving school to that time pretty much in solitude. My companions were chiefly books, or at most one or two living ones of my own book-loving and sober stamp. I rose early, went to bed betimes, and the faculties which God had given me, I have reason to think, did not rust in me unused.

About that time I fell in with some companions of a different order. They were men of boisterous spirits, sitters up a-nights, disputants, drunken; yet seemed to have something noble about them. We dealt about the wit, or what passes for it after midnight, jovially. Of the quality called fancy I certainly possessed a larger share than my companions. Encouraged by their applause, I set up for a profest joker! I, who of all men am least fitted for such an occupation, having, in addition to the greatest difficulty which I experience at all times of finding words to express my meaning, a natural nervous impediment in my speech!

Reader, if you are gifted with nerves like mine, aspire to any character but that of wit. When you find a tickling relish upon your tongue disposing you to that sort of conversation, especially if you find a preternatural flow of ideas setting in upon you at the sight of a bottle and fresh glasses, avoid giving way to it as

81

you would fly your greatest destruction. If you cannot crush the power of fancy, or that within you which you mistake for such, divert it, give it some other play. Write an essay, pen a character or description, – but not as I do now, with tears trickling down your cheeks.

To be an object of compassion to friends, of derision to foes; to be suspected by strangers, stared at by fools; to be esteemed dull when you cannot be witty, to be applauded for witty when you know that you have been dull; to be called upon for the extemporaneous exercise of that faculty which no premeditation can give; to be spurred on to efforts which end in contempt; to be set on to provoke mirth which procures the procurer hatred; to give pleasure and be paid with squinting malice; to swallow draughts of life-destroying wine which are to be distilled into airy breath to tickle vain auditors; to mortgage miserable morrows for nights of madness; to waste whole seas of time upon those who pay it back in little inconsiderable drops of grudging applause, – are the wages of buffoonery and death.

Time, which has a sure stroke at dissolving all connexions which have no solider fastening than this liquid cement, more kind to me than my own taste or penetration, at length opened my eyes to the supposed qualities of my first friends. No trace of them is left but in the vices which they introduced, and the habits they infixed. In them my friends survive still, and exercise ample retribution for any supposed infidelity that I may have been guilty of towards them.

My next more immediate companions were and are persons of such intrinsic and felt worth, that though accidentally their acquaintance has proved pernicious to me, I do not know that if the thing were to do over again, I should have the courage to eschew the mischief at the price of forfeiting the benefit. I came to them reeking from the steams of my late over-heated notions of companionship; and the slightest fuel which they unconsciously afforded, was sufficient to feed my old fires into a propensity.

They were no drinkers, but, one from professional habits, and another from a custom derived from his father, smoked tobacco. The devil could not have devised a more subtle trap to re-take a backsliding penitent. The transition, from gulping down draughts of liquid fire to puffing out innocuous blasts of dry smoke, was so like cheating him. But he is too hard for us when we hope to commute. He beats us at barter; and when we think to set off a new failing against an old infirmity, 'tis odds but he puts the trick upon us of two for one. That (comparatively) white devil of tobacco brought with him in the end seven worse than himself.

It were impertinent to carry the reader through all the processes by which, from smoking at first with malt liquor, I took my degrees through thin wines, through stronger wine and water, through small punch, to those juggling compositions, which, under the name of mixed liquors, slur a great deal of brandy or other poison under less and less water continually, until they come next to none, and so to none at all. But it is hateful to disclose the secrets of my Tartarus.

I should repel my readers, from a mere incapacity of believing me, were I to tell them what tobacco has been to me, the drudging service which I have paid, the slavery which I have vowed to it. How, when I have resolved to quit it, a feeling as of ingratitude has started up; how it has put on personal claims and made the demands of a friend upon me. How the reading of it casually in a book, as where Adams takes his whiff in the chimney-corner of some inn in Joseph Andrews, or Piscator in the Complete Angler breaks his fast upon a morning pipe in that delicate room *Piscatoribus Sacrum*, has in a moment broken down the resistance of weeks. How a pipe was ever in my midnight path before me, till the vision forced me to realise it, – how then its ascending vapours curled, its fragrance lulled, and the thousand delicious ministerings conversant about it, employing every faculty, extracted the sense of pain. How from illuminating it came to darken, from a quick solace it turned to a negative relief, thence to a restlessness and dissatisfaction, thence to a positive misery. How, even now, when the whole secret stands confessed in all its dreadful truth before me, I feel myself linked to it beyond the power of revocation. Bone of my bone—

Persons not accustomed to examine the motives of their actions, to reckon up the countless nails that rivet the chains of habit, or perhaps being bound by none so obdurate as those I have confessed to, may recoil from this as from an overcharged picture. But what short of such a bondage is it, which in spite of protesting friends, a weeping wife, and a reprobating world, chains down many a poor fellow, of no original indisposition to goodness, to his pipe and his pot?

I have seen a print after Correggio, in which three female figures are ministering to a man who sits fast bound at the root of a tree. Sensuality is soothing him, Evil Habit is nailing him to a branch, and Repugnance at the same instant of time is applying a snake to his side. In his face is feeble delight, the recollection of past rather than perception of present pleasures, languid enjoyment of evil with utter imbecility to good, a Sybaritic effeminacy, a submission to bondage, the springs of the will gone down like a broken clock, the sin and the suffering co-instantaneous, or the latter forerunning the former, remorse preceding action – all this represented in one point of time. – When I saw this, I admired the wonderful skill of the painter. But when I went away, I wept, because I thought of my own condition.

Of *that* there is no hope that it should ever change. The waters have gone over me. But out of the black depths, could I be heard, I would cry out to all those who have but set a foot in the perilous flood. Could the youth, to whom the flavor of his first wine is delicious as the opening scenes of life, or the entering upon some newly discovered paradise, look into my desolation, and be made to understand what a dreary thing it is when a man shall feel himself going down a precipice with open eyes and a passive will, – to see his destruction, and have no power to stop it, and yet to feel it all the way emanating from himself; to perceive all goodness emptied out of him, and yet not to be able to forget a time when it was otherwise; to bear about the piteous spectacle of his own self-ruins: – could he see my fevered eye, feverish with last night's drinking, and feverishly looking for this night's repetition of the folly; could he feel the body of the death out of which I cry hourly with feebler and feebler outcry to be delivered, – it were enough to make him dash the sparkling beverage to the earth in all the pride of its mantling temptation; to make him clasp his teeth,

84

and not undo 'em
To suffer WET DAMNATION to run through 'em.

Yea, but (methinks I hear somebody object) if sobriety be that fine thing you would have us to understand, if the comforts of a cool brain are to be preferred to that state of heated excitement which you describe and deplore, what hinders in your own instance that you do not return to those habits from which you would induce others never to swerve? if the blessing be worth preserving, is it not worth recovering?

Recovering! – O if a wish could transport me back to those days of youth, when a draught from the next clear spring could slake any heats which summer suns and youthful exercise had power to stir up in the blood, how gladly would I return to thee, pure element, the drink of children, and of child-like holy hermit. In my dreams I can sometimes fancy thy cool refreshment purling over my burning tongue. But my waking stomach rejects it. That which refreshes innocence, only makes me sick and faint.

But is there no middle way betwixt total abstinence and the excess which kills you? – For your sake, reader, and that you may never attain to my experience, with pain I must utter the dreadful truth, that there is none, none that I can find. In my stage of habit (I speak not of habits less confirmed – for some of them I believe the advice to be most prudential) in the stage which I have reached, to stop short of that measure which is sufficient to draw on torpor and sleep, the benumbing apoplectic sleep of the drunkard, is to have taken none at all. The pain of the self-denial is all one. And what that is, I had rather the reader should believe in my credit, than know from his own trial. He will come to know it, whenever he shall arrive at that state, in which, paradoxical as it may appear, *reason shall only visit him through intoxication*: for it is a fearful truth, that the intellectual faculties by repeated acts of intemperance may be driven from their orderly sphere of action, their clear day-light ministeries, until they shall be brought at last to depend, for the faint manifestation of their departing energies, upon the returning periods of the fatal madness to which they owe their devastation. The drinking man is never less himself than during his sober intervals. Evil is so far his good.

Behold me then, in the robust period of life, reduced to imbecility and decay. Hear me count my gains, and the profits which I have derived from the midnight cup.

Twelve years ago I was possessed of a healthy frame of mind and body. I was never strong, but I think my constitution (for a weak one) was as happily exempt from the tendency to any malady as it was possible to be. I scarce knew what it was to ail any thing. Now, except when I am losing myself in a sea of drink, I am never free from those uneasy sensations in head and stomach, which are so much worse to bear than any definite pains or aches.

At that time I was seldom in bed after six in the morning, summer and winter. I awoke refreshed, and seldom without some merry thoughts in my head, or some piece of a song to welcome the new-born day. Now, the first feeling which besets me, after stretching out the hours of recumbence to their last possible extent, is a forecast of the wearisome day that lies before me, with a secret wish that I could have lain on still, or never awaked.

Life itself, my waking life, has much of the confusion, the trouble, and obscure perplexity, of an ill dream. In the daytime I stumble upon dark mountains.

Business, which, though never particularly adapted to my nature, yet as something of necessity to be gone through, and therefore best undertaken with cheerfulness, I used to enter upon with some degree of alacrity, now wearies, affrights, perplexes me. I fancy all sorts of discouragements, and am ready to give up an occupation which gives me bread, from a harassing conceit of incapacity. The slightest commission given me by a friend, or any small duty which I have to perform for myself, as giving orders to a tradesman, &c. haunts me as a labour impossible to be got through. So much the springs of action are broken.

The same cowardice attends me in all my intercourse with mankind. I dare not promise that a friend's honour, or his cause, would be safe in my keeping, if I were put to the expense of any manly resolution in defending it. So much the springs of moral action are deadened within me.

My favourite occupations in times past, now cease to entertain. I can do nothing readily. Application for ever so short a time kills me. This poor abstract of my condition was penned at long intervals, with scarcely any attempt at connexion of thought, which is now difficult to me.

The noble passages which formerly delighted me in history or poetic fiction, now only draw a few weak tears, allied to dotage. My broken and dispirited nature seems to sink before any thing great and admirable.

I perpetually catch myself in tears, for any cause, or none. It is inexpressible how much this infirmity adds to a sense of shame, and a general feeling of deterioration.

These are some of the instances, concerning which I can say with truth, that it was not always so with me.

Shall I lift up the veil of my weakness any further? or is this disclosure sufficient?

I am a poor nameless egotist, who have no vanity to consult by these Confessions. I know not whether I shall be laughed at, or heard seriously. Such as they are, I commend them to the reader's attention, if he finds his own case any way touched. I have told him what I am come to. Let him stop in time.

Written in 1812.
Published in The Philanthropist, 1813.
Reprinted in Basil Montagu's 'Some
Enquiries into the Effects of Fermented
Liquors', 1814. Reprinted again as an
Elia essay, London Magazine, 1822,
with the note that follows:

Elia on his Confessions of a Drunkard

Many are the sayings of Elia, painful and frequent his lucubrations, set forth, for the most part (such is his modesty!), without a name, scattered about in obscure periodicals and forgotten miscellanies. From the dust of some of these it is our intention occasionally to revive a tract or two that shall seem worthy of a better fate, especially at a time like the present, when the pen of our industrious contributor, engaged in a laborious digest of his recent Continental tour, may haply want the leisure to expatiate in more miscellaneous speculations. We have been induced, in the first instance, to reprint a thing which he put forth in a friend's volume some years since, entitled 'The Confessions of a Drunkard', seeing that Messieurs the Quarterly Reviewers have chosen to embellish their last dry pages with fruitful quotations therefrom, adding, from their peculiar brains, the gratuitous affirmation that they have reason to believe that the describer (in his delineations of a drunkard, forsooth!) partly sat for his own picture. The truth is, that our friend had been reading among the essays of a contemporary, who has perversely been confounded with him, a paper in which Edax (or the Great Eater) humorously complaineth of an inordinate appetite; and it struck him that a better paper – of deeper interest and wider usefulness – might be made out of the imagined experiences of a Great Drinker. Accordingly he set to work, and, with that mock fervour and counterfeit earnestness with which he is too apt to over-realise his descriptions, has given us a frightful picture indeed, but no more resembling the man Elia than the fictitious Edax may be supposed to identify itself with Mr L., its author. It is indeed a compound extracted out of his long observations of the effects of drinking upon all the world about him; and this accumulated mass of misery he hath centred (as the custom is with judicious essayists) in a single figure. We deny not that a portion of his own experiences may have passed into the picture (as who, that is not a washy fellow, but must at some times have felt the after-operation of a too-generous cup?), but then how heightened? how exaggerated! how little within the sense of the Review, where a part, in their slanderous usage, must be understood to stand for the whole! But it is useless to expostulate with this Quarterly slime, brood of Nilus, watery heads with hearts of jelly, spawned under the sign of Aquarius, incapable of Bacchus, and therefore cold, washy, spiteful, bloodless. Elia shall string them up one day, and show their colours, – or rather how colourless and vapid the whole fry, – when he putteth forth his long-promised, but unaccountably hitherto delayed, 'Confessions of a Water-Drinker'.

London Magazine, 1822

An Autobiographical Sketch

Charles Lamb born in the Inner Temple 10 Feb. 1775 educated in Christ's Hospital afterwards a clerk in the Accountants office East India House pensioned off from that service 1825 after 33 years service, is now a Gentleman at large, can remember few specialities in his life worth noting except that he once caught a swallow flying (*teste suâ manu*); below the middle stature, cast of face slightly Jewish, with no Judaic tinge in his complexional religion; stammers abominably and is therefore more apt to discharge his occasional conversation in a quaint aphorism or a poor quibble than in set and edifying speeches; has consequently been libelled as a person always aiming at wit, which, as he told a dull fellow that charged him with it, is at least as good as aiming at dulness; a small eater but not drinker; confesses a partiality for the production of the juniper berry, was a fierce smoker of Tobacco, but may be resembled to a volcano burnt out, emitting only now and then a casual puff. Has been guilty of obtruding upon the Public a Tale in Prose, called Rosamund Gray, a Dramatic Sketch named John Woodvil, a Farewell Ode to Tobacco, with sundry other Poems and light prose matter, collected in Two slight crown Octavos and pompously christened his Works, tho' in fact they were his Recreations and his true works may be found on the shelves of Leadenhall Street, filling some hundred Folios. He is also the true Elia whose Essays are extant in a little volume published a year or two since; and rather better known from that name without a meaning, than from anything he has done or can hope to do in his own. He also was the first to draw the Public attention to the old English Dramatists in a work called 'Specimens of English Dramatic Writers who lived about the time of Shakespeare', published about 15 years since. In short all his merits and demerits to set forth would take to the end of Mr Upcott's book and then not be told truly. He died   18   much lamented.
Witness his hand, CHARLES LAMB, 10th Apr 1827.

The New Monthly Magazine, 1835

THE BLANK FILLED

On 27th December 1834, Charles Lamb died at Edmonton – 'much lamented'.

II

HE SERVES UP HIS FRIENDS

With what well-disguised humour he serves
up his friends.

William Hazlitt, *The Spirit of the Age*

The Old Familiar Faces

I have had playmates, I have had companions,
In my days of childhood, in my joyful school-days,
All, all are gone, the old familiar faces.

I have been laughing, I have been carousing,
Drinking late, sitting late, with my bosom cronies,
All, all are gone, the old familiar faces.

I loved a love once, fairest among women;
Closed are her doors on me, I must not see her –
All, all are gone, the old familiar faces.

I have a friend, a kinder friend has no man;
Like an ingrate, I left my friend abruptly;
Left him, to muse on the old familiar faces.

Ghost-like, I paced round the haunts of my childhood.
Earth seemed a desart I was bound to traverse,
Seeking to find the old familiar faces.

Friend of my bosom, thou more than a brother,
Why wert not thou born in my father's dwelling?
So might we talk of the old familiar faces –

How some they have died, and some they have left me,
And some are taken from me; all are departed;
All, all are gone, the old familiar faces.

Blank Verse, 1798

To Sarah Hutchinson

Thurs., 19 Oct., 1815.

Dear Miss H. – I am forced to be the replier to your letter, for Mary has been ill and gone from home these five weeks yesterday. She has left me very lonely and very miserable. I stroll about, but there is no rest but at one's own fireside, and there is no rest for me there now. I look forward to the worse half being past, and keep up as well as I can. She has begun to show some favorable symptoms. The return of her disorder has been frightfully soon this time, with scarce a six month's interval. I am almost afraid my worry of spirits about the E.I. House was partly the cause of her illness, but one always imputes it to the cause next at hand; more probably it comes from some cause we have no control over or conjecture of. It cuts sad great slices out of the time, the little time we shall have to live together. I don't know but the recurrence of these illnesses might help me to sustain her death better than if we had had no partial separations. But I won't talk of death. I will imagine us immortal, or forget that we are otherwise; by God's blessing in a few weeks we may be making our meal together, or sitting in the front row of the Pit at Drury Lane, or taking our evening walk past the theatres, to look at the outside of them at least, if not to be tempted in. Then we forget we are assailable, we are strong for the time as rocks, the wind is tempered to the shorn Lambs. Poor C. Lloyd, and poor Priscilla, I feel I hardly feel enough for him, my own calamities press about me and involve me in a thick integument not to be reached at by other folks' misfortunes. But I feel all I can, and all the kindness I can towards you all. God bless you. I hear nothing from Coleridge. Yours truly

C. LAMB.

To William Wordsworth

May, 1833

Mary is ill again. Her illnesses encroach yearly. The last was three months, followed by two of depression most dreadful. I look back upon her earlier attacks with longing. Nice little durations of six weeks or so, followed by complete restoration – shocking as they were to me then. In short, half her life she is dead to me, and the other half is made anxious with fears and lookings forward to the next shock. With such prospects, it seemed to me necessary that she should no longer live with me, and be fluttered with continual removals, so I am come to live with her, at a Mr Walden's, and his wife, who take in patients, and have arranged to lodge and board us only. They have had the care of her before. I see little of her: alas! I too often hear her. *Sunt lachrymæ rerum* – and you and I must bear it.

To lay a little more load on it, a circumstance has happened, *cujus pars magna fui*, and which at another crisis, I should have more rejoiced in. I am about to lose my old and only walk-companion, whose mirthful spirits were the 'youth of our house,' Emma Isola. I have her here now for a little while, but she is too nervous properly to be under such a roof, so she will make short visits, be no more an inmate. With my perfect approval, and more than concurrence, she is to be wedded to Moxon, at the end of August. So 'perish the roses and the flowers' – how is it?

Now to the brighter side. I am emancipated from most *hated* and *detestable* people, the Westwoods, and I am with attentive people, and younger – I am 3 or 4 miles nearer the Great City, Coaches half-price less, and going always, of which I will avail myself. I have few friends left there, one or two though most beloved. But London Streets and faces cheer me inexpressibly, though of the latter not one known one were remaining.

Thank you for your cordial reception of 'Elia'. Inter nos, the 'Ariadne' is not a darling with me; several incongruous things are in it, but in the composition it serve me as illustrative.

I want you in the 'Popular Fallacies' to like the *Home that is no home*, and *Rising with the lark*.

I am feeble, but cheerful in this my genial hot weather. Walked sixteen miles yesterday. I can't read much in summer time.

With my kindest love to all, and prayers for dear Dorothy.

I remain most affectionately yours,

C. LAMB.

Moxon has introduced Emma to Rogers, and he smiles upon the project. I have given E. my 'Milton', (will you pardon me?) in part of a *portion*. It hangs famously in his Murray-like shop.

GOD ALMIGHTY'S GENTLEMAN

To Thomas Manning

[P.M. August 28, 1800].
George Dyer is an Archimedes, and an Archimagus, and a Tycho
Brahé, and a Copernicus; and thou art the darling of the Nine,
and midwife to their wandering babe also! We take tea with that
learned poet and critic on Tuesday night, at half-past five, in his
neat library; the repast will be light and Attic, with criticism. If
thou couldst contrive to wheel up thy dear carcase on the Monday, and after dinner with us on tripe, calves' kidneys, or whatever else the Cornucopia of St Clare may be willing to pour out
on the occasion, might we not adjourn together to the Heathen's
– thou with thy Black Backs and I with some innocent volume of
the Bell Letters – Shenstone, or the like? It would make him wash
his old flannel gown (that has not been washed to my knowledge
since it has been *his* – Oh the long time!) with tears of joy. Thou
shouldst settle his scruples and unravel his cobwebs, and sponge
off the sad stuff that weighs upon his dear wounded pia mater;
thou shouldst restore light to his eyes, and him to his friends
and the public; Parnassus should shower her civic crowns upon
thee for saving the wits of a citizen! I thought I saw a lucid interval
in George the other night – he broke in upon my studies just at
tea-time, and brought with him Dr Anderson, an old gentleman
who ties his breeches' knees with packthread, and boasts that
he has been disappointed by ministers. The Doctor wanted to
see *me*: for, I being a Poet, he thought I might furnish him with
a copy of verses to suit his 'Agricultural Magazine'. The Doctor,
in the course of the conversation, mentioned a poem called
'Epigoniad' by one Wilkie, an epic poem, in which there is not
one tolerable good line all through, but every incident and speech
borrowed from Homer. George had been sitting inattentive seemingly to what was going on – hatching of negative quantities –
when, suddenly, the name of his old friend Homer stung his peri-
cranicks, and jumping up, he begged to know where he could

meet with Wilkie's work. 'It was a curious fact that there should be such an epic poem and he not know of it; and he *must* get a copy of it, as he was going to touch pretty deeply upon the subject of the Epic – and he was sure there must be some things good in a poem of 1400 lines!' I was pleased with this transient return of his reason and recurrence to his old ways of thinking: it gave me great hopes of a recovery, which nothing but your book can completely insure. Pray come on Monday if you *can*, and stay your own time. I have a good large room, with two beds in it, in the handsomest of which thou shalt repose a-nights, and dream of Spheroides. I hope you will understand by the nonsense of this letter that I am *not* melancholy at the thoughts of thy coming: I thought it necessary to add this, because you love *precision*. Take notice that our stay at Dyer's will not exceed eight o'clock, after which our pursuits will be our own. But indeed I think a little recreation among the Bell Letters and poetry will do you some service in the interval of severer studies. I hope we shall fully discuss with George Dyer what I have never yet heard done to my satisfaction, the reason of Dr Johnson's malevolent strictures on the higher species of the Ode.

C.L.

To Thomas Manning

27th December, 1800

At length George Dyer's phrenitis has come to a crisis; he is raging and furiously mad. I waited upon the heathen, Thursday was a se'nnight; the first symptom which struck my eye and gave me incontrovertible proof of the fatal truth was a pair of nankeen pantaloons four times too big for him, which the said Heathen did pertinaciously affirm to be new.

They were absolutely ingrained with the accumulated dirt of ages; but he affirmed them to be clean. He was going to visit a lady that was nice about those things, and that's the reason he wore nankeen that day. And then he danced, and capered, and fidgeted, and pulled up his pantaloons, and hugged his intolerable flannel vestment closer about his poetic loins; anon he gave it loose to the zephyrs which plentifully insinuate their tiny bodies through every crevice, door, window, or wainscot, expressly formed for the exclusion of such impertinents. Then he caught at a proof sheet, and catched up a laundress's bill instead – made a dart at Bloomfield's Poems, and threw them in agony aside. I could not bring him to one direct reply; he could not maintain his jumping mind in a right line for the tithe of a moment by Clifford's Inn clock. He must go to the printer's immediately – the most unlucky accident – he had struck off five hundred impressions of his Poems, which were ready for delivery to subscribers, and the Preface must all be expunged. There were eighty pages of Preface, and not till that morning had he discovered that in the very first page of said Preface he had set out with a principle of Criticism fundamentally wrong, which vitiated all his following reasoning. The Preface must be expunged, although it cost him £30 – the lowest calculation, taking in paper and printing! In vain have his real friends remonstrated against this Midsummer madness. George is as obstinate as a Primitive Christian and wards and parries off all our thrusts with one unanswerable fence: – 'Sir, 'tis of great consequence that the *world* is not *misled*!'

As for the other Professor, he has actually begun to dive into Tavernier and Chardin's *Persian* Travels for a story, to form a new drama for the sweet tooth of this fastidious age. Hath not Bethlehem College a fair action for non-residents against such professors? Are poets so *few* in *this age*, that He must write poetry? *Is morals* a subject so exhausted, that he must quit that line? Is the metaphysic well (without a bottom) drained dry?

If I can guess at the wicked pride of the Professor's heart, I would take a shrewd wager that he disdains ever again to dip his pen in *Prose*. Adieu, ye splendid theories! Farewell, dreams of political justice! Lawsuits, where I was council for Archbishop Fenelon *versus* my own mother, in the famous fire cause!

Vanish from my mind, professors, one and all! I have metal more attractive on foot.

Man of many snipes, – I will sup with thee, Deo volente et

diabolo nolente, on Monday night the 5th of January, in the new year, and crush a cup to the infant century.

A word or two of my progress. Embark at six o'clock in the morning, with a fresh gale, on a Cambridge one-decker; very cold till eight at night; land at St Mary's light-house, muffins and coffee upon table (or any other curious production of Turkey or both Indies), snipes exactly at nine, punch to commence at ten, with *argument*; difference of opinion is expected to take place about eleven; perfect unanimity, with some haziness and dimness, before twelve. – N.B. My single affection is not so singly wedded to snipes; but the curious and epicurean eye would also take a pleasure in beholding a delicate and well-chosen assortment of teals, ortolans, the unctuous and palate-soothing flesh of geese wild and tame, nightingales' brains, the sensorium of a young sucking pig, or any other Christmas dish, which I leave to the judgment of you and the cook of Gonville.

C. LAMB.

To Mrs Hazlitt

November, 1823

Sitting down to write a letter is such a painful operation to Mary, that you must accept me as her proxy. You have seen our house. What I now tell you is literally true. Yesterday week George Dyer called upon us, at one o'clock, (*bright noon day*) on his way to dine with Mrs Barbauld at Newington. He sat with Mary about half an hour, and took leave. The maid saw him go out, from her kitchen window, but suddenly losing sight of him, ran up in a fright to Mary. G.D., instead of keeping the slip that leads to the gate, had deliberately, staff in hand, in broad open day, marched into the New River. He had not his spectacles on, and you know his absence. Who helped him out, they can hardly tell; but between 'em they got him out, drenched thro' and thro'. A mob collected by that time and accompanied him in. 'Send for the

Doctor,' they said: and a one-eyed fellow, dirty and drunk, was fetched from the Public House at the end, where it seems he lurks, for the sake of picking up water practice, having formerly had a medal from the Humane Society for some rescue. By his advice, the patient was put between blankets; and when I came home at four to dinner, I found G.D. a-bed, and raving, light-headed with the brandy-and-water which the doctor had administered. He sang, laughed, whimpered, screamed, babbled of guardian angels, would get up and go home; but we kept him there by force; and by next morning he departed sober, and seems to have received no injury. All my friends are open-mouth'd about having paling before the river; but I cannot see, that because a lunatic chooses to walk into a river with his eyes open at mid day, I am any the more likely to be drowned in it, coming home at midnight.

I had the honour of dining at the Mansion House on Thursday last by special card from the Lord Mayor, who never saw my face, nor I his; and all from being a writer in a magazine. The dinner costly, served on massy plate; champagne, pines, &c.; 47 present, among whom the Chairman and two other directors of the India Company.

There's for you! and got away pretty sober. Quite saved my credit.

We continue to like our house prodigiously.

Does Mary Hazlitt go on with her novel? or has she began another? I would not discourage her, though we continue to think it (so far) in its present state not saleable. Our kind remembrances to her and hers, and you and yours,

Yours truly,

C. LAMB.

I am pleased that H. liked my letter to the Laureat.

Amicus Redivivus

Where were ye, Nymphs, when the remorseless deep
Clos'd o'er the head of your loved Lycidas?

I do not know when I have experienced a stranger sensation,
than on seeing my old friend G[eorge] D[yer], who had been
paying me a morning visit a few Sundays back, at my cottage at
Islington, upon taking leave, instead of turning down the right
hand path by which he had entered – with staff in hand, and at
noon day, deliberately march right forwards into the midst of
the stream that runs by us, and totally disappear.

A spectacle like this at dusk would have been appalling enough;
but, in the broad open daylight, to witness such an unreserved
motion towards self-destruction in a valued friend, took from me
all power of speculation.

How I found my feet, I know not. Consciousness was quite
gone. Some spirit, not my own, whirled me to the spot. I remember nothing but the silvery apparition of a good white head
emerging; nigh which a staff (the hand unseen that wielded it)
pointed upwards, as feeling for the skies. In a moment (if time
was in that time) he was on my shoulders, and I – freighted with
a load more precious than his who bore Anchises.

And here I cannot but do justice to the officious zeal of sundry
passers by, who, albeit arriving a little too late to participate in
the honours of the rescue, in philanthropic shoals came thronging
to communicate their advice as to the recovery; prescribing var-
iously the application, or non-application, of salt, &c., to the
person of the patient. Life meantime was ebbing fast away,
amidst the stifle of conflicting judgments, when one, more saga-
cious than the rest, by a bright thought, proposed sending for
the Doctor. Trite as the counsel was, and impossible, as one
should think, to be missed on, – shall I confess? – in this emergency, it was to me as if an Angel had spoken. Great previous
exertions – and mine had not been inconsiderable – are commonly
followed by a debility of purpose. This was a moment of irresolu-
tion.

MONOCULUS – for so, in default of catching his true name, I choose to designate the medical gentleman who now appeared – is a grave, middle-aged person, who, without having studied at the college, or truckled to the pedantry of a diploma, hath employed a great portion of his valuable time in experimental processes upon which the bodies of unfortunate fellow-creatures, in whom the vital spark, to mere vulgar thinking, would seem extinct, and lost for ever. He omitteth no occasion of obtruding his services, from a case of common surfeit-suffocation to the ignobler obstructions, sometimes induced by a too wilful application of the plant *Cannabis* outwardly. But though he declineth not altogether these drier extinctions, his occupation tendeth for the most part to water-practice; for the convenience of which, he hath judiciously fixed his quarters near the grand repository of the stream mentioned, where, day and night, from his little watch-tower, at the Middleton's-Head, he listeneth, to detect the wrecks of drowned mortality – partly, as he saith, to be upon the spot – and partly, because the liquids which he useth to prescribe to himself and his patients, on these distressing occasions, are ordinarily more conveniently to be found at these common hostelries, than in the shops and phials of the apothecaries. His ear hath arrived to such finesse by practice, that it is reported, he can distinguish a plunge at a half furlong distance; and can tell, if it be casual or deliberate. He weareth a medal, suspended over a suit, originally of a sad brown, but which, by time, and frequency of nightly divings, has been dinged into a true professional sable. He passeth by the name of Doctor, and is remarkable for wanting his left eye. His remedy – after a sufficient application of warm blankets, friction, &c., is a simple tumbler, or more, of the purest Cognac, with water, made as hot as the convalescent can bear it. Where he findeth, as in the case of my friend, a squeamish subject, he condescendeth to be the taster; and showeth, by his own example, the innocuous nature of the prescription. Nothing can be more kind or encouraging than this procedure. It addeth confidence to the patient, to see his medical adviser go hand in hand with himself in the remedy. When the doctor swalloweth his own draught, what peevish invalid can refuse to pledge him in the potion? In fine, MONOCULUS is a human, sensible man, who for a slender pittance, scarce enough to sustain life, is content to

103

wear it out in the endeavour to save the lives of others – his pretensions so moderate, that with difficulty I could press a crown upon him, for the price of restoring the existence of such an invaluable creature to society as G.D.

It was pleasant to observe the effect of the subsiding alarm upon the nerves of the dear absentee. It seemed to have given a shake to memory, calling up notice after notice, of all the providential deliverances he had experienced in the course of his long and innocent life. Sitting up in my couch – my couch which, naked and void of furniture hitherto, for the salutary repose which it administered, shall be honoured with costly valance, at some price, and henceforth be a state-bed at Colebrooke, – he discoursed of marvellous escapes – by carelessness of nurses – by pails of gelid, and kettles of the boiling element, in infancy – by orchard pranks, and snapping twigs, in schoolboy frolics – by descent of tiles at Trumpington, and of heavier tomes at Pembroke – by studious watchings, inducing frightful vigilance – by want, and the fear of want, and all the sore throbbings of the learned head. – Anon, he would burst out into little fragments of chaunting – of songs long ago – ends of deliverance-hymns, not remembered before since childhood, but coming up now, when his heart was made tender as a child's – for the *tremor cordis*, in the retrospect of a recent deliverance, as in a case of impending danger, acting upon an innocent heart, will produce a self-tenderness, which we should do ill to christen cowardice; and Shakespeare, in the latter crisis, has made his good Sir Hugh to remember the sitting by Babylon, and to mutter of shallow rivers.

Waters of Sir Hugh Middleton – what a spark you were like to have extinguished for ever! Your salubrious streams to this City, for now near two centuries, would hardly have atoned for what you were in a moment washing away. Mockery of a river – liquid artifice – wretched conduit! henceforth rank with canals, and sluggish aqueducts. Was it for this, that, smit in boyhood with the explorations of that Abyssinian traveller, I paced the vales of Amwell to explore your tributary springs, to trace your salutary waters sparkling through green Hertfordshire, and cultured Enfield parks? – Ye have no swans – no Naiads – no river God –

or did the benevolent hoary aspect of my friend tempt ye to suck him in, that ye also might have the tutelary genius of your waters?

Had he been drowned in Cam there would have been some consonancy in it; but what willows had yet to wave and rustle over his moist sepulture? – or, having no *name*, besides that ˈ unmeaning assumption of *eternal novity*, did ye think to get one by the noble prize, and henceforth to be termed the STREAM DYERIAN?

> And could such spacious virtue find a grave
> Beneath the imposthumed bubble of a wave?

I protest, George, you shall not venture out again – no, not by daylight – without a sufficient pair of spectacles – in your musing moods especially. Your absence of mind we have borne, till your presence of body came to be called in question by it. You shall not go wandering into Euripus with Aristotle, if we can help it. Fie, man, to turn dipper at your years, after your many tracts in favour of sprinkling only!

I have nothing but water in my head o' nights since this frightful accident. Sometimes I am with Clarence in his dream. At others, I behold Christian beginning to sink, and crying out to his good brother Hopeful (that is to me), 'I sink in deep waters; the billows go over my head, all the waves go over me. Selah.' Then I have before me Palinurus, just letting go the steerage. I cry out too late to save. Next follow – a mournful procession – *suicidal faces*, saved against their wills from drowning; dolefully trailing a length of reluctant gratefulness, with ropy weeds pendant from locks of watchet hue – constrained Lazari – Pluto's half-subjects – stolen fees from the grave – bilking Charon of his fare. At their head Arion – or is it G.D.? – in his singing garments marcheth singly, with harp in hand, and votive garland, which Machaon (or Dr Hawes) snatcheth straight, intending to suspend it to the stern God of Sea. Then follow dismal streams of Lethe, in which the half-drenched on earth are constrained to drown downright, by wharfs where Ophelia twice acts her muddy death.

And, doubtless, there is some notice in that invisible world, when one of us approacheth (as my friend did so lately) to their inexorable precincts. When a soul knocks once, twice, at death's

door, the sensation aroused within the palace must be considerable; and the grim Feature, by modern science so often disposses-
sed of his prey, must have learned by this time to pity Tantalus.

A pulse assuredly was felt along the line of the Elysian shades,
when the near arrival of G.D. was announced by no equivocal
indications. From their seats of Asphodel arose the gentler and
the graver ghosts – poet, or historian – of Grecian or of Roman
lore – to crown with unfading chaplets the half-finished love-
labours of their unwearied scholiast. Him Markland expected –
him Tyrwhitt hoped to encounter – him the sweet lyrist of Peter
House, whom he had barely seen upon earth, with newest airs
prepared to greet —; and, patron of the gentle Christ's boy, –
who should have been his patron through life – the mild Askew,
with longing aspirations, leaned foremost from his venerable
Æsculapian chair, to welcome into that happy company the
matured virtues of the man, whose tender scions in the boy he
himself upon earth had so prophetically fed and watered.

London Magazine, 1823

To George Dyer

22nd February, 1831

Dear Dyer,

Mr Rogers, and Mr Rogers's friends, are perfectly assured, that
you never intended any harm by an innocent couplet, and that
in the revivification of it by blundering Barker you had no hand
whatever. To imagine that, at this time of day, Rogers broods
over a fantastic expression of more than thirty years' standing,
would be to suppose him indulging his 'Pleasures of Memory'
with a vengeance. You never penned a line which for its own
sake you need, dying, wish to blot. You mistake your heart if
you think you *can* write a lampoon. Your whips are rods of roses.
Your spleen has ever had for its object vices, not the vicious,
abstract offences, not the concrete sinner. But you are sensitive;

and wince as much at the consciousness of having committed a compliment, as another man would at the perpetration of an affront. But do not lug me into the same soreness of conscience with yourself. I maintain, and will to the last hour, that I never writ of you but *con amore*. That if any allusion was made to your near-sightedness, it was not for the purpose of mocking an infirmity, but of connecting it with scholar-like habits: for is it not erudite and scholarly to be somewhat near of sight before age naturally brings on the malady? You could not then plead the *obrepens senectus*. Did I not moreover make it an apology for a certain *absence*, which some of our friends may have experienced, when you have not on a sudden made recognition of them in a casual street-meeting? and did I not strengthen your excuse for this slowness of recognition by further accounting morally for the present engagement of your mind in worthy objects? Did I not, in your person, make the handsomest apology for absent-of-mind people that was ever made? If these things be not so, I never knew what I wrote, or meant by my writing, and have been penning libels all my life without being aware of it. Does it follow that I should have exprest myself exactly in the same way of those dear old eyes of yours *now*, now that Father Time has conspired with a hard task-master to put a last extinguisher upon them? I should as soon have insulted the Answerer of Salmasius when he awoke up from his ended task and saw no more with mortal vision. But you are many films removed yet from Milton's calamity. You write perfectly intelligibly. Marry, the letters are not all of the same size or tallness; but that only shows your proficiency in the *hands*, text-german-hand, court-hand, sometimes Law-hand, and affords variety. You pen better than you did a twelvemonth ago, and if you continue to improve, you bid fair to win the golden pen which is the prize at your young Gentleman's academy. But you must be aware of Valpy, and his printing-house, that hazy cave of Trophonius, out of which it was a mercy that you escaped with a glimmer. Beware of MSS. – and Variæ Lectiones. Settle the text for once in your mind, and stick to it. You have some years' good sight in you yet, if you do not tamper with it. It is not for you (for *us* I should say) to go poring into Greek contractions, and star-gazing upon slim Hebrew points. We have yet the sight

– Of sun, and moon, and star, throughout the year
And man and woman –

you have vision enough to discern Mrs Dyer from the other
comely Gentlewoman who lives up at staircase No. 5; or, if you
should make a blunder in the twilight, Mrs Dyer has too much
good sense to be jealous for a mere effect of imperfect optics. But
don't try to write the Lord's Prayer, Creed, and Ten Commandments in the compass of a half-penny; nor run after a midge, or
a mote, to catch it, and leave off hunting for needles in bundles
of hay – for all these things strain the eyes.... The snow is six
feet deep in some parts here. I must put on jack-boots to get at
the post-office with this. It is not good for weak eyes to pore
upon snow too much. It lies in drifts. I wonder what its drift is,
only that it makes good pancakes, remind Mrs Dyer. It turns a
pretty green world into a white one. It glares too much for an
innocent colour, methinks. I wonder why you think I dislike gilt
edges. They set off a Letter marvellously. Yours, for instance
looks for all the world like a tablet of curious *hieroglyphics* in a
gold frame. But don't go and lay this to your eyes. You always
wrote hieroglyphically, yet not to come up to the mystical nota-
tions and conjuring characters of Dr Parr. You never wrote what
I call a school-master's hand, like Mrs Clarke; nor a woman's
hand, like Southey; nor a Missal hand, like Porson; nor an all-of-
the-wrong-side-sloping hand, like Miss Hayes; nor a dogmatic
Mede-and-Persian, peremptory hand, like Rickman; but you ever
wrote what I call a Grecian's hand – what the Grecians write (or
used) at Christ's Hospital; such as Whalley would have admired,
and Boyer have applauded, but Smith or Atwood (writing-
masters) would have horsed you for. Your boy-of-genius hand
and your mercantile hand are various. By your flourishes, I
should think you never learned to make eagles or corkscrews,
or flourish the governors' names in the writing-school; and by
the tenour and cut of your Letters I suspect you were never in it
at all. By the length of this scrawl you will think I have a design
upon your optics; but I have writ as large as I could, out of respect
to them, too large, indeed, for beauty. Mine is a sort deputy
Grecian's hand, a little better, and more of a worldly hand, than

a Grecian's, but still remote from the mercantile. I don't know how it is, but I keep my rank in fancy still since school-days. I can never forget I was a deputy Grecian! And writing to you, or to Coleridge, besides affection, I feel a reverential deference as to Grecians still – I keep my soaring way above the Great Erasmians yet far beneath the other: Alas! what am I now? what is a Leadenhall clerk, or India pensioner, to a deputy Grecian? How art thou fallen, O Lucifer! Just room for our loves to Mrs D., &c.

C. LAMB.

To Thomas Manning

[P.M. March, 17, 1800].

Dear Manning, – I am living in a continuous feast. Coleridge has been with me now for nigh three weeks, and the more I see of him in the quotidian undress and relaxation of his mind, the more cause I see to love him, and believe him a *very good man*, and all those foolish impressions to the contrary fly off like morning slumbers. He is engaged in translations, which I hope will keep him this month to come. He is uncommonly kind and friendly to me. He ferrets me day and night to *do something*. He tends me, amidst all his own worrying and heart-oppressing occupations, as a gardener tends his young *tulip*. Marry come up! what a pretty similitude, and how like your humble servant! He has lugged me to the brink of engaging to a newspaper, and has suggested to me for a first plan the forgery of a supposed manuscript of Burton the anatomist of melancholy. I have even written the introductory letter; and, if I can pick up a few guineas this way, I feel they will be most *refreshing*, bread being so dear. If I go on with it, I will apprise you of it, as you may like to see my things! and the *tulip*, of all flowers, loves to be admired most.

Pray pardon me, if my letters do not come very thick. I am so taken up with one thing or other, that I cannot pick out (I will not say time, but) fitting times to write to you. My dear love to Lloyd and Sophia, and pray split this thin letter into three parts, and present them with the *two biggest* in my name.

They are my oldest friends; but ever the new friend driveth out the old, as the ballad sings! God bless you all three! I would hear from Lloyd, if I could.

C.L.

Flour has just fallen nine shillings a sack! we shall be all too rich.

Tell Charles I have seen his Mamma, and am almost fallen in love with *her*, since I mayn't with Olivia. She is so fine and graceful,

110

a complete Matron-Lady-Quaker. She has given me two little books. Olivia grows a charming girl – full of feeling, and thinner than she was.

But I have not time to fall in love.

Mary presents her *general compliments*. She keeps in fine health! Huzza! boys,

and down with the Atheists.

To S.T. Coleridge

Autumn, 1820

Dear C.,

Why will you make your visits, which should give pleasure, matter of regret to your friends? You never come but you take away some folio that is part of my existence. With a great deal of difficulty I was made to comprehend the extent of my loss. My maid Becky brought me a dirty bit of paper, which contained her description of some book which Mr Coleridge had taken away. It was 'Luster's Tables,' which, for some time, I could not make out. 'What! has he carried away any of the *tables*, Becky?' 'No, it wasn't any tables, but it was a book that he called Luster's Tables.' I was obliged to search personally among my shelves, and a huge fissure suddenly disclosed to me the true nature of the damage I had sustained. That book, C., you should not have taken away, for it is not mine; it is the property of a friend, who does not know its value, nor indeed have I been very sedulous in explaining to him the estimate of it; but was rather contented in giving a sort of corroboration to a hint that he let fall, as to its being suspected to be not genuine, so that in all probability it would have fallen to me as a deodand; not but I am as sure it is Luther's as I am sure that Jack Bunyan wrote the *Pilgrim's Progress*; but it was not for me to pronounce upon the validity of testimony that had been disputed by learneder clerks than I. So I quietly let it occupy the place it had usurped upon my shelves, and

111

should never have thought of issuing an ejectment against it; for why should I be so bigoted as to allow rites of hospitality to none but my own books, children, &c.? – a species of egotism I abhor from my heart. No; let 'em all snug together, Hebrews and Proselytes of the gate; no selfish partiality of mine shall make distinction between them; I charge no warehouse room for my friends' commodities; they are welcome to come and stay as long as they like, without paying rent. I have several such strangers that I treat with more than Arabian courtesy; there's a copy of More's fine poem, which is none of mine; but I cherish it as my own; I am none of those churlish landlords that advertise the goods to be taken away in ten days' time, or then to be sold to pay expenses. So you see I had no right to lend you that book; I may lend you my own books, because it is at my hazard, but it is not honest to hazard a friend's property; I always make that distinction. I hope you will bring it with you, or send it by Hartley; or he can bring that, and you the *Polemical Discourses*, and come and eat some atoning mutton with us one of these days shortly. We are engaged two or three Sundays deep, but always dine at home on week-days at half-past four. So come all four – men and books I mean – my third shelf (northern compartment) from the top has two devilish gaps, where you have knocked out its two eye-teeth.

Your wronged friend,

C. LAMB.

The Two Races of Men

The human species, according to the best theory I can form of it, is composed of two distinct races, *the men who borrow, and the men who lend*. To these two original diversities may be reduced all those impertinent classifications of Gothic and Celtic tribes, white men, black men, red men. All the dwellers upon earth, 'Parthians, and Medes, and Elamites', flock hither, and do naturally fall in with one or other of these primary distinctions. The infinite superiority of the former, which I choose to designate as the *great race*, is discernible in their figure, port, and a certain instinctive sovereignty. The latter are born degraded. 'He shall serve his brethren.' There is something in the air of one of this cast, lean and suspicious; contrasting with the open, trusting, generous manners of the other.

Observe who have been the greatest borrowers of all ages – Alcibiades – Falstaff – Sir Richard Steele – our late incomparable Brinsley – what a family likeness in all four!

What a careless, even deportment hath your borrower! What rosy gills! what a beautiful reliance on Providence doth he manifest – taking no more thought than lilies! What contempt for money – accounting it (yours and mine especially) no better than dross! What a liberal confounding of those pedantic distinctions of *meum* and *tuum*! or rather, what a noble simplification of language (beyond Tooke), resolving these supposed opposites into one clear, intelligible pronoun adjective! – What near approaches doth he make to the primitive *community* – to the extent of one-half of the principle at least.

He is the true taxer who 'calleth all the world up to be taxed'; and the distance is as vast between him and *one of us*, as subsisted between the Augustan Majesty and the poorest obolary Jew that paid it tribute-pittance at Jerusalem! His exactions, too, have such a cheerful, voluntary air! So far removed from your sour parochial or state-gatherers – those ink-horn varlets, who carry their want of welcome in their faces! He cometh to you with a smile, and troubleth you with no receipt; confining himself to no set season. Every day is his Candlemas, or his feast of Holy Michael. He applieth the *lene tormentum* of a pleasant look to your purse – which to that gentle warmth expands her silken leaves, as naturally as the cloak of the traveller, for which sun and wind contended! He is the true Propontic which never ebbeth! The sea which taketh handsomely at each man's hand. In vain the victim, whom he delighteth to honour, struggles with destiny; he is in the net. Lend therefore cheerfully, O man ordained to lend – that thou lose not in the end, with thy worldly penny, the reversion promised. Combine not preposterously in thine own person the penalties of Lazarus and of Dives! – but, when thou seest the proper authority coming, meet it smilingly, as it were half-way. Come, a handsome sacrifice! See how light *he* makes of it! Strain not courtesies with a noble enemy.

Reflections like the foregoing were forced upon my mind by the death of my old friend, Ralph Bigod, Esq., who departed this life on Wednesday evening; dying, as he had lived, without much trouble. He boasted himself a descendant from mighty ancestors of that name, who heretofore held ducal dignities in this realm. In his actions and sentiments he belied not the stock to which he pretended. Early in life he found himself invested with ample revenues; which, with that noble disinterestedness which I have noticed as inherent in men of the *great race*, he took almost immediate measures entirely to dissipate and bring to nothing: for there is something revolting in the idea of being a king holding a private purse; and the thoughts of Bigod were all regal. Thus furnished, by the very act of disfurnishment; getting rid of the cumbersome luggage of riches, more apt (as one sings)

> To slacken virtue, and abate her edge,
> Than prompt her to do aught may merit praise,

he set forth, like some Alexander, upon his great enterprise, 'borrowing and to borrow!'

In his periegesis, or triumphant progress throughout this island, it has been calculated that he laid a tithe part of the inhabitants under contribution. I reject this estimate as greatly exaggerated: – but having had the honour of accompanying my friend, divers times in his perambulations about this vast city, I own I was greatly struck at first with the prodigious number of faces we met, who claimed a sort of respectful acquaintance with us. He was one day so obliging as to explain the phenomenon. It seems, these were his tributaries; feeders of his exchequer; gentlemen, his good friends (as he was pleased to express himself), to whom he had occasionally been beholden for a loan. Their multitudes did no way disconcert him. He rather took a pride in numbering them; and, with Comus, seemed pleased to be 'stocked with so fair a herd'.

With such sources, it was a wonder how he contrived to keep his treasury always empty. He did it by force of an aphorism, which he had often in his mouth, that 'money kept longer than three days stinks'. So he made use of it while it was fresh. A good part he drank away (for he was an excellent toss-pot), some he gave away, the rest he threw away, literally tossing and hurling it violently from him – as boys do burrs, or as if it had been infectious – into ponds, or ditches, or deep holes, inscrutable cavities of the earth; – or he would bury it (where he would never seek it again) by a river's side under some bank, which (he would facetiously observe) paid no interest – but out away from him it must go peremptorily, as Hagar's offspring into the wilderness, while it was sweet. He never missed it. The streams were perennial which fed his fisc. When new supplies became necessary, the first person that had the felicity to fall in with him, friend or stranger, was sure to contribute to the deficiency. For Bigod had an *undeniable* way with him. He had a cheerful, open exterior, a quick jovial eye, a bald forehead, just touched with grey (*cana fides*). He anticipated no excuse, and found none. And, waiving for a while my theory as to the *great race*, I would put it to the most untheorising reader, who may at times have disposable coin in his pocket, whether it is not more repugnant to the kindliness of his nature to refuse such a one as I am describing, than to say *no* to a poor petitionary rogue (your bastard borrower), who, by his mumping visnomy, tells you that he expects nothing better; and, therefore, whose preconceived notions and expectations you do in reality so much less shock in the refusal.

When I think of this man; his fiery glow of heart; his swell of feeling; how magnificent, how *ideal* he was; how great at the midnight hour; and when I compare with him the companions with whom I have associated since, I grudge the saving of a few idle ducats, and think that I am fallen into the society of *lenders*, and *little men*.

To one like Elia, whose treasures are rather cased in leather covers than closed in iron coffers, there is a class of alienators more formidable than that which I have touched upon; I mean your *borrowers of books* – those mutilators of collections, spoilers of the symmetry of shelves, and creators of odd volumes. There is Comberbatch, matchless in his depredations!

That foul gap in the bottom shelf facing you, like a great eye-tooth knocked out – (you are now with me in my little back study in Bloomsbury, Reader!) – with the huge Switzer-like tomes on each side (like the Guildhall giants, in their reformed posture, guardant of nothing) once held the tallest of my folios, *Opera Bonaventuræ*, choice and massy divinity, to which its two supporters (school divinity also, but of a lesser calibre, – Bellarmine, and Holy Thomas), showed but as dwarfs – itself an Ascapart! – *that* Comberbatch abstracted upon the faith of a theory he holds, which is more easy, I confess, for me to suffer by than to refute, namely that 'the title to property in a book (my Bonaventure, for instance) is in exact ratio to the claimant's powers of understanding and appreciating the same.' Should he go on acting upon this theory, which of our shelves is safe?

The slight vacuum in the left-hand case – two shelves from the ceiling – scarcely distinguishable but by the quick eye of a loser, was whilom the commodious resting-place of Browne on Urn Burial. C. will hardly allege that he knows more about that treatise than I do, who introduced it to him, and was indeed the first (of the moderns) to discover its beauties – but so have I known a foolish lover to praise his mistress in the presence of a rival more qualified to carry her off than himself. Just below, Dodsley's dramas want their fourth volume, where Vittoria Corombona is! The remainder nine are as distasteful as Priam's refuse sons, when the Fates *borrowed* Hector. Here stood the Anatomy of Melancholy, in sober state. – There loitered the Complete Angler; quiet as in life, by some stream side. In yonder nook, John Buncle, a widower-volume, with 'eyes closed', mourns his ravished mate.

One justice I must do my friend, that if he sometimes, like the sea, sweeps away a treasure, at another time, sea-like, he throws up as rich an equivalent to match it. I have a small under-collection of this nature (my friend's gatherings in his various calls), picked up, he has forgotten at what odd places, and deposited with as little memory at mine. I take in these orphans, the twice-deserted. These proselytes of the gate are welcome as the true Hebrews. There they stand in conjunction; natives, and naturalised. The latter seem as little disposed to inquire out their true lineage as I am. – I charge no warehouse-room for these deodands, nor shall ever put myself to the ungentlemanly trouble of advertising a sale of them to pay expenses.

To lose a volume to C. carries some sense and meaning in it. You are sure that he will make one hearty meal on your viands, if he can give no account of the platter after it. But what moved thee, wayward, spiteful K[enney], to be so importunate to carry off with thee, in spite of tears and adjurations to thee to forbear, the Letters of that princely woman, the thrice noble Margaret Newcastle? – knowing at the time, and knowing that I knew also, thou most assuredly wouldst never turn over one leaf of the illustrious folio: – what but the mere spirit of contradiction, and childish love of getting the better of thy friend? – Then, worst cut of all! to transport it with thee to the Gallican land –

Unworthy land to harbour such a sweetness,
A virtue in which all ennobling thoughts dwelt,
Pure thoughts, kind thoughts, high thoughts, her sex's wonder!

– hadst thou not thy play-books, and books of jests and fancies, about thee, to keep thee merry, even as thou keepest all companies with thy quips and mirthful tales? Child of the Greenroom, it was unkindly done of thee. Thy wife too, that part-French, better-part-English-woman! – that *she* could fix upon no other treatise to bear away, in kindly token of remembering us, than the works of Fulke Greville, Lord Brook[e] – of which no Frenchman, nor woman of France, Italy, or England, was ever by nature constituted to comprehend a tittle! *Was there not Zimmerman On Solitude?*

Reader, if haply thou art blessed with a moderate collection, be shy of showing it; or, if thy heart over-floweth to lend them, lend thy books; but let it be to such a one as S[amuel] T[aylor] C[oleridge] – he will return them (generally anticipating the time appointed) with usury; enriched with annotations, tripling their value. I have had experience. Many are these precious MSS. of his – (in *matter* oftentimes, and almost in *quantity* not infrequently, vying with the originals) in no very clerkly hand – legible in my Daniel, in old Burton, in Sir Thomas Browne, and those abstruser cogitations of the Greville, now, alas! wandering in Pagan lands. – I counsel thee, shut not thy heart, nor thy library, against S.T.C.

London Magazine, 1820

To J. Payne Collier

The Garden of England, Dec. 10, 1829

Dear J.P.C.,

– I know how zealously you feel for our friend S.T. Coleridge; and I know that you and your family attended his lectures four or five years ago. He is in bad health, and worse mind: and unless something is done to lighten his mind he will soon be reduced to his extremities; and even these are not in the best condition. I am sure that you will do for him what you can; but at present he seems to be in a mood to do for himself. He projects a new course, not of physic, nor of metaphysic, nor a new course of life, but a new course of lectures on Shakespeare and Poetry. There is no man better qualified (always excepting number one); but I am pre-engaged for a series of dissertations on Indian and Indiapendance, to be completed, at the expense of the Company, in I know not (yet) how many volumes foolscap folio. I am busy getting up my Hindoo mythology; and, for the purpose, I am once more enduring Southey's curse (of 'Kehama'). To be serious, Coleridge's state and affairs make me so, and there are particular reasons just now, and have been any time for the last twenty years, why he should succeed. He will do so with a little encouragement. I have not seen him lately; and he does not know that I am writing.

Yours (for Coleridge's sake) in haste,

C. LAMB.

The Death of Coleridge

When I heard of the death of Coleridge, it was without grief. It seemed to me that he long had been on the confines of the next world, – that he had a hunger for eternity. I grieved then that I could not grieve. But since, I feel how great a part he was of me.

118

His great and dear spirit haunts me. I cannot think a thought, I cannot make a criticism on men or books, without an ineffectual turning and reference to him. He was the proof and touchstone of all my cogitations. He was a Grecian (or in the first form) at Christ's Hospital, where I was deputy Grecian; and the same subordination and deference to him I have preserved through a life-long acquaintance. Great in his writings, he was greatest in his conversation. In him was disproved that old maxim, that we should allow every one his share of talk. He would talk from morn to dewy eve, nor cease till far midnight, yet who ever would interrupt him, – who would obstruct that continuous flow of converse, fetched from Helicon to Zion? He had the tact of making the unintelligible seem plain. Many who read the abstruser parts of his 'Friend' would complain that his works did not answer to his spoken wisdom. They were identical. But he had a tone in oral delivery, which seemed to convey sense to those who were otherwise imperfect recipients. He was my fifty years old friend without a dissension. Never saw I his likeness, nor probably the world can see again. I seemed to love the house he died at more passionately than when he lived. I love the faithful Gilmans more than while they exercised their virtues towards him living. What was his mansion is consecrated to me a chapel.

EDMONTON. *November 21. 1834*
CHS. LAMB.

Written by Lamb in the album of the bookseller Keymer and included by John Forster in his obituary notice of Lamb, *The New Monthly Magazine*, 1835

In a letter to Manning in March, 1803, Lamb writes: 'Dear Manning, – I send you some verses I have made on the death of a young Quaker you may have heard me speak of as being in love with for some years while I lived at Pentonville, though I had never spoken to her in my life. She died about a month since...'. The verses form one of Lamb's best-known poems.

Hester

When maidens such as Hester die,
Their place ye may not well supply,
Though ye among a thousand try,
   With vain endeavour.

A month or more hath she been dead,
Yet cannot I by force be led
To think upon the wormy bed,
   And her together.

A springy motion in her gait,
A rising step, did indicate
Of pride and joy no common rate,
   That flushed her spirit.

I know not by what name beside
I shall it call: – if 'twas not pride,
It was a joy to that allied
   She did inherit.

Her parents held the Quaker rule,
Which doth the human feeling cool,
But she was trained in Nature's school,
   Nature had blest her.

A waking eye, a prying mind,
A heart that stirs, is hard to bind,
A hawk's keen sight ye cannot blind,
    Ye could not Hester.

My sprightly neighbour, gone before
To that unknown and silent shore,
Shall we not meet, as heretofore,
    Some summer morning,

When from thy cheerful eyes a ray
Hath struck a bliss upon the day,
A bliss that would not go away,
    A sweet forewarning?

Works, 1818

To Jacob Vale Asbury

April, 1830

Dear Sir
– Some draughts and boluses have been brought here which
we conjecture were meant for the young lady whom you saw
this morning, though they are labelled for

MISS ISOLA LAMB.

No such person is known on the Chase Side, and she is fearful
of taking medicines which may have been made up for another
patient. She begs me to say that she was born an *Isola* and christened *Emma*. Moreover that she is Italian by birth, and that her
ancestors were from Isola Bella (Fair Island) in the kingdom of
Naples. She has never changed her name and rather mournfully
adds that she has no prospect at present of doing so. She is
literally 'I. Sola', or single, at present. Therefore she begs that

the obnoxious monosyllable may be omitted on future Phials, – an innocent syllable enough, you'll say, but she has no claim to it. It is the bitterest pill of the seven you have sent her. When a lady loses her good *name*, what is to become of her? Well she must swallow it as well as she can, but begs the dose may not be repeated.

Yours faithfully,
CHARLES LAMB (not Isola.)

To Edward Moxon

July 24th, 1833

For God's sake give Emma no more watches; *one* has turned her head. She is arrogant and insulting. She said something very unpleasant to our old clock in the passage, as if he did not keep time, and yet he had made her no appointment. She takes it out every instant to look at the moment-hand. She lugs us out into the fields, because there the bird-boys ask you, 'Pray, Sir, can you tell us what's o'clock?' and she answers them punctually. She loses all her time looking to see 'what the time is'. I overheard her whispering, 'Just so many hours, minutes, &c., to Tuesday; I think St George's goes too slow'. This little present of Time! – why, – 'tis Eternity to her!

What can make her so fond of a gingerbread watch?

She has spoiled some of the movements. Between ourselves, she has kissed away 'half-past twelve', which I suppose to be the canonical hour in Hanover Square.

Well, if 'love me love my watch' answers, she will keep time to you.

It goes right by the Horse Guards.

Dearest M., – Never mind opposite nonsense. She does not love you for the watch, but the watch for you. I will be at the wedding, and keep the 30th July, as long as my poor months last me, as a festival, gloriously.

Yours ever,

ELIA.

We have not heard from Cambridge. I will write the moment we do.

Edmonton, 24th July, twenty minutes past three by Emma's watch.

To Fanny Kelly

20 July, 1819

Dear Miss Kelly,

– We had the pleasure, *pain* I might better call it, of seeing you last night in the new Play. It was a most consummate piece of Acting, but what a task for you to undergo! at a time when your heart is sore from real sorrow! it has given rise to a train of thinking, which I cannot suppress.

Would to God you were released from this way of life; that you could bring your mind to consent to take your lot with us, and throw off for ever the whole burden of your Profession. I neither expect or wish you to take notice of this which I am writing, in your present over occupied & hurried state. – But to think of it at your leisure. I have quite income enough, if that were all, to justify for me making such a proposal with what I may call even a handsome provision for my survivor. What you possess of your own would naturally be appropriated to those, for whose sake chiefly you have made so many hard sacrifices. I am not so foolish as not to know that I am a most unworthy match for such a one as you, but you have for years been a principal object in my mind. In many a sweet assumed character I have learned to love you, but simply as F.M. Kelly I love you better than them all. Can you quit these shadows of existence, & come & be a reality to us? can you leave off harassing yourself to please a

123

thankless multitude, who know nothing of you, and begin at last to live to yourself and your friends?

As plainly and frankly as I have seen you give or refuse assent in some feigned scene, so frankly do me the justice to answer me. It is impossible I should feel injured or aggrieved by your telling me at once, that the proposal does not suit you. It is impossible that I should ever think of molesting you with idle importunity and persecution after your mind [is] once firmly spoken – but happier, far happier, could I have leave to hope a time might come, when our friends might be your friends, our interests yours; our book-knowledge, if in that inconsiderable particular we have any little advantage, might impart something to you, which you would every day have it in your power ten thousand fold to repay by the added cheerfulness and joy which you could not fail to bring as a dowry into whatever family should have the honor and happiness of receiving *you*, the most welcome accession that could be made to it.

In haste, but with entire respect and deepest affection, I subscribe myself

C. LAMB.

From Fanny Kelly

Henrietta Street, July 20th, 1819

An early and deeply rooted attachment has fixed my heart on one from whom no worldly prospect can well induce me to withdraw it, but while I thus frankly and decidedly decline your proposal, believe me, I am not insensible to the high honour which the preference of such a mind as yours confers upon me – let me, however, hope that all thought upon this subject will end with this letter, and that you will henceforth encourage no other sentiment towards me than esteem in my private character and a continuance of that approbation of my humble talents which you have already expressed so much and so often to my advantage and gratification.

Believe me I feel proud to acknowledge myself,
Your obliged friend,

F.M. KELLY.

To Fanny Kelly

20 July, 1819

Dear Miss Kelly,
– *Your injunctions shall be obeyed to a tittle.* I feel myself in a lacka-daisacal no-how-ish kind of a humour. I believe it is the rain or something. I had thought to have written seriously, but I fancy I succeed best in epistles of mere fun; puns and *that* nonsense. You will be good friends with us, will you not? let what has past 'break no bones' between us. You will not refuse us them next time we send for them?

C.L.

Do you observe the delicacy of not signing my full name?
N.B. Do not paste that last letter of mine into your Book.

To Mrs Wordsworth

18th February, 1818

My Dear Mrs Wordsworth,

I have repeatedly taken pen in hand to answer your kind letter. My sister should more properly have done it, but she having failed, I consider myself answerable for her debts. I am now trying to do it in the midst of Commercial noises, and with a quill which seems more ready to glide into arithmetical figures and names of Goods, Cassia, Cardemoms, Aloes, Ginger, Tea, than into kindly responses and friendly recollections.

The reason why I cannot write letters at home is, that I am never alone. Plato's (I write to *W.W.* now) Plato's double-animal parted never longed more to be reciprocally re-united in the system of its first creation, than I sometimes do to be but for a moment single and separate. Except my morning's walk to the office, which is like treading on sands of gold for that reason, I am never so. I cannot walk home from office but some officious friend offers his unwelcome courtesies to accompany me. All the morning I am pestered. I could sit and gravely cast up sums in great Books, or compare sum with sum, and write 'paid' against this, and 'unpaid' against t'other, and yet reserve in some corner of my mind some darling thoughts all my own – faint memory of some passage in a Book or the tone of an absent friend's voice – a snatch of Miss Burrell's singing – a gleam of Fanny Kelly's divine plain face – The two operations might be going on at the same time without thwarting, as the sun's two motions (earth's I mean,) or as I sometimes turn round till I am giddy, in my back parlour, while my sister is walking longitudinally in the front – or as the shoulder of veal twists round with the spit, while the smoke wreathes up the chimney – but there are a set of amateurs of the Belles Lettres – the gay science – who come to me as a sort of rendezvous, putting questions of criticism, of British Institutions,

126

Lalla Rookhs &c. – what Coleridge said at the Lecture last night – who have the form of reading men, but, for any possible use Reading can be to them, but to talk of, might as well have been Ante-Cadmeans born, or have lain sucking out the sense of an Egyptian hieroglyph as long as the pyramids will last before they should find it. These pests worrit me at business, and in all its intervals, perplexing my accounts, poisoning my little salutary warming-time at the fire, puzzling my paragraphs if I take a newspaper, cramming in between my own free thoughts and a column of figures which had come to an amicable compromise but for them. Their noise ended, one of them, as I said, accompanys me home, lest I should be solitary for a moment; he at length takes his welcome leave at the door, up I go, mutton on table, hungry as hunter, hope to forget my cares, and bury them in the agreeable abstraction of mastication, knock at the door, in comes Mrs Hazlitt, or M. Burney, or Morgan, or Demogorgon, or my brother, or somebody, to prevent my eating alone, a Process absolutely necessary to my poor wretched digestion. O the pleasure of eating alone! – eating my dinner alone! let me think of it. But in they come, and make it absolutely necessary that I should open a bottle of orange – for my meat turns into stone when any one dines with me, if I have not wine – wine can mollify stones. Then *that* wine turns into acidity, acerbity, misanthropy, a hatred of my interrupters (God bless 'em! I love some of 'em dearly), and with the hatred a still greater aversion to their going away. Bad is the dead sea they bring upon me, choking and death-doing, but worse is the deader dry sand they leave me on if they go before bed-time. Come never, I would say to these spoilers of my dinner, but if you come, never go! The fact is, this interruption does not happen very often, but every time it comes by surprise, that present bane of my life, orange wine, with all its dreary stifling consequences, follows. Evening Company I should always like had I any mornings, but I am saturated with human faces (*divine* forsooth) and voices all the golden morning, and five evenings in a week would be as much as I should covet to be in company, but I assure you that is a wonderful week in which I can get two, or one, to myself, I am never C.L., but always C.L. & Co.

He who thought it not good for man to be alone, preserve me from the more prodigious monstrosity of being never by myself. I forget bed-time, but even there these sociable frogs clamber up to annoy me. Once a week, generally some singular evening that, being alone, I go to bed at the hour I ought always to be a-bed, just close to my bed-room window, is the club-room of a public-house, where a set of singers, I take them to be chorus singers of the two theatres, (it must be *both of them*), begin their orgies. They are a set of fellows (as I conceive) who being limited by their talents to the burthen of the song at the play-houses, in revenge have got the common popular airs by Bishop or some cheap composer arranged for choruses, that is, to be sung all in chorus. At least I never can catch any of the text of the plain song, nothing but the Bablyonish choral howl at the tail on't. 'That fury being quenched' – the howl I mean – a curseder burden succeeds, of shouts and clapping and knocking of the table. At length over tasked nature drops under it and escapes for a few hours into the society of the sweet silent creatures of Dreams, which so away with mocks and mows at cockcrow. And then I think of the words Christabel's father used (bless me, I have dipt in the wrong ink) to say every morning by way of variety when he awoke:

> *Every knell, the Baron saith,*
> *Wakes us up to a world of death –*

or something like it. All I mean by this senseless interrupted tale is that by my central situation I am a little over-companied. Not that I have any animosity against the good creatures that are so anxious to drive away the Harpy solitude from me. I like 'em, and cards, and a chearful glass, but I mean merely to give you an idea, between office confinement and after-office society, how little time I can call my own. I mean only to draw a picture, not to make an inference. I would not that I know of have it otherwise. I only wish sometimes I could exchange some of my faces and voices for the faces and voices which a late visitation brought most welcome and carried away leaving regret, but more plea-sure, even a kind of gratitude at being so often favoured with that kind northern visitation. My London faces and noises don't

128

hear me – I mean no disrespect – or I should explain myself that instead of their return 220 times a year, and the return of W.W., &c., 7 times in 104 weeks, some more equal distribution might be found. I have scarce room to put in Mary's kind love and my poor name,

C. LAMB

This to be read last.

W[illiam] H[azlitt] goes on lecturing against W[illiam] W[ordsworth] and making copious use of quotations from said W.W. to give a zest to said lectures. S[amuel] T[aylor] C[oleridge] is lecturing with success. I have not heard either him or H. but I dined with S.T.C. at Gilman's a Sunday or two since and he was well and in good spirits. I mean to hear some of the course, but lectures are not much to my taste, whatever the lecturer may be. If *read*, they are dismal flat, and you can't think why you are brought together to hear a man read his works which you could read so much better at leisure yourself; if delivered extempore, I am always in pain lest the gift of utterance should suddenly fail the orator in the middle, as it did me at the dinner given in honour of me at the London Tavern. 'Gentlemen,' said I, and there I stopped, – the rest my feelings were under the necessity of supplying. Mrs Wordsworth *will* go on, kindly haunting us with visions of seeing the lakes once more which never can be realised. Between us there is a great gulf – not of inexplicable moral antipathies and distances, I hope (as there seemed to be between me and that Gentleman concerned in the Stamp Office, that I so strangely coiled up from at Haydon's). I think I had an instinct that he was the head of an office. I hate all such people – Accountants, Deputy Accountants. The dear abstract notion of the East India Company, as long as she is unseen, is pretty, rather Poetical; but as SHE makes herself manifest by the persons of such Beasts, I loathe and detest her as the Scarlet what-do-you-call-her of Babylon. I thought, after abridging us of all our red-letter days, they had done their worst; but I was deceived in the length to which Heads of offices, those true liberty-haters, can go. They are the tyrants, not Ferdinand, nor Nero – by a decree passed this week, they have abridged us of the immemorially-observed custom of going at one o'clock of a Saturday, the little shadow of a holiday left us. Blast them. I speak it soberly. Dear W.W., be thankful for your Liberty.

Many Friends

Unfortunate is the lot of that man, who can look round about the wide world, and exclaim with truth, *I have no friend!* Do you know any such lonely sufferer? For mercy sake send him to me. I can afford him plenty. He shall have them good, cheap. I have enough and to spare. Truly society is the balm of human life. But you may take a surfeit from sweetest odours administered to satiety. Hear my case, dear 'Variorum', and pity me. I am an elderly gentleman – not old – a sort of middle-aged-gentleman-and-a-half – with a tolerable larder, cellar, &c.; and a most unfortunately easy temper for the callous front of impertinence to try conclusions on. My day times are entirely engrossed by the business of a public office, where I am any thing but alone from nine till five. I have forty fellow-clerks about me during those hours; and, though the human face be divine, I protest that so many faces seen every day do very much diminish the homage I am willing to pay to that divinity. It fares with these divine resemblances as with a Polytheism. Multiply the object and you infallibly enfeeble the adoration. 'What a piece of work is Man! how excellent in faculty,' &c. But a great many men together – a hot huddle of rational creatures – Hamlet himself would have lowered his contemplation a peg or two in my situation. *Tædet me harum quotidianarum formarum.* I go home every day to my late dinner, absolutely famished and face-sick. I am sometimes fortunate enough to go off unaccompanied. The relief is restorative like sleep; but far oftener, alas! some one of my fellows, who lives *my way* (as they call it) does me the sociality of walking with me. He sees me to the door; and now I figure to myself a snug fire-side – comfortable meal – a respiration from the burthen of society –

130

and the blessedness of a single knife and fork. I sit down to my solitary mutton, happy as Adam when a bachelor. I have not swallowed a mouthful, before a startling ring announces the visit of *a friend*. O! for an everlasting muffle upon that appalling instrument of torture! A knock makes me nervous; but a ring is a positive fillip to all the sour passions of my nature: – and yet such is my effeminacy of temperament, I neither tie up the one nor dumbfound the other. But these accursed friends, or fiends, that torture me thus! They come in with a full consciousness of their being unwelcome – with a sort of grin of triumph over your weakness. My soul sickens within when they enter. I can scarcely articulate a 'how d'ye'. My digestive powers fail. I have enough to do to maintain them in any healthiness when alone. Eating is a solitary function; you may drink in company. Accordingly the bottle soon succeeds; and such is my infirmity, that the reluctance soon subsides before it. The visitor becomes agreeable. I find a great deal that is good in him; wonder I should have felt such aversion on his first entrance; we get chatty, conversible; insensibly comes midnight; and I am dismissed to the cold bed of celibacy (the only place, alas! where I am suffered to be alone) with the reflection that another day has gone over my head without the possibility of enjoying my own free thoughts in solitude even for a solitary moment. O for a Lodge in some vast wilderness! the den of those Seven Sleepers (conditionally the other six were away) – a *Crusoe* solitude!

What most disturbs me is, that my chief annoyers are mostly young men. Young men, let them think as they please, are no company *singly* for a gentleman of my years. They do mighty well in a mixed society, and where there are females to take them off, as it were. But to have the load of one of them to one's own self for successive hours conversation is unendurable.

There was my old friend Captain Beacham – he died some six years since, bequeathing to my friendship three stout young men, his sons, and seven girls, the tallest in the land. Pleasant, excellent young women they were, and for their sakes I did, and could endure much. But they were too tall. I am superstitious in that respect, and think that to a just friendship, something like proportion in stature as well as mind is desirable. Now I am five feet and a trifle more. Each of these young women rose to six, and one exceeded by two inches. The brothers are proportionably taller. I have sometimes taken the altitude of this friendship; and on a modest computation I may be said to have known at one time a whole furlong of Beachams. But the young women are married off, and dispersed among the provinces. The brothers are left. Nothing is more distasteful than these relics and parings of past friendships – unmeaning records of agreeable hours flown. There are three of them. If they hunted in triples, or even couples, it were something; but by a refinement of persecution, they contrive to come singly; and so spread themselves out into three evenings molestation in a week. Nothing is so distasteful as the sight of their long legs, couched for continuance upon my fender. They have been mates of India-men; and one of them in particular has a story of a shark swallowing a boy in the bay of Calcutta. I wish the shark had swallowed *him*. Nothing can be more useless than their conversation to me, unless it is mine to them. We have no ideas (save of eating and drinking) in common. The shark story has been told till it cannot elicit a spark of attention; but it goes on just as usual. When I try to introduce a point of literature, or common life, the mates gape at me. When I fill a glass, they fill one too. Here is sympathy. And for this poor correspondency of having a gift of swallowing and retaining liquor in common with my fellow-creatures, I am to be tied up to an ungenial intimacy, abhorrent from every sentiment, and every sympathy besides. But I cannot break the bond. They are sons of my old friend.

LEPUS.

The New Times, 1825

III

THE IRATE ST CHARLES

...My gentle Charles, to whom
No sound is dissonant which tells of Life.

Coleridge, 'This Lime-Tree Bower My Prison'.
(Addressed to Charles Lamb of the India
House, London.) *Annual Anthology*, 1800

In the new edition of the 'Anthology'...please
to blot out *gentle-hearted*, and substitute drunken dog, ragged-head, seld-shaven, odd-
eyed, stuttering, or any other epithet which
truly and properly belongs to the gentleman
in question.

Lamb to Coleridge, 14 August 1806

Almost all who wrote obituary notices for Charles Lamb confirmed the canonisation already conferred on him in his lifetime by a Congregation of Rites of impeccable authority and possessed of such awesome powers of public persuasion that its unanimous verdict made virtually inaudible the opposition of a few malicious dissenters – most of them Scotsmen. Carlyle, Byron, Christopher North and the entourage of *Blackwood's* were no match for the combined voices of Coleridge, Wordsworth, Hazlitt, Hood, Leigh Hunt, De Quincey, Southey, Cary, Clare and Crabb Robinson.

Two there were, Lamb himself and his *alter ego* Elia, who served, persistently and consistently, as devil's advocates, who might have been thought to be more knowledgeable about Lamb's character than all those who were forever lauding his gentleness, his generous spirit and his unfailing loyalty. But as witness in their own cause, both were notoriously unreliable, the vices which both ascribed to Lamb were shrugged off as no more than eccentricities which made him all the more lovable because human in his sainthood, and his occasional flares of private irritability and public anger were dismissed as responses, essential and inevitable, to the ever-present burdens of family life.

It is not surprising that Lamb rejected the sainthood that was thrust upon him, frequently by those who knew him best, and it is understandable that he resented above all else the term 'gentle' which was regularly coupled with his name. Gentleness is too often equated with weakness, and weakness is not an attribute that any man – and least of all any man who is a writer – likes to have applied to himself.

Yet, seen in the perspective allowed by almost two centuries of detachment from Lamb's lifetime, most of the evidence supports the conclusion of a majority of his literary contemporaries and friends. His life-long dedication to the care of Mary is undeniable, and so also is his record of unwavering loyalty to his friends. The impression remains vivid that he was seldom other than good-humoured and that, though his opinions, especially on matters political or literary, were unambiguous and firmly-held, he seldom allowed his objections to other men's views or actions to explode into malice.

Lamb's tenets of literary criticism were clear in his mind. He was shrewd, he was clever, and he was undoubtedly capable of slaughtering any work that in his opinion merited such treatment, but he refused to waste his skills or his energy on indifferent performance or worthless writing. Instead he set himself to the task of making quality better known and more widely appreciated than it would have been without his intervention.

Similarly, and though his political stance was solid, his political writings were not often cruel to those who did not share his convictions. As writer of epigrams it was not often his intention to inflict serious wounds on an opponent, in epigram after epigram it is obvious that all is designed as preface to a pun or some other witty criticism.

Perhaps because in rank, political pretension and moral turpitude the Regent epitomised all that Lamb found most repugnant in the Carlton House cronies, which by his reckoning then dominated British social and political life, perhaps because he was encouraged so to do by his friend and editor, Leigh Hunt (a critic of the Prince and his party even more perfervid than Lamb), and perhaps because he estimated that this target was far beyond the range of his lighter darts, Lamb brought up his heavy artillery. 'The Triumph of the Whale' is for its vehemence unique in Lamb's writings. Indeed, as a sustained exercise in personal abuse it has few equals in all English verse.

There were other occasions when Lamb spluttered angrily. Most were, like the diatribe levelled at the Prince Regent, sparked off by some offence to his intellectual convictions. Twice, however, the hurt was heartfelt. Coleridge and Southey were his friends, when they offended him he judged them guilty of a much more heinous crime: they had abandoned the principle which he honoured more than the Ten Commandments, the principle of unqualified loyalty between friends.

The first round in the skirmish between Lamb and Coleridge was fired by Coleridge but once Charles Lloyd had passed on to Lamb that unfortunate, probably idle but certainly arrogant remark, 'Poor Lamb, if he wants any knowledge, he may apply to me', all the rest of the shots came from Lamb – in furious fusillade. The reason for the quarrel was private, Lamb expressed his resentment ferociously but in private correspondence, Coleridge was contrite, and peace between them was restored. Coleridge was again Lamb's 'dearest friend', though ever after Coleridge was for Lamb 'an archangel a little damaged', the fact that there had ever been dissension between them was decently buried in the subconscious of both men.

A quarter of a century later, when Lamb quarrelled with Coleridge's brother-in-law, Robert Southey, the catalyst was again a chance remark, but this time the remark was given the authority of print. Even so, Southey's comment that the *Essays of Elia* lacked religious feeling might have passed unanswered by Lamb had it not been printed in *The Quarterly Review*.

The Quarterly was stridently Tory and its Editor, William Gifford, was in Lamb's eye twice-damned because he had come to his post from another Tory journal, the *Anti-Jacobin* where he had collaborated with George Canning, one of Lamb's chosen *bêtes noires*. The journal's political bias soured all its literary judgements; as almost all the 'Cockney' writers were liberals, so were almost all the 'Cockney' writers dismissed as worthless – or worse – by *The Quarterly*.

But, as it seemed to Lamb, *The Quarterly* had consistently selected him for particularly vicious and patently personal abuse. It was *The Quarterly* which had called his *Specimens* the 'blasphemies of a maniac'. It was *The Quarterly* that had insisted that *Confessions of a Drunkard* was testimony to his viciousness, entire and unqualified, by an impenitent dipsomaniac. It was the influence of the hierarchs of *The Quarterly* which persuaded its publisher, John Murray (himself a Tory but a man who did not allow his political prejudice to colour his literary or commercial judgements) to reject *Essays of Elia*. And, on the one occasion when Lamb was persuaded to write for the enemy, his review of Wordsworth's *Excursion* was subbed so ruthlessly by Gifford that 'more than a third of the substance is cut away, and that not all from one place but *passim* so as to make rather nonsense', changing 'every warm expression for a cold one' and 'putting his damn'd shoemaker's phraseology 'in place of the reviewer's'. (Lamb gave most ungentle return for this outrage in a sonnet contributed to *The Examiner*. See p.152)

Southey, himself a regular contributor to *The Quarterly* and an adviser to its editorial board, had offered no protest against this persecution of his friend. Already he had offended Lamb's susceptibilities by accepting first a Government pension and then the office of Poet Laureate, and now, in his article 'The Progress of Infidelity', Southey came into the open as one of Lamb's *Quarterly* persecutors.

Lamb's capacity for forbearance was exhausted. Southey had insulted him publicly and in print; publicly and in print he would be answered. (See Letter of Elia to Robert Southey, Esquire', p.139) Southey did his limited best to explain away the passage that had occasioned Lamb's outburst but his explanation was not a recantation; he wrote privately and he did not withdraw so much as one comma of what he had said in print. Nevertheless, his protestation of friendship was adamant and Lamb forgave him though he could never forgive 'the accurs'd Quarterly'. When Lamb was attacked in the Press, this time in 1830 in the *Literary Gazette*, although Lamb proved quite capable of handling his own defence (see p.152) Southey moved to exorcise his guilt in not having made his apology public. He submitted to *The Times* a poem honouring Lamb and denigrating his assailant:

Charles Lamb, to those who know thee justly dear
For rarest genius, and for sterling worth,
Unchanging friendship, warmth of heart sincere,
And wit that never gave an ill thought birth...

and so on for another twenty-three lines, except when the Poet Laureate broke off to cuff the Editor of *The Literary Gazette*, so fulsome that, had Elia's gods allowed it, the poem must have served not only as expiation for Southey's offence against Lamb but also for all the sins of *The Quarterly Review*. It was not, of course, too fulsome for that unwavering champion of Charles Lamb, the Editor of *The Times*, Thomas Barnes.

His poem in *The Times* was Southey's first public comment on Lamb since the publication of 'Elia's Letter' seven years previously. It sparked off in Lamb a response which in the last resort must be measured as more true to his nature than all the occasional outbursts of fury added together. 'How noble... in RS', he wrote to Bernard Barton, 'to come forward for an old friend who has treated him so unworthily'.

As for the critics: for them he did not give 'the five hundred thousandth part of the tythe of a half-farthing'.

Perhaps by 1830 it was true.

To S.T. Coleridge

May, 1798

THESES QUÆDAM THEOLOGICÆ

1. Whether God loves a lying angel better than a true man?

2. Whether the Archangel Uriel *could* affirm an untruth? and if he *could*, whether he *would*?

3. Whether honesty be an angelic virtue? or not rather to be reckoned among those qualities which the schoolmen term '*virtutes minus splendidæ et terræ et hominis participes*'?

4. Whether the higher order of Seraphim Illuminati ever sneer?

5. Whether pure intelligences can love?

6. Whether the Seraphim Ardentes do not manifest their virtue by the way of vision and theory? and whether practice be not a sub-celestial and merely human virtue?

138

7. Whether the Vision Beatific by any thing more or less than a perpetual representment to each individual Angel of his own present attainments and future capabilities, somehow in the manner of mortal looking-glasses, reflecting a perpetual complacency and self-satisfaction?

8, and last, Whether an immortal and amenable soul may not come to be condemned at last, and the man never suspect it beforehand?

Learned Sir, my Friend,

Presuming on our long habits of friendship, and emboldened further by your late liberal permission to avail myself of your correspondence in case I want any knowledge, (which I intend to do when I have no Encyclopædia or Ladies' Magazine at hand to refer to in any matter of science,) I now submit to your inquiries the above theological propositions, to be by you defended or oppugned, or both, in the Schools of Germany, whither, I am told, you are departing, to the utter dissatisfaction of your native Devonshire and regret of universal England, but to my own individual consolation if through the channel of your wished return, Learned Sir, my Friend, may be transmitted to this our Island, from those famous Theological Wits of Leipsic and Gottingen, any rays of illumination, in vain to be derived from the home growth of our English Halls and Colleges. Finally wishing, Learned Sir, that you may see Schiller, and swing in a wood, (*vide* Poems,) and sit upon a Tun, and eat fat hams of Westphalia,

I remain
Your friend and docile pupil to instruct,
CHARLES LAMB.

Letter of Elia to Robert Southey, Esquire

Sir, – You have done me an unfriendly office, without perhaps much considering what you were doing. You have give an ill name to my poor Lucubrations. In a recent Paper on Infidelity, you usher in a conditional commendation of them with an exception; which, preceding the encomium, and taking up nearly the same space with it, must impress your readers with the notion, that the objectionable parts in them are at least equal in quantity to the pardonable. The censure is in fact the criticism; the praise – a concession merely. Exceptions usually follow, to qualify praise or blame. But there stands your reproof, in the very front of your notice, in ugly characters, like some bugbear, to frighten all good Christians from purchasing. Through you I am become an object of suspicion to preceptors of youth, and fathers of families. '*A book, which wants only a sounder religious feeling to be as delightful as it is original.*' With no further explanation, what must your readers conjecture, but that my little volume is some vehicle for heresy or infidelity? The quotation, which you honour me by subjoining, oddly enough, is of a character, which bespeaks a temperament in the writer the very reverse of *that* your reproof goes to insinuate. Had you been taxing me with superstition, the passage would have been pertinent to the censure. Was it worth your while to go so far out of your way to affront the feelings of an old friend, and commit yourself by an irrelevant quotation, for the pleasure of reflecting upon a poor child, an exile at Genoa?

I am at a loss what particular Essay you had in view (if my poor ramblings amount to that appellation) when you were in such a hurry to thrust in your objection, like bad news, foremost. – Perhaps the Paper on 'Saying Graces' was the obnoxious feature. I have endeavoured there to rescue a voluntary duty – good in place, but never, as I remember, literally commanded – from the charge of an undecent formality. Rightly taken, Sir, that Paper was not against Graces, but Want of Grace; not against the ceremony, but the carelessness and slovenliness so often observed in the performance of it.

Or was it *that* on the 'New Year' – in which I have described the feelings of the merely natural man, on a consideration of the amazing change, which is supposable to take place on our removal from this fleshly scene? – If men would honestly confess their misgivings (which few men will) there are times when the strongest Christians of us, I believe, have reeled under questionings of such staggering obscurity. I do not accuse you of this weakness. There are some who tremblingly reach out shaking hands to the guidance of Faith – Others who stoutly venture into the dark (their Human Confidence their leader, whom they mistake for Faith); and, investing themselves beforehand with Cherubic wings, as they fancy, find their new robes as familiar, and fitting to their supposed growth and stature in godliness, as the coat they left off yesterday – Some whose hope totters upon crutches – Others who stalk into futurity upon stilts.

The contemplation of a spiritual World, – which, without the addition of a misgiving conscience, is enough to shake some natures to their foundation – is smoothly got over by others, who shall float over the black billows, in their little boat of No-Distrust, as unconcernedly as over a summer sea. The difference is chiefly constitutional.

One man shall love his friends and his friends' faces; and, under the uncertainty of conversing with them again, in the same manner and familiar circumstances of sight, speech, &c., as upon earth – in a moment of no irreverent weakness – for a dream-while – no more – would be almost content, for a reward of a life of virtue (if he could ascribe such acceptance to his lame performances), to take up his portion with those he loved, and was made to love, in this good world, which he knows – which was created so lovely, beyond his deservings. Another, embracing a more exalted vision – so that he might receive indefinite additaments of power, knowledge, beauty, glory, &c. – is ready to forego the recognition of humbler individualities of earth, and the old familiar faces. The shapings of our heavens are the modifications of our constitution; and Mr Feeble Mind, or Mr Great Heart, is born in every one of us.

Some (and such have been accounted the safest divines) have shrunk from pronouncing upon the final state of any man; nor dare they pronounce the case of Judas to be desperate. Others (with stronger optics), as plainly as with the eye of flesh, shall behold a *given king* in bliss, and a *given chamberlain* in torment; even to the eternising of a cast of the eye in the latter, his own self-mocked and good-humouredly-borne deformity on earth, but supposed to aggravate the uncouth and hideous expression of his pangs in the other place. That one man can presume so far, and that another would with shuddering disclaim such

141

confidences, is, I believe, an effect of the nerves purely.

If in either of these Papers, or elsewhere, I have been betrayed into some levities – not affronting the sanctuary, but glancing perhaps at some of the out-skirts and extreme edges, the debateable land between the holy and the profane regions – (for the admixture of man's inventions twisting themselves with the name of religion itself, has artfully made it difficult to touch even the alloy, without, in some men's estimation, soiling the fine gold) – if I have sported within the purlieus of serious matter – it was, I dare say, a humour – be not startled, Sir – which I have unwittingly derived from yourself. You have all your life been making a jest of the Devil. Not of the scriptural meaning of that dark essence – personal or allegorical; for the nature is no where plainly delivered. I acquit you of intentional irreverence. But indeed you have made wonderfully free with, and been mighty pleasant upon, the popular idea and attributes of him. A noble Lord, your brother Visionary, has scarcely taken greater liberties with the material keys, and merely Catholic notion of St Peter. – You have flattered him in prose: you have chanted him in goodly odes. You have been his Jester; Volunteer Laureat, and self-elected Court Poet to Beëlzebub.

You have never ridiculed, I believe, what you thought to be religion, but you are always girding at what some pious, but perhaps mistaken folks, think to be so. For this reason I am sorry to hear, that you are engaged upon a life of George Fox. I know you will fall into the error of intermixing some comic stuff with your seriousness. The Quakers tremble at the subject in your hand. The Methodists are shy of you, upon account of *their* founder. But, above all, our Popish brethren are most in your debt. The errors of that church have proved a fruitful source to your scoffing vein. Their Legend has been a golden one to you. And here, your friends, Sir, have noticed a notable inconsistency. To the imposing rites, the solemn penances, devout austerities of that communion; the affecting though erring piety of their hermits; the silence and solitude of the Chartreux – their crossings, their holy waters – their Virgin, and their saints – to these, they say, you have been indebted for the best feelings, and the richest imagery, of your Epic poetry. You have drawn copious drafts upon Loretto. We thought at one time you were going to post to

142

Rome – but that in the facetious commentaries, which it is your custom to append so plentifully, and (some say) injudiciously, to your loftiest performances in this kind, you spurn the uplifted toe, which you but just now seemed to court; leave his holiness in the lurch; and show him a fair pair of Protestant heels under your Romish vestment. When we think you already at the wicket, suddenly a violent cross wind blows you transverse –

> ten thousand leagues awry.
> Then might we see
> Cowls, hoods, and habits, with their wearers, tost
> And flutter'd into rags; then reliques, beads,
> Indulgences, dispenses, pardons, bulls,
> The sport of winds.

You pick up pence by showing the hallowed bones, shrine, and crucifix; and you take money a second time by exposing the trick of them afterwards. You carry your verse to Castle Angelo for sale in a morning; and, swifter than a pedlar can transmute his pack, you are at Canterbury with your prose ware before night.

Sir, is it that I dislike you in this merry vein? The very reverse. No countenance becomes an intelligent jest better than your own. It is your grave aspect, when you look awful upon your poor friends, which I would deprecate.

In more than one place, if I mistake not, you have been pleased to compliment me at the expence of my companions. I cannot accept your compliment at such a price. The upbraiding a man's poverty naturally makes him look about him, to see whether he be so poor indeed as he is presumed to be. You have put me upon counting my riches. Really, Sir, I did not know I was so wealthy in the article of friendships. There is —, and —, whom you never heard of, but exemplary characters both, and excellent church-goers; and [Randall] N[orris], mine and my father's friend for nearly half a century; and the enthusiast for Wordsworth's poetry, T[homas] N[oon] T[alfourd], a little tainted with Socinianism, it is to be feared, but constant in his attachments, and a capital critic; and —, a sturdy old Athanasian, so that sets all to rights again; and W[ainwright], the light, and warm-as-light hearted, Janus of the London; and the translator of Dante, still

143

a curate, modest and amiable C[ary]; and Allan C[unningham],
the large-hearted Scot; and P[rocte]r, candid and affectionate as
his own poetry; and A[lso]p, Coleridge's friend; and G[illma]n,
his more than friend; and Coleridge himself, the same to me still,
as in those old evenings, when we used to sit and speculate (do
you remember them, Sir?) at our old Salutation tavern, upon
Pantisocracy and golden days to come on earth; and W[ordswor]th
(why, Sir, I might drop my rent-roll here; such goodly farms and
manors have I reckoned up already. In what possessions has not
this last name alone estated me! – but I will go on) – and M[onk-
house], the noble-minded kinsman, by wedlock, of W—th; and
H[enry] C[rabb] R[obinson], unwearied in the offices of a friend;
and Clarkson, almost above the narrowness of that relation, yet
condescending not seldom heretofore from the labours of his
world-embracing charity to bless my humble roof; and the gall-
less and single-minded Dyer; and the high-minded associate of
Cook, the veteran Colonel, with his lusty heart still sending car-
tels of defiance to old Time; and, not least, W[illiam] A[yrton],
the last and steadiest left to me of that little knot of whist-players,
that used to assemble weekly, for so many years, at the Queen's
Gate (you remember them, Sir?) and called Admiral Burney friend.

I will come to the point at once. I believe you will not make
many exceptions to my associates so far. But I have purposely
omitted some intimacies, which I do not yet repent of having
contracted, with two gentlemen, diametrically opposed to yourself in principles. You will understand me to allude to the authors
of Rimini and of the Table Talk. And first, of the former. –

It is an error more particularly incident to persons of the correctest
principles and habits, to seclude themselves from the rest of mankind, as from another species; and form into knots and clubs. The
best people, herding thus exclusively, are in danger of contracting
a narrowness. Heat and cold, dryness and moisture, in the natural
world, do not fly asunder, to split the globe into sectarian parts and
separations; but mingling, as they best may, correct the malignity
of any single predominance. The analogy holds, I suppose, in the
moral world. If all the good people were to ship themselves off to
Terra Incognitas, what, in humanity's name, is to become of the
refuse? If the persons, whom I chiefly have in view, have not

pushed matters to this extremity yet, they carry them as far as they can go. Instead of mixing with the infidel and the freethinker – in the room of opening a negociation, to try at least to find out at which gate the error entered – they huddle close together, in a weak fear of infection, like that pusillanimous underling in Spenser –

> This is the wandering wood, this Error's den;
> A monster vile, whom God and man does hate:
> Therefore, I reed, beware. Fly, fly, quoth then
> The fearful Dwarf,

and, if they be writers in orthodox journals – addressing themselves only to the irritable passions of the unbeliever – they proceed in a safe system of strengthening the strong hands, and confirming the valiant knees; of converting the already converted, and proselyting their own party. I am the more convinced of this from a passage in the very Treatise which occasioned this letter. It is where, having recommended to the doubter the writings of Michaelis and Lardner, you ride triumphant over the necks of all infidels, sceptics, and dissenters, from this time to the world's end, upon the wheels of two unanswerable deductions. I do not hold it meet to set down, in a Miscellaneous Compilation like this, such religious words as you have thought fit to introduce into the pages of a petulant Literary Journal. I therefore beg leave to substitute *numerals*, and refer to the Quarterly Review (for July) for filling of them up. 'Here,' you say, 'as in the history of 7, if these books are authentic, the events which they relate must be true; if they were written by 8, 9 is 10 and 11.' Your first deduction, if it means honestly, rests upon two identical propositions; though I suspect an unfairness in one of the terms, which this would not be quite the proper place for explicating. At all events *you* have no cause to triumph; you have not been proving the premises, but refer for satisfaction therein to very long and laborious works, which may well employ the sceptic a twelvemonth or two to digest, before he can possibly be ripe for your conclusion. When he has satisfied himself about the premises, he will concede to you the inference, I dare say, most readily. – But your latter deduction, *viz.* that because 8 has written a book concerning 9, therefore 10 and 11 was certainly his meaning, is one of the most

145

extraordinary conclusions *per saltum* that I have had the good fortune to meet with. As far as 10 is verbally asserted in the writings, all sects must agree with you; but you cannot be ignorant of the many various ways in which the doctrine of the * * * * * * * * * has been understood, from a low figurative expression (with the Unitarians) up to the most mysterious actuality; in which highest sense alone you and your church take it. And for 11, that there is *no other possible conclusion* – to hazard this in the face of so many thousands of Arians and Socinians, &c., who have drawn so opposite a one, is such a piece of theological hardihood, as, I think, warrants me in concluding that, when you sit down to pen theology, you do not at all consider your opponents; but have in your eye, merely and exclusively, readers of the same way of thinking with yourself, and therefore have no occasion to trouble yourself, with the quality of the logic, to which you treat them.

Neither can I think, if you had had the welfare of the poor child – over whose hopeless condition you whine so lamentably and (I must think) unseasonably – seriously at heart, that you could have taken the step of sticking him up *by name* – T[hornton] H[unt] is as good as *naming* him – to perpetuate an outrage upon the paternal feelings, as long as the Quarterly Review shall last. – Was it necessary to specify an individual case, and give to Christian compassion the appearance of personal attack? Is this the way to conciliate unbelievers, or not rather to widen the breach irreparably?

I own I could never think so considerably of myself as to decline the society of an agreeable or worthy man upon difference of opinion only. The impediments and the facilitations to a sound belief are various and inscrutable as the heart of man. Some believe upon weak principles. Others cannot feel the efficacy of the strongest. One of the most candid, most upright, and single-meaning men, I ever knew, was the late Thomas Holcroft. I believe he never said one thing and meant another, in his life; and, as near as I can guess, he never acted otherwise than with the most scrupulous attention to conscience. Ought we to wish the character false, for the sake of a hollow compliment to Christianity?

Accident introduced me to the acquaintance of Mr L[eigh] H[unt] – and the experience of his many friendly qualities confirmed a friendship between us. You, who have been misrepresented

146

yourself, I should hope, have not lent an idle ear to the calumnies which have been spread abroad respecting this gentle-man. I was admitted to his household for some years, and do most solemnly aver that I believe him to be in his domestic relations as correct as any man. He chose an ill-judged subject for a poem; the peccant humours of which have been visited on him tenfold by the artful use, which his adversaries have made, of an *equivocal term*. The subject itself was started by Dante, but better because brieflier treated of. But the crime of the Lovers, in the Italian and the English poet, with its aggravated enormity of circumstance, is not of a kind (as the critics of the latter well knew) with those conjunctions, for which Nature herself has provided no excuse, because no temptation. – It has nothing in common with the black horrors, sung by Ford and Massinger. The familiarising of it in tale or fable may be for that reason incidentally more contagious. In spite of Rimini, I must look upon its author as a man of taste, and a poet. He is better than so, he is one of the most cordial-minded men I ever knew, and matchless as a fire-side companion. I mean not to affront or wound your feelings when I say that, in his more genial moods, he has often reminded me of you. There is the same air of mild dogmatism – the same condescending to a boyish sportiveness – in both your conversations. His hand-writing is so much the same with your own, that I have opened more than one letter of his, hoping, nay, not doubting, but it was from you, and have been disappointed (he will bear with my saying so) at the discovery of my error. L.H. is unfortunate in holding some loose and not very definite speculations (for at times I think he hardly knows whither his premises would carry him) on marriage – the tenets, I conceive, of the Political Justice, carried a little further. For anything I could discover in his practice, they have reference, like those, to some future possible condition of society, and not to the present times. But neither for these obliquities of thinking (upon which my own conclusions are as distant as the poles asunder) – nor for his political asperities and petulancies, which are wearing out with the heats and vanities of youth – did I select him for a friend; but for qualities which fitted him for that relation. I do not know whether I flatter myself with being the occasion, but certain it is, that, touched with some misgivings for sundry harsh things which

147

he had written aforetime against our friend C[oleridge], – before he left this country he sought a reconciliation with that gentleman (himself being his own introducer), and found it.

L.H. is now in Italy; on his departure to which land with much regret I took my leave of him and of his little family – seven of them, Sir, with their mother – and as kind a set of little people (T[hornton] H[unt] and all), as affectionate children, as ever blessed a parent. Had you seen them, Sir, I think you could not have looked upon them as so many little Jonases – but rather as pledges of the vessel's safety, that was to bear such a freight of love.

I wish you would read Mr H.'s lines to that same T.H., 'six years old, during a sickness':

> Sleep breaks at last from out thee,
> My little patient boy –

(they are to be found on the 47th page of 'Foliage') – and ask yourself how far they are out of the spirit of Christianity. I have a letter from Italy, received but the other day, into which L.H. has put as much heart, and as many friendly yearnings after old associates, and native country, as, I think, paper can well hold. It would do you no hurt to give that the perusal also.

From the *other gentleman* I neither expect nor desire (as he is well assured) any such concessions as L.H. made to C. What hath soured him, and made him to suspect his friends of infidelity towards him, when there was no such matter, I know not. I stood well with him for fifteen years (the proudest of my life), and have ever spoke my full mind of him to some, to whom his panegyric must naturally be least tasteful. I never in thought swerved from him, I never betrayed him, I never slackened in my admiration of him, I was the same to him (neither better nor worse) though he could not see it, as in the days when he thought fit to trust me. At this instant, he may be preparing for me some compliment, above my deserts, as he has sprinkled many such among his admirable books, for which I rest his debtor; or, for any thing I know, or can guess to the contrary, he may be about to read a lecture on my weaknesses. He is welcome to them (as he was to my humble hearth), if they can divert a spleen, or ventilate a fit of sullenness. I wish he would not quarrel with the world at the rate he does;

but the reconciliation must be effected by himself, and I despair of living to see that day. But, protesting against much that he has written, and some things which he chooses to do; judging him by his conversation which I enjoyed so long, and relished so deeply; or by his books, in those places where no clouding passion intervenes – I should belie my own conscience, if I said less, than that I think W[illiam] H[azlitt] to be, in his natural and healthy state, one of the wisest and finest spirits breathing. So far from being ashamed of that intimacy, which was betwixt us, it is my boast that I was able for so many years to have preserved it entire; and I think I shall go to my grave without finding, or expecting to find, such another companion. But I forget my manners – you will pardon me, Sir – I return to the correspondence. —

Sir, you were pleased (you know where) to invite me to a compliance with the wholesome forms and doctrines of the Church of England. I take your advice with as much kindness, as it was meant. But I must think the invitation rather more kind than seasonable. I am a Dissenter. The last sect, with which you can remember me to have made common confession, were the Unitarians. You would think it not very pertinent, if (fearing that all was not well with you), I were gravely to invite you (for a remedy) to attend with me a course of Mr Belsham's Lectures at Hackney. Perhaps I have scruples to some of your forms and doctrines. But if I come, am I secure of civil treatment? – The last time I was in any of your places of worship was on Easter Sunday last. I had the satisfaction of listening to a very sensible sermon of an argumentative turn, delivered with great propriety, by one of your bishops. The place was Westminster Abbey. As such religion, as I have, has always acted on me more by way of sentiment than argumentative process, I was not unwilling, after sermon ended, by no unbecoming transition, to pass over to some serious feelings, impossible to be disconnected from the sight of those old tombs, &c. But, by whose order I know not, I was debarred that privilege even for so short a space as a few minutes; and turned, like a dog or some profane person, out into the common street; with feelings, which I could not help, but not very congenial to the day or the discourse. I do not know that I shall ever venture myself again into one of your Churches.

You had your education at Westminster; and doubtless among those dim aisles and cloisters, you must have gathered much of that devotional feeling in those young years, on which your purest mind feeds still – and may it feed! The antiquarian spirit, strong in you, and gracefully blending ever with the religious, may have been sown in you among those wrecks of splendid mortality. You owe it to the place of your education; you owe it to your learned fondness for the architecture of your ancestors; you owe it to the venerableness of your ecclesiastical establishment, which is daily lessened and called in question through these practices – to speak aloud your sense of them; never to desist raising your voice against them, till they be totally done away with and abolished; till the doors of Westminster Abbey be no longer closed against the decent, though low-in-purse, enthusiast, or blameless devotee, who must commit an injury against his family economy, if he would be indulged with a bare admission within its walls. You owe it to the decencies, which you wish to see maintained in its impressive services, that our Cathedral be no longer an object of inspection to the poor at those times only, in which they must rob from their attendance on the worship every minute which they can bestow upon the fabrick. In vain the public prints have taken up this subject, in vain such poor nameless writers as myself express their indignation. A word from you, Sir – a hint in your Journal – would be sufficient to fling open the doors of the Beautiful Temple again, as we can remember them when we were boys. At that time of life, what would the imaginative faculty (such as it is) in both of us, have suffered, if the entrance to so much reflection had been obstructed by the demand of so much silver! – If we had scraped it up to gain an occasional admission (as we certainly should have done) would the sight of those old tombs have been as impressive to us (while we had been weighing anxiously prudence against sentiment) as when the gates stood open, as those of the adjacent Park; when we could walk in at any time, as the mood brought us, for a shorter or longer time, as *that* lasted? Is the being shown over a place the same as silently for ourselves detecting the genius of it? In no part of our beloved Abbey now can a person find entrance (out of service time) under the sum of *two shillings*. The rich and the great will smile at the anticlimax, presumed to lie in these two short words. But you can tell them, Sir, how much quiet worth, how much capacity for enlarged feeling, how much taste and genius, may coexist, especially in youth, with a purse incompetent to this demand. – A respected friend of ours, during his late visit to the metropolis, presented himself for admission to Saint Paul's. At the same time a decently clothed man, with as decent a wife and child, were bargaining for the same indulgence. The price was only two-pence each person. The poor but decent man hesitated, desirous to go in; but there were three of them, and he turned away reluctantly. Perhaps he wished to have seen the tomb of Nelson. Perhaps the Interior of the Cathedral was his object. But in the state of his finances, even sixpence might reasonably seem too much. Tell the Aristocracy of the country (no man can do it more impressively); instruct them of what value these insignificant pieces of money, these minims to their sight, may be to their humbler brethren. Shame these Sellers out of the Temple. Show the poor, that you can sometimes think of them in some other light than as mutineers and mal-contents. Conciliate them by such kind methods to their superiors, civil and ecclesiastical. Stop the mouths of the railers; and suffer your old friends, upon the old terms, again to honour and admire you. Stifle not the suggestions of your better nature with the stale evasion, that an indiscriminate admission would expose the Tombs to violation. Remember your boy-days. Did you ever see, or hear, of a mob in the Abbey, while it was free to all? Did the rabble come there, or trouble their heads about such speculations? It is all that you can do to drive them into your churches; they do not voluntarily offer themselves. They have, alas! no passion for antiquities; for tomb of king or prelate, sage or poet. If they had, they would be no longer the rabble.

For forty years that I have known the Fabrick, the only well-attested charge of violation adduced, has been – a ridiculous dismemberment committed upon the effigy of that amiable spy Major André. And is it for this – the wanton mischief of some school-boy, fired perhaps with raw notions of Transatlantic Freedom – or the remote possibility of such a mischief occurring again, so easily to be prevented by stationing a constable within the walls, if the vergers are incompetent to the duty – is it upon such

151

wretched pretences, that the people of England are made to pay a new Peter's Pence, so long abrogated; or must content themselves with contemplating the ragged Exterior of their Cathedral? The mischief was done about the time that you were a scholar there. Do you know any thing about the unfortunate relic? – can you help us in this emergency to find the nose? – or can you give Chantry a notion (from memory) of its pristine life and vigour? I am willing for peace' sake to subscribe my guinea towards a restoration of the lamented feature.

I am, Sir,

Your humble servant,

ELIA.

Printed in *The London Magazine* in 1823 and republished ten years later, much amended, in *The Last Essays of Elia* under the title 'The Tombs in The Abbey'.

On the Literary Gazette

In merry England I computed once
The number of the dunces – dunce for dunce;
There were *four hundred*, if I don't forget,
All readers of the L[iterar]y G[azett]e;
But if the author to himself keep true,
In some short months they'll be reduced to *two*.

The Examiner, 1830

Sonnet

St Crispin to Mr Gifford

All unadvised, and in an evil hour,
    Lured by aspiring thoughts, my son, you daft
    The lowly labours of the Gentle Craft

152

For learned toils, which blood and spirits sour.
All things, dear pledge, are not in all men's power;
 The wiser sort of shrub affects the ground;
 And sweet content of mind is oftener found
In cobbler's parlour, than in critic's bower.
The sorest work is what doth cross the grain;
 And better to this hour you had been plying
 The obsequious awl with well-waxed finger flying,
Than ceaseless thus to till a thankless vein;
 Still teazing Muses, which are still denying;
Making a stretching-leather of your brain.

The Examiner, 1810

The Triumph of the Whale

Io! Pæan! Io! sing
To the finny people's King.
Not a mightier Whale than this
In the vast Atlantic is;
Not a fatter fish than he
Flounders round the polar sea.
See his blubber – at his gills
What a world of drink he swills,
From his trunk, as from a spout,
Which next moment he pours out.
 Such his person – next declare,
Muse, who his companions are. –
Every fish of generous kind
Scuds aside, or slinks behind;
But about his presence keep
All the Monsters of the Deep;
Mermaids, with their tails and singing
His delighted fancy stinging;
Crooked Dolphins, they surround him,
Dog-like Seals, they fawn around him.
Following hard the progress mark,

153

Of the intolerant salt sea Shark.
For his solace and relief,
Flat-fish are his courtiers chief.
Last and lowest in his train,
Ink-fish (libellers of the main)
Their black liquor shed in spite:
(Such on earth *the things that write*.)
In his stomach, some do say,
No good thing can ever stay.
Had it been the fortune of it
To have swallowed that old Prophet,
Three days there he'd not have dwell'd,
But in one have been expell'd.
Hapless mariners are they,
Who beguil'd (as seamen say),
Deeming him some rock or island,
Footing sure, safe spot, and dry land,
Anchor in his scaly rind;
Soon the difference they find
Sudden plumb he sinks beneath them;
Does to ruthless seas bequeathe them.

   Name or title, what has he?
Is he Regent of the Sea?
From this difficulty free us,
Buffon, Banks, or sage Linnæus.
With his wondrous attributes
Say, what appellation suits?
By his bulk, and by his size,
By his oily qualities,
This (or else my eyesight fails),
This should be the PRINCE OF WHALES.

The Examiner, 1812.

IV

MORE HOUSE LAMB THAN GRASS LAMB

Elia – much more of house Lamb than
of grass Lamb – avowedly caring little
or nothing for pastoral.

Thomas Hood (in a description of a
London Magazine dinner),
London Magazine, 1822.

To Thomas Manning

[P.M. Nov. 28, 1800.]

Dear Manning,

– I have received a very kind invitation from Lloyd and Sophia to go and spend a month with them at the Lakes. Now it fortunately happens (which is so seldom the case!) that I have spare cash by me, enough to answer the expenses of so long a journey; and I am determined to get away from the office by some means. The purpose of this letter is to request of you (my dear friend) that you will not take it unkind if I decline my proposed visit to Cambridge *for the present*. Perhaps I shall be able to take Cambridge *in my way*, going or coming. I need not describe to you the expectations which such an one as myself, pent up all my life in a dirty city, have formed of a tour to the Lakes. Consider Grasmere! Ambleside! Wordsworth! Coleridge! I hope you will. Hills, woods, lakes, and mountains, to the eternal devil. I will eat snipes with thee, Thomas Manning. Only confess, confess, a *bite*.

P.S. I think you named the 16th; but was it not modest of Lloyd to send such an invitation! It shows his knowledge of *money* and *time*. I would be loth to think he meant

> 'Ironic satire sidelong sklented
> On my poor pursie.' – BURNS.

For my part, with reference to my friends northward, I must confess that I am not romance-bit about *Nature*. The earth, and sea, and sky (when all is said) is but as a house to dwell in. If the inmates be courteous, and good liquors flow like the conduits at an old coronation; if they can talk sensibly and feel properly; I have no need to stand staring upon the gilded looking-glass (that strained my friend's purse-strings in the purchase), nor his five-shilling print over the mantelpiece of old Nabbs the carrier

157

(which only betrays his false taste). Just as important to me (in a sense) is all the furniture of my world – eye-pampering, but satisfies no heart. Streets, streets, streets, markets, theatres, churches, Covent Gardens, shops sparkling with pretty faces of industrious milliners, neat sempstresses, ladies cheapening, gentlemen behind counters lying, authors in the street with spectacles, George Dyers (you may know them by their gait), lamps lit at night, pastry-cooks' and silver-smiths' shops, beautiful Quakers of Pentonville, noise of coaches, drowsy cry of mechanic watchman at night, with bucks reeling home drunk; if you happen to wake at midnight, cries of Fire and Stop thief; inns of court, with their learned air, and halls, and butteries, just like Cambridge colleges; old book-stalls, Jeremy Taylors, Burtons on Melancholy, and Religio Medicis on every stall. These are thy pleasures, O London with-the-many-sins. For these may Keswick and her giant brood go hang!

C.L.

To William Wordsworth

[P.M. January 30, 1801.]
Thanks for your Letter and Present. I had already borrowed your second volume. What most please me are, the Song of Lucy.... *Simon's sickly daughter* in the Sexton made me *cry*. Next to these are the description of the continuous Echoes in the story of Joanna's laugh, where the mountains and all the scenery absolutely seem alive – and that fine Shakesperian character of the Happy Man, in the Brothers,

> — that creeps about the fields,
> Following his fancies by the hour, to bring
> Tears down his cheek, or solitary smiles
> Into his face, *until the Setting Sun*
> *Write Fool upon his forehead.*

I will mention one more: the delicate and curious feeling in the wish for the Cumberland Beggar, that he may have about him the melody of Birds, altho' he hear them not. Here the mind knowingly passes a fiction upon herself, first substituting her own feelings for the Beggar's, and, in the same breath detecting the fallacy, will not part with the wish. – The Poet's Epitaph is disfigured, to my taste by the vulgar satire upon parsons and lawyers in the beginning, and the coarse epithet of pin point in the 6th stanza. All the rest is eminently good, and your own. I will just add that it appears to me a fault in the Beggar, that the instructions conveyed in it are too direct and like a lecture: they don't slide into the mind of the reader, while he is imagining no such matter. An intelligent reader finds a sort of insult in being told, I will teach you how to think upon this subject. This fault, if I am right, is in a ten-thousandth worse degree to be found in Sterne and many many novelists and modern poets, who continually put a sign post up to shew where you are to feel. They set out with assuming their readers to be stupid. Very different from Robinson Crusoe, the Vicar of Wakefield, Roderick Random, and other beautiful bare narratives. There is implied an unwritten compact between Author and reader; I will tell you a story, and I suppose you will understand it. Modern novels 'St Leons' and the like are full of such flowers as these 'Let not my reader suppose', 'Imagine, *if you can*' – modest! – &c. – I will here have done with praise and blame. I have written so much, only that you may not think I have passed over your book without observation. – I am sorry that Coleridge has christened his Ancient Marinere 'a poet's Reverie' – it is as bad as Bottom the Weaver's declaration that he is not a Lion but only the scenical representation of a Lion. What new idea is gained by this Title, but one subversive of all credit, which the tale should force upon us, of its truth? For me, I was never so affected with any human Tale. After first reading it, I was totally possessed with it for many days – I dislike all the miraculous part of it, but the feelings of the man under the operation of such scenery dragged me along like Tom Piper's magic whistle. I totally differ from your idea that the Marinere should have had a character and profession. This is a Beauty in Gulliver's Travels, where the mind is kept in a placid state of little wonderments; but the Ancient Marinere undergoes such trials, as overwhelm and bury all individuality or memory of what he was, like the state of a man in a Bad dream, one terrible peculiarity of which is: that all consciousness of personality is gone. Your other observation is I think as well a little unfounded: the Marinere from being conversant in supernatural events *has* acquired a supernatural and strange cast of *phrase*, eye, appearance, &c. which frighten the wedding guest. You will excuse my remarks, because I am hurt and vexed that you should think it necessary, with a prose apology, to open the eyes of dead men that cannot see. To sum up a general opinion of the second vol. – I do not feel any one poem in it so forcibly as the Ancient Marinere, the Mad Mother, and the Lines at Tintern Abbey in the first. – I could, too, have wished the Critical preface had appeared in a separate treatise. All its dogmas are true and just, and most of them new, *as* criticism. But they associate a *diminishing* idea with the Poems which follow, as having been written for *Experiment* on the public taste, more than having sprung (as they must have done) from living and daily circumstances. – I am prolix, because I am gratifyed in the opportunity of writing to you, and I don't well know when to leave off. I ought before this to have reply'd to your very kind invitation into Cumberland. With you and your Sister I could gang any where. But I am afraid whether I shall ever be able to afford so desperate a Journey. Separate from the pleasure of your company, I don't much care if I never see a mountain in my life. I have passed all my days in London, until I have formed as many and intense local attachments, as any of you mountaineers can have done with dead nature.

The Lighted shops of the Strand and Fleet Street, the innumerable trades, tradesmen and customers, coaches, waggons, playhouses, all the bustle and wickedness round about Covent Garden, the very women of the Town, the Watchmen, drunken scenes, rattles, – life awake, if you awake, at all hours of the night, the impossibility of being dull in Fleet Street, the crowds, the very dirt & mud, the Sun shining upon houses and pavements, the print shops, the old book stalls, parsons cheap'ning books, coffee houses, steams of soup from kitchens, the pantomimes,

London itself a pantomime and a masquerade, – all these things work themselves into my mind and feed me, without a power of satiating me. The wonder of these sights impells me into night-walks about her crowded streets, and I often shed tears in the motley Strand from fulness of joy at so much Life. – All these emotions must be strange to you. So are your rural emotions to me. But consider, what must I have been doing all my life, not to have lent great portions of my heart with usury to such scenes? –

My attachments are all local, purely local. I have no passion (or have had none since I was in love, and then it was the spurious engendering of poetry & books) to groves and vallies. The rooms where I was born, the furniture which has been before my eyes all my life, a book case which has followed me about (like a faithful dog, only exceeding him in knowledge) wherever I have moved – old chairs, old tables, streets, squares, where I have sunned myself, my old school, – these are my mistresses. Have I not enough, without your mountains? I do not envy you. I should pity you, did I not know, that the Mind will make friends of any thing. Your sun & moon and skys and hills & lakes affect me no more, or scarcely come to me in more venerable characters, than as a gilded room with tapestry and tapers, where I might live with handsome visible objects. I consider the clouds above me but as a roof, beautifully painted but unable to satisfy the mind, and at last, like the pictures of the apartment of a connoisseur, unable to afford him any longer a pleasure. So fading upon me, from disuse, have been the Beauties of Nature, as they have been confinedly called; so ever fresh & green and warm are all the inventions of men and assemblies of men in this great city. I should certainly have laughed with dear Joanna.

Give my kindest love, *and my sister's*, to D[orothy] & your*self* and a kiss from me to little Barbara Lewthwaite.

C. LAMB.

Thank you for Liking my Play!!

The Londoner

I was born under the shadow of St Dunstan's steeple, just where the conflux of the eastern and western inhabitants of this twofold city meet and jostle in friendly opposition at Temple Bar. The same day which gave me to the world saw London happy in the celebration of her great annual feast. This I cannot help looking upon as a lively omen of the future great good-will which I was destined to bear toward the city, resembling in kind that solicitude which every chief magistrate is supposed to feel for whatever concerns her interests and well-being. Indeed, I consider myself in some sort a speculative Lord Mayor of London; for though circumstances unhappily preclude me from the hope of ever arriving at the dignity of a gold chain and Spital sermon, yet thus much will I say of myself in truth, that Whittington with his cat (just emblem of vigilance and a furred gown) never went beyond me in affection which I bear to the citizens.

I was born, as you have heard, in a crowd. This has begot in me an entire affection for that way of life, amounting to an almost insurmountable aversion from solitude and rural scenes. This aversion was never interrupted or suspended except for a few years in the younger part of my life, during a period in which I had set my affections upon a charming young woman. Every man, while the passion is upon him, is for a time at least addicted to groves and meadows and purling streams. During this short period of my existence, I contracted just familiarity enough with rural *objects* to understand tolerably well ever after the *poets* when they declaim in such passionate terms in favour of a country life.

For my own part, now the fit is past, I have no hesitation in declaring that a mob of happy faces crowding up at the pit-door of Drury Lane Theatre, just at the hour of six, gives me ten thousand sincerer pleasures than I could ever receive from all the flocks of silly sheep that ever whitened the plains of Arcadia or Epsom Downs.

This passion for crowds is nowhere feasted so full as in London. The man must have a rare recipe for melancholy who can be dull in Fleet Street. I am naturally inclined to Hypochondria, but in London it vanishes, like all other ills. Often, when I have felt a

162

weariness or distaste at home, have I rushed out into her crowded Strand and fed my humour, till tears have wetted my cheek for unutterable sympathies with the multitudinous moving picture, which she never fails to present at all hours, like the scenes of a shifting pantomime.

The very deformities of London, which give distaste to others, from habit do not displease me. The endless succession of shops, where *fancy, miscalled folly*, is supplied with perpetual gauds and toys, excite in me no puritanical aversion. I gladly behold every appetite supplied with its proper food. The obliging customer and the obliged tradesman – things which live by bowing and things which exist but for homage – do not affect me with disgust; from habit I perceive nothing but urbanity, where other men, more refined, discover meanness. I love the very smoke of London because it has been the medium most familiar in my vision. I see grand principles of honour at work in the dirty ring which encompasses two combatants with fists, and principles of no less eternal justice in the detection of a pick-pocket. The salutary astonishment with which an execution is surveyed convinces me, more forcibly than a hundred volumes of abstract polity, that the universal instinct of man in all ages has leaned to order and good government.

Thus an art of extracting morality from the commonest incidents of a town life is attained by the same well-natured alchemy with which the foresters of Arden, in a beautiful country –

Found tongues in trees, books in the running brooks,
Sermons in stones, and good in everything.

Where has Spleen her food but in London? Humour, Interest, Curiosity, suck at her measureless breasts without a possibility of being satiated. Nursed amid her noise, her crowds, her beloved smoke, what have I been doing all my life, if I have not lent out my heart with usury to such scenes!

This essay was collected in the 1818 edition of Lamb's works as addressed to the Editor of the *Reflector*. In fact it had been published in the *Morning Post*, eight years before the birth of Leigh Hunt's short-lived quarterly, in February 1802, and did not appear in the pages of the *Reflector*.

To Thomas Manning

My dear Manning,
– Since the date of my last letter, I have been a traveller. A strong
desire seized me of visiting remote regions. My first impulse was
to go and see Paris. It was a trivial objection to my aspiring mind,
that I did not understand a word of the language, since I certainly
intend some time in my life to see Paris, and equally certainly never
intend to learn the language; therefore that could be no objection.
However, I am very glad I did not go, because you had left Paris
(I see) before I could have set out. I believe, Stoddart promising
to go with me another year prevented that plan. My next scheme,
(for to my restless, ambitious mind London was become a bed
of thorns) was to visit the far-famed Peak in Derbyshire, where
the Devil sits, they say, without breeches. *This* my purer mind
rejected as indelicate. And my final resolve was a tour to the Lakes.
I set out with Mary to Keswick, without giving Coleridge any
notice; for my time being precious did not admit of it. He received
us with all the hospitality in the world, and gave up his time to
show us all the wonders of the country. He dwells upon a small
hill by the side of Keswick, in a comfortable house, quite enveloped
on all sides by a net of mountains: great floundering bears and
monsters they seemed, all couchant and asleep. We got in in the
evening, travelling in a post-chaise from Penrith, in the midst of
a gorgeous sunshine, which transmuted all the mountains into
colours, purple, &c., &c. We thought we had got into fairyland.
But that went off (as it never came again – while we stayed we had
no more fine sunsets); and we entered Coleridge's comfortable
study just in the dusk, when the mountains were all dark with
clouds upon their heads. Such an impression I never received from
objects of sight before, nor do I suppose I can ever again. Glorious
creatures, fine old fellows, Skiddaw, &c., I never shall forget ye,
how ye lay about that night, like an intrenchment; gone to bed, as
it seemed for the night, but promising that ye were to be seen in
the morning. Coleridge had got a blazing fire in his study; which
is a large, antique, ill-shaped room, with an old-fashioned organ,

never played upon, big enough for a church, shelves of scattered folios, an Æolian harp, and an old sofa, half-bed, &c. And all looking out upon the last fading view of Skiddaw and his broad-breasted brethren: what a night! Here we stayed three full weeks, in which time I visited Wordsworth's cottage, where we stayed a day or two with the Clarksons (good people and most hospitable, at whose house we tarried one day and night), and saw Lloyd. The Wordsworths were gone to Calais. They have since been in London and past much time with us: he is now gone into Yorkshire to be married to a girl of small fortune, but he is in expectation of augmenting his own in consequence of the death of Lord Lonsdale, who kept him out of his own in conformity with a plan my lord had taken up in early life of making everybody unhappy. So we have seen Keswick, Grasmere, Ambleside, Ulswater (where the Clarksons live), and a place at the other end of Ulswater – I forget the name – to which we travelled on a very sultry day, over the middle of Helvellyn. We have clambered up to the top of Skiddaw, and I have waded up the bed of Lodore. In fine, I have satisfied myself, that there is such a thing as that which tourists call *romantic*, which I very much suspected before: they make such a spluttering about it, and toss their splendid epithets around them, till they give as dim a light as at four o'clock next morning the lamps do after an illumination. Mary was excessively tired, when she got about half-way up Skiddaw, but we came to a cold rill (than which nothing can be imagined more cold, running over cold stones), and with the reinforcement of a draught of cold water she surmounted it most manfully. Oh, its fine black head, and the bleak air atop of it, with a prospect of mountains all about, and about, making you giddy; and then Scotland afar off, and the border countries so famous in song and ballad! It was a day that will stand out, like a mountain, I am sure, in my life. But I am returned (I have now been come home near three weeks – I was a month out), and you cannot conceive the degradation I felt at first, from being accustomed to wander free as air among mountains, and bathe in rivers without being controlled by any one, to come home and *work*. I felt very *little*. I had been dreaming I was a very great man. But that is going off, and I find I shall conform in time to that state of life to which it has pleased God to call me. Besides, after all, Fleet-Street and the

165

Strand are better places to live in for good and all than among Skiddaw. Still, I turn back to those great places where I wandered about, participating in their greatness. After all, I could not *live* in Skiddaw. I could spend a year – two, three years – among them, but I must have a prospect of seeing Fleet-Street at the end of that time, or I should mope and pine away, I know. Still, Skiddaw is a fine creature. My habits are changing, I think: *i.e.* from drunk to sober. Whether I shall be happier or not remains to be proved. I shall certainly be more happy in a morning; but whether I shall not sacrifice the fat, and the marrow, and the kidneys, *i.e.* the night, the glorious care-drowning night, that heals all our wrongs, pours wine into our mortifications, changes the scene from indifferent and flat to bright and brilliant! – O Manning, if I should have formed a diabolical resolution, by the time you come to England, of not admitting any spiritous liquors into my house, will you be my guest on such shame-worthy terms? Is life, with such limitations, worth trying? The truth is, that my liquors bring a nest of friendly harpies about my house, who consume me. This is a pitiful tale to be read at St Gothard; but it is just now nearest my heart. Fenwick is a ruined man. He is hiding himself from his creditors, and has sent his wife and children into the country. Fell, my other drunken companion (that has been: nam hic cæstus artemque repono), is turned editor of a 'Naval Chronicle'. Godwin (with a pitiful artificial wife) continues a steady friend, though the same facility does not remain of visiting him often. That Bitch has detached Marshall from his house, Marshall the man who went to sleep when the 'Ancient Mariner' was reading; the old, steady, unalterable friend of the Professor. Holcroft is not yet come to town. I expect to see him, and will deliver your message. How I hate *this part* of a letter. Things come crowding in to say, and no room for 'em. Some things are too little to be told, *i.e.* to have a preference; some are too big and circumstantial. Thanks for yours, which was most delicious. Would I had been with you, benighted &c. I fear my head is turned with wandering. I shall never be the same acquiescent being. Farewell; write again quickly, for I shall not like to hazard a letter, not knowing where the fates have carried you. Farewell, my dear fellow.

C. LAMB.

To William Wordsworth

[Dated at end: August 9, 1814.]

Dear Wordsworth,

I cannot tell you how pleased I was at the receit of the great Armful of Poetry which you have sent me, and to get it before the rest of the world too! I have gone quite through with it, and was thinking to have accomplished that pleasure a second time before I wrote to thank you, but M. Burney came in the night (while we were out) and made holy theft of it, but we expect restitution in a day or two. It is the noblest conversational poem I ever read. A day in heaven. The part (or rather main body) which has left the sweetest odour on my memory (a bad term for the remains of an impression so recent) is the Tales of the Churchyard. The only girl among seven brethren, born out of due time and not duly taken away again – the deaf man and the blind man – the Jacobite and the Hanoverian whom antipathies reconcile – the Scarron-entry of the rusticating parson upon his solitude – these were all new to me too. My having known the story of Margaret (at the beginning), a very old acquaintance, even as long back as I saw you first at Stowey, did not make her reappearance less fresh. I don't know what to pick out of this Best of Books upon the best subjects for partial naming.

That gorgeous Sunset is famous, I think it must have been the identical one we saw on Salisbury plain five years ago, that drew Phillips from the card table where he had sat from rise of that luminary to its unequall'd set, but neither he nor I had gifted eyes to see those symbols of common things glorified such as the prophets saw them, in that sunset – the wheel – the potter's clay – the wash pot – the wine press – the almond tree rod – the baskets of figs – the four-fold visaged head, the throne and him that sat thereon.

One feeling I was particularly struck with as what I recognised so very lately at Harrow Church on entering in it after a hot and secular day's pleasure, – the instantaneous coolness and calming, almost transforming, properties of a country church just entered – a certain fragrance which it has – either from its holiness, or

167

being kept shut all the week, or the air that is let in being pure country – exactly what you have reduced into words but I am feeling I cannot. The reading your lines about it fixed me for a time, a monument, in Harrow Church, (do you know it?) with its fine long Spire white as washd marble, to be seen by vantage of its high site as far as Salisbury spire itself almost.

I shall select a day or two very shortly when I am coolest in brain to have a steady second reading, which I feel will lead to many more, for it will be a stock book with me while eyes or spectacles shall be lent me.

There is a deal of noble matter about mountain scenery, yet not so much as to overpower and discountenance a poor Londoner or South country man entirely, though Mary seems to have felt it occasionally a little too powerfully, for it was her remark during reading it that by your system it was doubtful whether a Liver in Towns had a Soul to be Saved. She almost trembled for that invisible part of us in her.

Save for a late excursion to Harrow and a day or two on the banks of the Thames this Summer, rural images were fast fading from my mind, and by the wise provision of the Regent all that was countryfy'd in the Parks is all but obliterated. The very colour of green is vanishd, the whole surface of Hyde Park is dry crumbling sand (Arabia Arenosa), not a vestige or hint of grass ever having grown there, booths and drinking places go all round it for a mile and half I am confident – I might say two miles in circuit – the stench of liquors, *bad* tobacco, dirty people and provisions, conquers the air and we are stifled and suffocated in Hyde Park.

Order after Order has been issued by L^d. Sidmouth in the name of the Regent (acting in behalf of his Royal father) for the dispersion of the varlets, but in vain. The vis unita of all the Publicans in London, Westm^r·, Marybone, and miles round is too powerful a force to put down. The Regent has rais'd a phantom which he cannot lay. There they'll stay probably for ever. The whole beauty of the Place is gone – that lake-look of the Serpentine – it has got foolish ships upon it – but something whispers to have confidence in nature and its revival –

at the coming of the *milder day*
These monuments shall all be overgrown.

Meantime I confess to have smoked one delicious Pipe in one of the cleanliest and goodliest of the booths – a tent rather, 'O call it not a booth!' – erected by the public Spirit of Watson, who keeps the Adam and Eve at Pancras (the ale houses have all emigrated with their train of bottles, mugs, corkscrews, waiters, into Hyde Park – whole Ale houses with all their Ale!) in company with some of the guards that had been in France and a fine French girl (habited like a Princess of Banditti) which one of the dogs had transported from the Garonne to the Serpentine. The unusual scene in H. Park, by Candlelight in open air, good tobacco, bottled stout, made it look like an interval in a campaign, a repose after battle, I almost fancied scars smarting and was ready to club a story with my comrades of some of my lying deeds.

After all, the fireworks were splendid – the Rockets in clusters, in trees and all shapes, spreading about like young stars in the making, floundering about in Space (like unbroke horses) till some of Newton's calculations should fix them, but then they went out. Any one who could see 'em and the still finer showers of gloomy rain fire that fell sulkily and angrily from 'em, and could go to bed without dreaming of the Last Day, must be as hardened an Atheist as * * * * * *.

Again let me thank you for your present and assure you that fireworks and triumphs have not distracted me from receiving a calm and noble enjoyment from it (which I trust I shall often), and I sincerely congratulate you on its appearance.

With kindest remembrances to you & household, we remain – yours sincerely

C. LAMB and sister.

9 Aug., 1814.

169

Written at Cambridge, August 15, 1819

I was not train'd in Academic bowers
And to those learned streams I nothing owe
Which copious from those twin fair founts do flow;
Mine have been anything but studious hours.
Yet can I fancy, wandering 'mid thy towers,
Myself a nursling, Granta, of thy lap;
My brow seems tightening with the Doctor's cap
And I walk gownéd; feel unusual powers.
Strange forms of logic clothe my admiring speech,
Old Ramus' ghost is busy at my brain;
And my skull teems with notions infinite.
Be still ye reed of Camus, while I teach
Truths, which transcend the searching schoolman's vein
And half had stagger'd that stout Stagirite!

Examiner, 1819

Oxford in the Vacation

Casting a preparatory glance at the bottom of this article – as the wary connoisseur in prints, with cursory eye (which, while it reads, seems as though it read not), never fails to consult the *quis sculpsit* in the corner, before he pronounces some rare piece to be a Vivares, or a Woollet – methinks I hear you exclaim, Reader, *Who is Elia?*

Because in my last I tried to divert thee with some half-forgotten humours of some old clerks defunct, in an old house of business, long since gone to decay, doubtless you have already set me down in your mind as one of the self-same college – a votary of the desk – a notched and cropt scrivener – one that sucks his sustenance, as certain sick people are said to do, through a quill.

Well, I do agnize something of the sort. I confess that it is my humour, my fancy – in the fore-part of the day, when the mind of your man of letters requires some relaxation – (and none better than such as at first sight seems most abhorrent from his beloved studies) – to while away some good hours of my time in the contemplation of indigos, cottons, raw silks, piece-goods, flowered or otherwise. In the first place * * * and then it sends you home with such increased appetite to your books * * * not to say, that your outside sheets, and waste wrappers of foolscap, do receive into them, most kindly and naturally, the impression of sonnets, epigrams, *essays* – so that the very parings of a counting-house are, in some sort, the settings up of an author. The enfranchised quill, that has plodded all the morning among the cart-rucks of figures and ciphers, frisks and curvets so at its ease over the flowery carpet-ground of a midnight dissertation. – It feels its promotion. * * * * * So that you see, upon the whole, the literary dignity of *Elia* is very little, if at all, compromised in the condescension.

Not that, in my anxious detail of the many commodities incidental to the life of a public office, I would be thought blind to certain flaws, which a cunning carper might be able to pick in this Joseph's vest. And here I must have leave, in the fulness of my soul, to regret the abolition, and doing-away-with altogether, of those consolatory interstices, and sprinklings of freedom, through the four seasons, – the *red-letter days*, now become, to all intents and purposes, *dead-letter* days. There was Paul, and Stephen, and Barnabas –

Andrew and John, men famous in old times

– we were used to keep all their days holy, as long back as I was at school at Christ's. I remember their effigies, by the same token, in the old *Baskett* Prayer Book. There hung Peter in his uneasy posture – holy Bartlemy in the troublesome act of flaying, after the famous Marsyas by Spagnoletti. – I honoured them all, and could almost have wept the defalcation of Iscariot – so much did we love to keep holy memories sacred: – only methought I a little grudged at the coalition of the *better Jude* with Simon – clubbing (as it were) their sanctities together, to make up one poor gaudy-day between them – as an economy unworthy of the dispensation.

171

These were bright visitations in a scholar's and a clerk's life – 'far off their coming shone'. I was as good as an almanac in those days. I could have told you such a saint's-day falls out next week, or the week after. Peradventure the Epiphany, by some periodical infelicity, would, once in six years, merge in a Sabbath. Now am I little better than one of the profane. Let me not be thought to arraign the wisdom of my civil superiors, who have judged the further observation of these holy tides to be papistical, superstitious. Only in a custom of such long standing, methinks, if their Holinesses the Bishops had, in decency, been first sounded – but I am wading out of my depths. I am not the man to decide the limits of civil and ecclesiastical authority – I am plain Elia – no Selden, nor Archbishop Usher – though at present in the thick of their books, here in the heart of learning, under the shadow of the mighty Bodley.

I can here play the gentleman, enact the student. To such a one as myself, who has been defrauded in his young years of the sweet food of academic institution, nowhere is so pleasant, to while away a few idle weeks at, as one or other of the Universities. Their vacation, too, at this time of the year, falls in so pat with *ours*. Here I can take my walks unmolested, and fancy myself at what degree or standing I please. I seem admitted *ad eundem*. I fetch up past opportunities. I can rise at the chapel-bell, and dream that it rings for *me*. In moods of humility I can be a Sizar, or a Servitor. When the peacock vein rises, I strut a Gentleman Commoner. In graver moments, I proceed Master of Arts. Indeed I do not think I am much unlike that respectable character. I have seen your dim-eyed vergers, and bed-makers in spectacles, drop a bow or a curtsy, as I pass, wisely mistaking me for something of the sort. I go about in black, which favours the notion. Only in Christ Church reverend quadrangle I can be content to pass for nothing short of a Seraphic Doctor.

The walks at these times are so much one's own – the tall trees of Christ's, the groves of Magdalen! The halls deserted, and with open doors, inviting one to slip in unperceived, and pay a devoir to some Founder, or noble or royal Benefactress (that should have been ours) whose portrait seems to smile upon their overlooked beadsman, and to adopt me for their own. Then, to take a peep in by the way at the butteries, and sculleries, redolent of antique hospitality: the immense caves of kitchens, kitchen fire-places, cordial recesses; ovens whose first pies were baked four centuries ago; and spits which have cooked for Chaucer! Not the meanest minister among the dishes but is hallowed to me through his imagination, and the Cook goes forth a Manciple.

Antiquity! thou wondrous charm, what art thou? that, being nothing, art everything! When thou *wert*, thou wert not antiquity – then thou wert nothing, but hadst a remoter *antiquity*, as thou calledst it, to look back to with blind veneration; thou thyself being to thyself flat, jejune, *modern!* What mystery lurks in this retroversion? or what half Januses[1] are we, that cannot look for-ward with the same idolatry with which we for ever revert! The mighty future is as nothing, being everything! the past is every-thing, being nothing!

What were thy *dark ages?* Surely the sun rose as brightly then as now, and man got him to his work in the morning. Why is it we can never hear mention of them without an accompanying feeling, as though a palpable obscure had dimmed the face of things, and that our ancestors wandered to and fro groping!

Above all thy rarities, old Oxenford, what do most arride and solace me, are thy repositories of mouldering learning, thy shelves –

What a place to be in is an old library! It seems as though all the souls of all the writers, that have bequeathed their labours to these Bodleians, were reposing here, as in some dormitory, or middle state. I do not want to handle, to profane the leaves, their winding-sheets. I could as soon dislodge a shade. I seem to inhale learning, walking amid their foliage; and the odour of their old moth-scented coverings is fragrant as the first bloom of those sciential apples which grew amid the happy orchard.

Still less have I curiosity to disturb the elder repose of MSS. Those *variæ lectiones*, so tempting to the more erudite palates, do but disturb and unsettle my faith. I am no Herculean raker. The credit of the three witnesses might have slept unimpeached for

---

[1] Januses of one face. – SIR THOMAS BROWNE.

me. I leave these curiosities to Porson, and to G[eorge] D[yer] – whom, by the way, I found busy as a moth over some rotten archive, rummaged out of some seldom-explored press, in a nook at Oriel. With long poring, he is grown almost into a book. He stood as passive as one by the side of the old shelves. I longed to new-coat him in Russia, and assign him his place. He might have mustered for a tall Scapula.

D. is assiduous in his visits to these seats of learning. No inconsiderable portion of his moderate fortune, I apprehend, is consumed in journeys between them and Clifford's Inn – where, like a dove on the asp's nest, he has long taken up his unconscious abode, amid an incongruous assembly of attorneys, attorneys' clerks, apparitors, promoters, vermin of the law, among whom he sits, 'in calm and sinless peace'. The fangs of the law pierce him not – the winds of litigation blow over his humble chambers – the hard sheriff's officer moves his hat as he passes – legal nor illegal discourtesy touches him – none thinks of offering violence or injustice to him – you would as soon 'strike an abstract idea'.

D. has been engaged, he tells me, through a course of laborious years, in an investigation into all curious matters connected with the two Universities; and has lately lit upon a MS. collection of charters, relative to C[ambridge], by which he hopes to settle some disputed points – particularly that long controversy between them as to priority of foundation. The ardour with which he engages in these liberal pursuits, I am afraid, has not met with all the encouragement it deserved, either here or at C—. Your caputs and heads of colleges care less than anybody else about these questions. – Contented to suck the milky fountains of their Alma Maters, without inquiring into the venerable gentlewomen's years, they rather hold such curiosities to be impertinent – unreverend. They have their good glebe lands *in manu*, and care not much to rake into the title-deeds. I gather at least so much from other sources, for D. is not a man to complain.

D. started like an unbroken heifer, when I interrupted him. *A priori* it was not very probable that we should have met in Oriel. But D. would have done the same, had I accosted him on the sudden in his own walks in Clifford's Inn, or in the Temple. In addition to a provoking short-sightedness (the effect of late studies and watchings at the midnight oil) D. is the most absent of men. He made a call the other morning at our friend M[ontagu]'s in Bedford Square; and, finding nobody at home, was ushered into the hall, where, asking for pen and ink, with great exactitude of purpose he enters me his name in the book, which ordinarily lies about in such places, to record the failures of the untimely or unfortunate visitor – and takes his leave with many cere-monies, and professions of regret. Some two or three hours after, his walking destinies returned him into the same neighbourhood again, and again the quiet image of the fireside circle at M[on-tagu]'s – Mrs M. presiding at it like a Queen Lar, with pretty A[nne] S[kepper] at her side – striking irresistibly on his fancy, he makes another call (forgetting that they were 'certainly not to return from the country before that day week'), and disappointed a second time, inquires for pen and paper as before: again the book is brought, and in the line just above that in which he is about to print his second name (his re-script) – his first name (scarce dry) looks out upon him like another Sosia, or as if a man should suddenly encounter his own duplicate! – The effect may be conceived. D. made many a good resolution against any such lapses in future. I hope he will not keep them too rigorously.

For with G.D. – to be absent from the body, is sometimes (not to speak it profanely) to be present with the Lord. At the very time when, personally encountering thee, he passes on with no recognition – or, being stopped, starts like a thing surprised – at that moment, Reader, he is on Mount Tabor – or Parnassus – or co-sphered with Plato – or, with Harrington, framing 'immortal commonwealths' – devising some plan of amelioration to thy country, or thy species – peradventure meditating some indi-vidual kindness or courtesy, to be done to *thee thyself*, the return-ing consciousness of which made him to start so guiltily at thy obtruded personal presence.

D. is delightful anywhere, but he is at the best in such places as these. He cares not much for Bath. He is out of his element at Buxton, at Scarborough, or Harrowgate. The Cam and the Isis are to him 'better than all the waters of Damascus'. On the Muses' hill he is happy, and good, as one of the Shepherds on the Delect-able Mountains; and, when he goes about with you to show you

175

the halls and colleges, you think you have with you the Interpreter at the House Beautiful.

London Magazine, 1820

The Old Margate Hoy

I am fond of passing my vacations (I believe I have said so before) at one or other of the Universities. Next to these my choice would fix me at some woody spot, such as the neighbourhood of Henley affords in abundance, on the banks of my beloved Thames. But somehow or other my cousin contrives to wheedle me, once in three or four seasons, to a watering-place. Old attachments cling to her in spite of experience. We have been dull at Worthing one summer, duller at Brighton another, dullest at Eastbourn a third, and are at this moment doing dreary penance at – Hastings! – and all because we were happy many years ago for a brief week at Margate. That was our first seaside experiment, and many circumstances combined to make it the most agreeable holiday of my life. We had neither of us seen the sea, and we had never been from home so long together in company.

Can I forget thee, thou old Margate Hoy, with thy weather-beaten, sun-burnt captain, and his rough accommodations – ill exchanged for the foppery and fresh-water niceness of the modern steam-packet? To the winds and waves thou committedst thy goodly freightage, and didst ask no aid of magic fumes, and spells, and boiling cauldrons. With the gales of heaven thou wentest swimmingly; or, when it was their pleasure, stoodest still with sailor-like patience. Thy course was natural, not forced, as in a hotbed; nor didst thou go poisoning the breath of ocean with sulphureous smoke – a great sea chimera, chimneying and furnacing the deep; or liker to that fire-god parching up Scamander.

Can I forget thy honest, yet slender crew, with their coy reluctant responses (yet to the suppression of anything like contempt)

176

to the raw questions, which we of the great city would be ever and anon putting to them, as to the uses of this or that strange naval implement? 'Specially can I forget thee, thou happy medium, thou shade of refuge between us and them, conciliating interpreter of their skill to our simplicity, comfortable ambassador between sea and land! – whose sailor-trousers did not more convincingly assure thee to be an adopted denizen of the former, than thy white cap, and whiter apron over them, with thy neat-fingered practice in thy culinary vocation, bespoke thee to have been of inland nurture heretofore – a master cook of Eastcheap? How busily didst thou ply thy multifarious occupation, cook, mariner, attendant, chamberlain; here, there, like another Ariel, flaming at once about all parts of the desk, yet with kindlier ministrations – not to assist the tempest, but, as if touched with a kindred sense of our infirmities, to soothe the qualms which that untried motion might haply raise in our crude land-fancies. And when the o'er-washing billows drove us below deck (for it was far gone in October, and we had stiff and blowing weather), how did thy officious ministerings, still catering for our comfort, with cards, and cordials, and thy more cordial conversation, alleviate the closeness and the confinement of thy else (truth to say) not very savoury, nor very inviting, little cabin!

With these additaments to boot, we had on board a fellow-passenger, whose discourse in verity might have beguiled a longer voyage than we meditated, and have made mirth and wonder abound as far as the Azores. He was a dark, Spanish-complexioned young man, remarkably handsome, with an officer-like assurance, and an insuppressible volubility of assertion. He was, in fact, the greatest liar I had met with then, or since. He was none of your hesitating, half story-tellers (a most painful description of mortals) who go on sounding your belief, and only giving you as much as they see you can swallow at a time – the nibbling pickpockets of your patience – but one who committed downright, daylight depredations upon his neighbour's faith. He did not stand shivering upon the brink, but was a hearty, thorough-paced liar, and plunged at once into the depth of your credulity. I partly believe, he made pretty sure of his company. Not many rich, not many wise, or learned, composed at that time

177

the common stowage of a Margate packet. We were, I am afraid, a set of as unseasoned Londoners (let our enemies give it a worse name) as Aldermanbury, or Watling Street, at that time of day could have supplied. There might be an exception or two among us, but I scorn to make any invidious distinctions among such a jolly, companionable ship's company as those were whom I sailed with. Something too must be conceded to the *Genius Loci*. Had the confident fellow told us half the legends on land which he favoured us with on the other element, I flatter myself the good sense of most of us would have revolted. But we were in a new world, with everything unfamiliar about us, and the time and place disposed us to the reception of any prodigious marvel whatsoever. Time has obliterated from my memory much of his wild fablings; and the rest would appear but dull, as written, and to be read on shore. He had been Aide-de-camp (among other rare accidents and fortunes) to a Persian Prince, and at one blow had stricken off the head of the King of Carimania on horseback. He, of course, married the Prince's daughter. I forget what unlucky turn in the politics of that court, combining with the loss of his consort, was the reason of his quitting Persia; but, with the rapidity of a magician, he transported himself, along with his hearers, back to England, where we still found him in the confidence of great ladies. There was some story of a princess – Elizabeth, if I remember – having intrusted to his care an extraordinary casket of jewels, upon some extraordinary occasion – but, as I am not certain of the name or circumstance at this distance of time, I must leave it to the Royal daughters of England to settle the honour among themselves in private.

I cannot call to mind half his pleasant wonders; but I perfectly remember that, in the course of his travels, he had seen a phœnix; and he obligingly undeceived us of the vulgar error, that there is but one of that species at a time, assuring us that they were not uncommon in some parts of Upper Egypt. Hitherto he had found the most implicit listeners. His dreaming fancies had transported us beyond the 'ignorant present'. But when (still hardying more and more in his triumphs over our simplicity) he went on to affirm that he had actually sailed through the legs of the Colossus at Rhodes, it really became necessary to make a stand.

And here I must do justice to the good sense and intrepidity of one of our party, a youth, that had hitherto been one of his most deferential auditors, who, from his recent reading, made bold to assure the gentleman, that there must be some mistake, as 'the Colossus in question had been destroyed long since'; to whose opinion, delivered with all modesty, our hero was obliging enough to concede thus much, that 'the figure was indeed a little damaged'. This was the only opposition he met with, and it did not at all seem to stagger him, for he proceeded with his fables, which the same youth appeared to swallow with still more complacency than ever – confirmed, as it were, by the extreme candour of that concession. With these prodigies he wheedled us on till we came in sight of the Reculvers, which one of our own company (having been the voyage before) immediately recognising, and pointing out to us, was considered by us as no ordinary seaman.

All this time sat upon the edge of the deck quite a different character. It was a lad, apparently very poor, very infirm, and very patient. His eye was ever on the sea, with a smile; and, if he caught now and then some snatches of these wild legends, it was by accident, and they seemed not to concern him. The waves to him whispered more pleasant stories. He was as one being with us, but not of us. He heard the bell of dinner ring without stirring; and when some of us pulled out our private stores – our cold meat and our salads – he produced none, and seemed to want none. Only a solitary biscuit he had laid in; provision for the one or two days and nights, to which these vessels then were oftentimes obliged to prolong their voyage. Upon a nearer acquaintance with him, which he seemed neither to court nor decline, we learned that he was going to Margate, with the hope of being admitted into the Infirmary there for sea-bathing. His disease was a scrofula, which appeared to have eaten all over him. He expressed great hopes of a cure; and when we asked him whether he had any friends where he was going, he replied, 'he *had* no friends'.

These pleasant, and some mournful passages, with the first sight of the sea, co-operating with youth, and a sense of holidays, and out-of-door adventure, to me that had been pent up in populous cities for many months before, – have left upon my mind the fragrance as of summer days gone by, bequeathing nothing but their remembrance for cold and wintry hours to chew upon.

Will it be thought a digression (it may spare some unwelcome comparisons) if I endeavour to account for the *dissatisfaction* which I have heard so many persons confess to have felt (as I did myself feel in part on this occasion), *at the sight of the sea for the first time*? I think the reason usually given – referring to the incapacity of actual objects for satisfying our preconceptions of them – scarcely goes deep enough into the question. Let the same person see a lion, an elephant, a mountain for the first time in his life, and he shall perhaps feel himself a little mortified. The things do not fill up that space which the idea of them seemed to take up in his mind. But they have still a correspondency to his first notion, and in time grow up to it, so as to produce a very similar impression: enlarging themselves (if I may say so) upon familiarity. But the sea remains a disappointment. Is it not, that in *the latter* we had expected to behold (absurdly, I grant), but, I am afraid, by the law of imagination, unavoidably) not a definite object, as those wild beasts, or that mountain compassable by the eye, but *all the sea at once*, 'the commensurate antagonist of the earth'? I do not say we tell ourselves so much, but the craving of the mind is to be satisfied with nothing less. I will suppose the case of a young person of fifteen (as I then was) knowing nothing of the sea, but from description. He comes to it for the first time – all that he has been reading of it all his life, and *that* the most enthusiastic part of life, – all he has gathered from narratives of wandering seamen, – what he has gained from true voyages, and what he cherishes as credulously from romance and poetry, – crowding their images, and exacting strange tributes from expectation. – He thinks of the great deep, and of those who go down unto it; of its thousand isles, and of the vast continents it washes; of its receiving the mighty Plata, or Orellana, into its bosom, without disturbance, or sense of augmentation; of Biscay swells, and the mariner

> For many a day, and many a dreadful night,
> Incessant labouring round the stormy Cape;

180

of fatal rocks, and the 'still-vexed Bermoothes'; of great whirl-pools, and the water-spout; of sunken ships, and sumless treasures swallowed up in the unrestoring depths; of fishes and quaint monsters, to which all that is terrible on earth –

> Be but as buggs to frighten babes withal,
> Compared with the creatures in the sea's entral;

of naked savages, and Juan Fernandez; of pearls, and shells; of coral beds, and of enchanted isles; of mermaids' grots –

I do not assert that in sober earnest he expects to be shown all these wonders at once, but he is under the tyranny of a mighty faculty, which haunts him with confused hints and shadows of all these; and when the actual object opens first upon him, seen (in tame weather, too, most likely) from our unromantic coasts – a speck, a slip of sea-water, as it shows to him – what can it prove but a very unsatisfying and even diminutive entertainment? Or if he has come to it from the mouth of a river, was it much more than the river widening? and, even out of sight of land, what had he but a flat watery horizon about him, nothing comparable to the vast o'er-curtaining sky, his familiar object, seen daily without dread or amazement? – Who, in similar circumstances, has not been tempted to exclaim with Charoba, in the poem of Gebir,

> Is this the mighty ocean? is this *all*?

I love town or country; but this detestable Cinque Port is neither. I hate these scrubbed shoots, thrusting out their starved foliage from between the horrid fissures of dusty innutritious rocks; which the amateur calls 'verdure to the edge of the sea'. I require woods, and they show me stunted coppices. I cry out for the water-brooks, and pant for fresh streams, and inland murmurs. I cannot stand all day on the naked beach, watching the capricious hues of the sea, shifting like the colours of a dying mullet. I am tired of looking out at the windows of this island-prison. I would fain retire into the interior of my cage. While I gaze upon the sea, I want to be on it, over it, across it. It binds me in with chains, as of iron. My thoughts are abroad. I should not so feel in Staffordshire. There is no home for me here. There is no sense of home at Hastings. It is a place of fugitive resort, an heterogeneous assemblage of sea-mews and stock-brokers, Amphitrites of the town, and misses that coquet with the Ocean. If it were what it was in its primitive shape, and what it ought to have remained, a fair, honest, fishing-town, and no more, it were something – with a few straggling fishermen's huts scattered about, artless as its cliffs, and with their materials filched from them, it were something. I could abide to dwell with Meshek; to assort with fisher-swains, and smugglers. There are, or I dream there are, many of this latter occupation here. Their faces become the place. I like the smuggler. He is the only honest thief. He robs nothing but the revenue – an abstraction I never greatly cared about. I could go out with them in their mackerel boats, or about their less ostensible business, with some satisfaction. I can even tolerate those poor victims to monotony, who from day to day pace along the beach, in endless progress and recurrence, to watch their illicit countrymen – townsfolk or brethren, perchance – whistling to the sheathing and unsheathing of their cutlasses (their only solace), who, under the mild name of preventive service, keep up a legitimated civil warfare in the deplorable absence of a foreign one, to show their detestation of run hollands, and zeal for Old England. But it is the visitants from town, that come here to *say* that they have been here, with no more relish of the sea than a pond-perch or a dace might be supposed to have, that are my aversion. I feel like a foolish dace in these regions, and have as little toleration for myself here as for them. What can they want here? If they had a true relish of the ocean, why have they brought all this land luggage with them? or why pitch their civilised tents in the desert? What mean these scanty book-rooms – marine libraries as they entitle them – if the sea were, as they would have us believe, a book 'to read strange matter in'? what are their foolish concert-rooms, if they come, as they would fain be thought to do, to listen to the music of the waves? All is false and hollow pretension. They come because it is the fashion, and to spoil the nature of the place. They are, mostly, as I have said, stock-brokers; but I have watched the better sort of them – now and then, an honest citizen (of the old stamp), in the simplicity of his heart, shall bring down his wife and daughters to taste the sea breezes. I always know the date of their arrival. It is easy to see it in their countenance. A day or two they go wandering on the shingles, picking up cockleshells, and thinking them great things; but, in a poor week, imagination slackens: they begin to discover that cockles produce no pearls, and then – O then! – if I could interpret for the pretty creatures (I know they have not the courage to confess it themselves), how gladly would they exchange their seaside rambles for a Sunday walk on the green sward of their accustomed Twickenham meadows!

I would ask one of these sea-charmed emigrants, who think they truly love the sea, with its wild usages, what would their feelings be if some of the unsophisticated aborigines of this place, encouraged by their courteous questionings here, should venture, on the faith of such assured sympathy between them, to return the visit, and come up to see – London. I must imagine them with their fishing-tackle on their back, as we carry our town necessaries. What a sensation would it cause in Lothbury! What vehement laughter would it not excite among

The daughters of Cheapside, and wives of Lombard-street!

I am sure that no town-bred or inland-born subjects can feel their true and natural nourishment at these sea-places. Nature, where she does not mean us for mariners and vagabonds, bids us stay at home. The salt foam seems to nourish a spleen. I am not half so good-natured as by the milder waters of my natural river. I would exchange these sea-gulls for swans, and scud a swallow for ever about the banks of Thamesis.

ELIA.
London Magazine, 1823

To Barron Field

Sept. 22nd., 1822.

My dear F.,

– I scribble hastily at office. Frank wants my letter presently. I and sister are just returned from Paris!! We have eaten frogs. It has been such a treat. You know our monotonous tenor. Frogs are the nicest little delicate things – rabbity-flavoured. Imagine a Lilliputian rabbit! They fricassee them; but in my mind, drest, seethed, plain, with parsley and butter, would have the decision of Apicius. Shelley the great Atheist has gone down by Water to Eternal fire. Hunt and his young fry are left stranded at Pisa, to be adopted by the remaining duumvir Lord Bryon, he, wife and six children and their maid. What a cargo of Jonases, if they had founder'd too. The only use I can find of friends, is that they do borrow money of you – Henceforth I will consort with none but rich rogues. Paris is a glorious picturesque old city. London looks mean and new to it, as the town of Washington would, seen after it. But they have no St Paul's, or Westminster Abbey. The Seine, so much despised by Cockneys, is exactly the size to run through a magnificent street; palaces a mile long on one side, lofty Edin-boro' stone (O the glorious antiques!) houses on the other. The Thames disunites London and Southwark. I had Talma to supper with me. He has picked up, as I believe, an authentic portrait of Shakespeare. He paid a broker about 40L. English for it. It is painted on the one half of a pair of bellows, – a lovely picture, corresponding with the folio head. The bellows has old carved *wings* round it, and round the visnomy is inscribed, as near as I remember, not divided into rhyme – I found out the rhyme

> Whom have we here
> Stuck on the bellows,
> But the Prince of good fellows,
>   Willy Shakespeare?

>   At top –

> O base and coward luck
> To be here stuck! – *Poins.*

At bottom –

Nay! rather a glorious lot is to him assign'd,
Who, like the Almighty, rides upon the *wind. – Pistol*.

This is all in old carved wooden letters. The countenance smiling, sweet, and intellectual beyond measure, even as he was
immeasurable. It may be a forgery. They laugh at me and tell me
Ireland is in Paris, and has been putting off a portrait of the Black
Prince. How far old wood may be imitated I cannot say. Ireland
was not found out by his parchments, but by his poetry. I am
confident no painter on either side the Channel could have
painted anything near like the face I saw. Again, would such a
painter and forger have taken 40L. for a thing, if authentic, worth
4000L.? Talma is not in the secret, for he had not even found out
the rhymes in the first inscription. He is coming over with it,
and, my life to Southey's 'Thalaba', it will gain universal faith.

The letter is wanted, and I am wanted. Imagine the blank filled
up with all kind things.

Our joint hearty remembrances to both of you.

Yours, as ever,

C. LAMB.

V

JUICES OF MEATS, INNOCENT VANITIES AND JESTS

Sun, and sky, and breeze and solitary walks, and summer holidays, and the greenness of fields, and the delicious juices of meats and fishes, and society, and the cheerful glass, and candlelight, and fireside conversations, and innocent vanities and jests, and *irony itself* – do these things go out with life?

'New Year's Eve',
London Magazine, 1821.

Grace Before Meat

The custom of saying grace at meals had, probably, its origin in the early times of the world and the hunter-state of man, when dinners were precarious things, and a full meal was something more than a common blessing; when a belly-full was a wind-fall, and looked like a special providence. In the shouts and triumphal songs with which, after a season of sharp abstinence, a lucky booty of deer's or goat's flesh would naturally be ushered home, existed, perhaps, the germ of the modern grace. It is not otherwise easy to be understood, why the blessing of food – the act of eating – should have had a particular expression of thanksgiving annexed to it, distinct from that implied and silent gratitude with which we are expected to enter upon the enjoyment of the many other various gifts and good things of existence.

I own that I am disposed to say grace upon twenty other occasions in the course of the day besides my dinner. I want a form for setting out upon a pleasant walk, for a moonlight ramble, for a friendly meeting, or a solved problem. Why have we none for books, those spiritual repasts – a grace before Milton – a grace before Shakespeare – a devotional exercise proper to be said before reading *The Faery Queene*? but, the received ritual having prescribed these forms to the solitary ceremony of manducation, I shall confine my observations to the experience which I have had of the grace properly so called: commending my new scheme for extension to a niche in the grand philosophical, poetical, and perchance in part heretical, liturgy now compiling by my friend Homo Humanus for the use of a certain snug congregation of Utopian Rabelæsian Christians, no matter where assembled.

The form then of the benediction before eating has its beauty at a poor man's table or at the simple and unprovocative repast of children. It is here that the grace becomes exceedingly graceful. The indigent man, who hardly knows whether he shall have a

189

meal the next day or not, sits down to his fare with a present sense of the blessing, which can be but feebly acted by the rich, into whose minds the conception of wanting a dinner could never, but by some extreme theory, have entered. The proper end of food – the animal sustenance – is barely contemplated by them. The poor man's bread is his daily bread, literally his bread for the day. Their courses are perennial.

Again, the plainest diet seems the fittest to be preceded by the grace. That which is least stimulative to appetite leaves the mind most free for foreign considerations. A man may feel thankful, heartily thankful, over a dish of plain mutton with turnips, and have leisure to reflect upon the ordinance and institution of eating; when he shall confess a perturbation of mind, inconsistent with the purposes of the grace, at the presence of venison or turtle. When I have sate (a *rarus hospes*) at rich men's tables with the savoury soup and messes steaming up the nostrils and moistening the lips of the guests with desire and a distracted choice, I have felt the introduction of that ceremony to be unseasonable. With the ravenous orgasm upon you, it seems impertinent to interpose a religious sentiment. It is a confusion of purpose to mutter out praises from a mouth that waters. The heats of epicurism put out the gentle flame of devotion. The incense which rises round is pagan, and the bellygod intercepts it for its own. The very excess of the provision beyond the needs takes away all sense of proportion between the end and means. The giver is veiled by his gifts. You are startled at the injustice of returning thanks – for what? for having too much while so many starve. It is to praise the Gods amiss.

I have observed this awkwardness felt, scarce consciously perhaps, by the good man who says the grace. I have seen it in clergymen and others – a sort of shame, a sense of the co-presence of circumstances which unhallow the blessing. After a devotional tone put on for a few seconds, how rapidly the speaker will fall into his common voice, helping himself or his neighbour as if to get rid of some uneasy sensation of hypocrisy. Not that the good man was a hypocrite, or was not most conscientious in the discharge of the duty; but he felt in his inmost mind the incompatability of the scene and the viands before him with the exercise of a calm and rational gratitude.

I hear somebody exclaim, – Would you have Christians sit down at table like hogs to their troughs, without remembering the Giver? – No, I would have them sit down as Christians, remembering the Giver, and less like hogs. Or, if their appetites must run riot and they must pamper themselves with delicacies for which east and west are ransacked, I would have them postpone their benediction to a fitter season, when appetite is laid, when the still small voice can be heard, and the reason of the grace returns – with temperate diet and restricted dishes. Gluttony and surfeiting are no proper occasions for thanksgiving. When Jeshurun waxed fat, we read that he kicked. Virgil knew the harpy-nature better when he put into the mouth of Celæno anything but a blessing. We may be gratefully sensible of the deliciousness of some kinds of food beyond others, though that is a meaner and inferior gratitude: but the proper object of the grace is sustenance not relishes; daily bread, not delicacies; the means of life and not the means of pampering the carcass. With what frame or composure, I wonder, can a city chaplain pronounce his benediction at some great Hall-feast, when he knows that his last concluding pious word – and that in all probability, the sacred name which he preaches – is but the signal for so many impatient harpies to commence their foul orgies with as little sense of true thankfulness (which is temperance) as those Virgilian fowl! It is well if the good man himself does not feel his devotions a little clouded, those foggy sensuous streams mingling with and polluting the pure altar sacrifice.

The severest satire upon full tables and surfeits is the banquet which Satan, in the *Paradise Regained*, provides for a temptation in the wilderness:

> A table richly spread in regal mode,
> With dishes piled, and meats of noblest sort
> And savour; beasts of chase, or fowl of game,
> In pastry built, or from the spit, or boiled,
> Gris-amber-steamed; all fish from sea or shore,
> Freshet or purling brook, for which was drained
> Pontus, and Lucrine bay, and Afric coast.

The Tempter, I warrant you, thought these cates would go

down without the recommendatory preface of a benediction.
They are like to be short graces where the devil plays the host.
I am afraid the poet wants his usual decorum in this place. Was
he thinking of the old Roman luxury, or of a gaudy day at Cambridge? This was a temptation fitter for a Heliogabalus. The whole
banquet is too civic and culinary, and the accompaniments altogether a profanation of that deep, abstracted, holy scene. The
mighty artillery of sauces which the cook-fiend conjures up is
out of proportion to the simple wants and plain hunger of the
guest. He that disturbed him in his dreams, from his dreams
might have been taught better. To the temperate fantasies of the
famished Son of God, what sort of feasts presented themselves?
– He dreamed indeed

———— As appetite is wont to dream,
Of meats and drinks, nature's refreshment sweet.

But what meats? –

Him thought, he by the brook of Cherith stood,
And saw the ravens with their horny beaks
Food to Elijah bringing, even and morn;
Though ravenous, taught to abstain from what they brought:
He saw the prophet also how he fled
Into the desert, and how there he slept
Under a juniper; then how awaked
He found his supper on the coals prepared,
And by the angel was bid rise and eat,
And ate the second time after repose,
The strength whereof sufficed him forty days:
Sometimes, that with Elijah he partook,
Or as a guest with Daniel at his pulse.

Nothing in Milton is finelier fancied than these temperate dreams
of the divine Hungerer. To which of these two visionary banquets, think you, would the introduction of what is called the
grace have been the most fitting and pertinent?

Theoretically I am no enemy to graces; but practically I own
that (before meat especially) they seem to involve something awkward and unseasonable. Our appetites, of one or another kind,

192

are excellent spurs to our reason, which might otherwise but feebly set about the great ends of preserving and continuing the species. They are fit blessings to be contemplated at a distance with a becoming gratitude; but the moment of appetite (the judicious reader will apprehend me) is, perhaps, the least fit season for that exercise. The Quakers, who go about their business of every description with more calmness than we, have more title to the use of these benedictory prefaces. I have always admired their silent grace, and the more because I have observed their applications to the meat and drink following to be less passionate and sensual than ours. They are neither gluttons nor wine-bibbers as a people. They eat, as a horse bolts his chopt hay, with indifference, calmness, and cleanly circumstances. They neither grease nor slop themselves. When I see a citizen in his bib and tucker, I cannot imagine it a surplice.

I am no Quaker at my food. I confess I am not indifferent to the kinds of it. Those unctuous morsels of deer's flesh were not made to be received with dispassionate services. I hate a man who swallows it, affecting not to know what he is eating. I suspect his taste in higher matters. I shrink instinctively from one who professes to like minced veal. There is a physiognomical character in the tastes for food. C[oleridge] holds that a man cannot have a pure mind who refuses apple-dumplings. I am not certain but he is right. With the decay of my first innocence, I confess a less and less relish daily for those innocuous cates. The whole vegetable tribe have lost their gust with me. Only I stick to asparagus, which still seems to inspire gentle thoughts. I am impatient and querulous under culinary disappointments, as to come home at the dinner hour, for instance, expecting some savoury mess, and to find one quite tasteless and sapidless. Butter ill melted – that commonest of kitchen failures – puts me beside my tenor. – The author of the *Rambler* used to make inarticulate animal noises over a favourite food. Was this the music quite proper to be preceded by the grace? or would the pious man have done better to postpone his devotions to a season when the blessing might be contemplated with less perturbation? I quarrel with no man's tastes, nor would set my thin face against those excellent things, in their way, jollity and feasting. But as these exercises, however laudable, have little in them of grace or gracefulness, a man should be sure, before he ventures so to grace them, that while he is pretending his devotions otherwise, he is not secretly kissing his hand to some great fish – his Dagon – with a special consecration of no art but the fat tureen before him. Graces are the sweet preluding strains to the banquets of angels and children; to the roots and severer repasts of the Chartreuse; to the slender, but not slenderly acknowledged, refection of the poor and humble man: but at the heaped-up boards of the pampered and the luxurious they become of dissonant mood, less timed and tuned to the occasion, methinks, than the noise of those better befitting organs would be which children hear tales of, at Hog's Norton. We sit too long at our meals, or are too curious in the study of them, or too disordered in our application to them, or engross too great a portion of those good things (which should be common) to our share, to be able with any grace to say grace. To be thankful for what we grasp exceeding our proportion is to add hypocrisy to injustice. A lurking sense of this truth is what makes the performance of this duty so cold and spiritless a service at most tables. In houses where the grace is as indispensable as the napkin, who has not seen that never-settled question arise, as to *who shall say it?* while the good man of the house and the visitor clergyman or some other guest belike of next authority from years or gravity, shall be bandying about the office between them as a matter of compliment, each of them not unwilling to shift the awkward burthen of an equivocal duty from his own shoulders?

I once drank tea in company with two Methodist divines of different persuasions, whom it was my fortune to introduce to each other for the first time that evening. Before the first cup was handed round, one of these reverend gentlemen put it to the other, with all due solemnity, whether he chose to *say any thing*. It seems it is the custom with some sectaries to put up a short prayer before this meal also. His reverend brother did not at first quite apprehend him, but upon an explanation with little less importance he made answer that it was not a custom known in his church: in which courteous evasion the other acquiescing for good manners' sake, or in compliance with a weak brother, the supplementary or tea grace was waived altogether. With what spirit might not Lucian have painted two priests, of *his* religion, playing into each others' hands the compliment of performing or omitting a sacrifice – the hungry God meantime, doubtful of his incense, with expectant nostrils hovering over the two flamens, and (as between two stools) going away in the end without his supper?

A short form upon these occasions is felt to want reverence; a long one, I am afraid, cannot escape the charge of impertinence. I do not quite approve of the epigrammatic conciseness with which that equivocal wag (but my pleasant school-fellow) C.V. L[e Grice], when importuned for grace, used to inquire, first shyly leering down the table, 'Is there no clergyman here?' – significantly adding 'Thank G—.' Nor do I think our old form at school quite pertinent, where we used to preface our bald bread and cheese suppers with a preamble, connecting with that humble blessing a recognition of benefits the most awful and overwhelming to the imagination which religion has to offer. *Non tunc illis erat locus.* I remember we were put to it to reconcile the phrase, 'good creatures', upon which the blessing rested, with the fare set before us, wilfully understanding that expression in a low and animal sense, till some one recalled a legend which told how in the golden days of Christ's the young Hospitallers were wont to have smoking joints of roast meat upon their nightly boards, till some pious benefactor, commiserating the decencies, rather than the palates, of the children, commuted our flesh for garments, and gave us – *horresco referens* – trousers instead of mutton.

London Magazine, 1821

To S.T. Coleridge

March 9th, 1822.

Dear C.,

– It gives me great satisfaction to hear that the pig turned out so well – they are interesting creatures at a certain age – what a pity such buds should blow out into the maturity of rank bacon! You had all some of the crackling – and brain sauce – did you remember to rub it with butter, and gently dredge it a little, just before the crisis? Did the eyes come away kindly with no Œdipean avulsion? Was the crackling the colour of the ripe pomegranate? Had you no complement of boiled neck of mutton before it, to blunt the edge of delicate desire? Did you flesh maiden teeth in it? Not that I sent the pig, or can form the remotest guess what part Owen could play in the business. I never knew him give anything away in my life. He would not begin with strangers. I suspect the pig, after all, was meant for me; but at the unlucky juncture of time being absent, the present somehow went round to Highgate. To confess an honest truth, a pig is one of those things I could never think of sending away. Teals, wigeons, snipes, barndoor fowl, ducks, geese – your tame villatic things – Welsh mutton, collars of brawn, sturgeon, fresh or pickled, your potted char, Swiss cheeses, French pies, early grapes, muscadines, I impart as freely unto my friends as to myself. They are but self-extended; but pardon me if I stop somewhere – where the fine feeling of benevolence giveth a higher smack than the sensual rarity – there my friends (or any good man) may command me; but pigs are pigs, and I myself therein am nearest to myself. Nay, I should think it an affront, an undervaluing done to Nature who bestowed such a boon upon me, if in a churlish mood I parted with the precious gift. One of the bitterest pangs of remorse I ever felt was when a child – when my kind old aunt had strained her pocket-strings to bestow a sixpenny whole plum-cake upon me. In my way home through the Borough, I met a venerable old man, not a mendicant, but thereabouts – a look-beggar, not a verbal petitionist; and in the coxcombry of taught-charity I gave away the cake to him. I walked on a little in all the pride of an

196

Evangelical peacock, when of a sudden my old aunt's kindness crossed me – the sum it was to her – the pleasure she had a right to expect that I – not the old impostor – should take in eating her cake – the cursed ingratitude by which, under the colour of a Christian virtue, I had frustrated her cherished purpose. I sobbed, wept, and took it to heart so grievously, that I think I never suffered the like – and I was right. It was a piece of unfeeling hypocrisy, and proved a lesson to me ever after. The cake has long been masticated, consigned to dunghill with the ashes of that unseasonable pauper.

But when Providence, who is better to us all than our aunts, gives me a pig, remembering my temptation and my fall, I shall endeavour to act towards it more in the spirit of the donor's purpose.

Yours (short of pig) to command in everything.

C.L.

A Dissertation Upon Roast Pig

Mankind, says a Chinese manuscript, which my friend M[anning] was obliging enough to read and explain to me, for the first seventy thousand ages ate their meat raw, clawing or biting it from the living animal, just as they do in Abyssinia to this day. This period is not obscurely hinted at by their great Confucius in the second chapter of his Mundane Mutations, where he designates a kind of golden age by the term Cho-fang, literally the Cooks' holiday. The manuscript goes on to say that the art of roasting, or rather broiling (which I take to be the elder brother), was accidentally discovered in the manner following: The swine-herd Ho-ti having gone out into the woods one morning, as his manner was, to collect mast for his hogs, left his cottage in the care of his eldest son Bo-bo, a great lubberly boy, who, being fond of playing with fire, as younkers of his age commonly are, let some sparks escape into a bundle of straw, which kindling quickly spread the conflagration

197

over every part of their poor mansion, till it was reduced to ashes. Together with the cottage (a sorry antediluvian make-shift of a building, you may think it), what was of much more importance, a fine litter of new-farrowed pigs, no less than nine in number, perished. China pigs have been esteemed a luxury all over the East from the remotest periods that we read of. Bo-bo was in the utmost consternation, as you may think, not so much for the sake of the tenement, which his father and he could easily build up again with a few dry branches and the labour of an hour or two at any time, as for the loss of the pigs. While he was thinking what he should say to his father, and wringing his hands over the smoking remnants of one of those untimely sufferers, an odour assailed his nostrils unlike any scent which he had before experienced. What could it proceed from? Not from the burnt cottage – he had smelt that smell before – indeed, this was by no means the first accident of the kind which had occurred through the negligence of this unlucky young firebrand. Much less did it resemble that of any known herb, weed, or flower. A premonitory moistening at the same time overflowed his nether lip. He knew not what to think. He next stooped down to feel the pig, if there were any signs of life in it. He burnt his fingers, and to cool them he applied them in his booby fashion to his mouth. Some of the crumbs of the scorched skin had come away with his fingers, and for the first time in his life (in the world's life indeed, for before him no man had known it) he tasted – *crackling*! Again he felt and fumbled at the pig. It did not burn him so much now – still he licked his fingers from a sort of habit. The truth at length broke into his slow understanding that it was the pig that smelt so, and the pig that tasted so delicious; and, surrendering himself up to the new-born pleasure, he fell to tearing up whole handfuls of the scorched skin with the flesh next to it, and was cramming it down his throat in his beastly fashion when his sire entered amid the smoking rafters, armed with retributory cudgel, and, finding how affairs stood, began to rain blows upon the young rogue's shoulders as thick as hail-stones, which Bo-bo heeded not any more than if they had been flies. The tickling pleasure which he experienced in his lower regions had rendered him quite callous to any inconveniences he might feel in those remote quarters. His father might lay on, but he could not beat him from his pig till he had fairly made an end of it, when, becoming a little more sensible of his situation, something like the following ensued.

'You graceless whelp, what have you got there devouring? Is it not enough that you have burnt me down three houses with your dog's tricks, and be hanged to you, but you must be eating fire, and I know not what – what have you got there, I say?'

'O father, the pig, the pig! Do come and taste how nice the burnt pig eats.'

The ears of Ho-ti tingled with horror. He cursed his son, and he curseth himself that ever he should beget a son that should eat burnt pig.

Bo-bo, whose scent was wonderfully sharpened since morning, soon raked out another pig, and fairly rending it asunder, thrust the lesser half by main force into the fists of Ho-ti, still shouting out, 'Eat, eat, eat the burnt pig, father, only taste – O Lord,' – with suchlike barbarous ejaculations, cramming all the while as if he would choke.

Ho-ti trembled every joint while he grasped the abominable thing, wavering whether he should not put his son to death for an unnatural young monster when, the crackling scorching his fingers as it had done his son's, and applying the same remedy to them, he in his turn tasted some of its flavour, which, make what sour mouths he would for a pretence, proved not altogether displeasing to him. In conclusion (for the manuscript here is a little tedious), both father and son fairly set down to the mess, and never left off till they had despatched all that remained of the litter.

Bo-bo was strictly enjoined not to let the secret escape, for the neighbours would certainly have stoned them for a couple of abominable wretches who could think of improving upon the good meat which God had sent them. Nevertheless, strange stories got about. It was observed that Ho-ti's cottage was burnt down now more frequently than ever. Nothing but fires from this time forward. Some would break out in broad day, others in the night-time. As often as the sow farrowed, so sure was the house of Ho-ti to be in a blaze; and Ho-ti himself, which was the more remarkable, instead of chastising his son, seemed to grow more indulgent to him than ever. At length they were watched, the terrible mystery discovered, and father and son summoned to take their trial at Pekin, then an inconsiderable assize town. Evidence was given, the obnoxious food itself produced in court, and verdict about to be pronounced, when the foreman of the jury begged that some of the burnt pig of which the culprits stood accused might be handed into the box. He handled it, and they all handled it, and, burning their fingers as Bo-bo and his father had done before them, and nature prompting to each of them the same remedy, against the face of all the facts, and the clearest charge which judge had ever given, – to the surprise of the whole court, townsfolk, strangers, reporters, and all present – without leaving the box or any manner of consultation whatever, they brought in a simultaneous verdict of Not Guilty.

The judge, who was a shrewd fellow, winked at the manifest iniquity of the decision: and when the court was dismissed went privily and bought up all the pigs that could be had for love or money. In a few days his lordship's town-house was observed to be on fire. The thing took wing, and now there was nothing to be seen but fires in every direction. Fuel and pigs grew enormously dear all over the district. The insurance-offices one and all shut up shop. People built slighter and slighter every day, until it was feared that the very science of architecture would in no long time be lost to the world. Thus this custom of firing houses continued till in process of time, says my manuscript, a sage arose, like our Locke, who made a discovery that the flesh of swine, or indeed of any other animal, might be cooked (*burnt*, as they called it) without the necessity of consuming a whole house to dress it. Then first began the rude form of a gridiron. Roasting by the string or spit came in a century or two later, I forget in whose dynasty. By such slow degrees, concludes the manuscript, do the most useful, and seemingly the most obvious, arts make their way among mankind –

Without placing too implicit faith in the account above given, it must be agreed that if a worthy pretext for so dangerous an experiment as setting houses on fire (especially in these days) could be assigned in favour of any culinary object, that pretext and excuse might be found in ROAST PIG.

200

Of all the delicacies in the whole *mundus edibilis*, I will maintain it to be the most delicate – *princeps obsoniorum*.

I speak not of your grown porkers – things between pig and pork – those hobblehoys – but a young and tender suckling – under a moon old – guiltless as yet of the sty – with no original speck of the *amor immunditiæ*, the hereditary failing of the first parent, yet manifest – his voice as yet not broken, but something between a childish treble and a grumble – the mild forerunner or *præludium* of a grunt.

He must be roasted. I am not ignorant that our ancestors ate them seethe, or boiled – but what a sacrifice of the exterior tegument!

There is no flavour comparable, I will contend, to that of the crisp, tawny, well-watched, not over-roasted, *crackling*, as it is well called – the very teeth are invited to their share of the pleasure of this banquet in overcoming the coy, brittle resistance – with the adhesive oleaginous – O call it not fat – but an indefinable sweetness growing up to it – the tender blossoming of fat – fat cropped in the bud – taken in the shoot – in the first innocence – the cream and quintessence of the child-pig's yet pure food – the lean, no lean, but a kind of animal manna, or, rather, fat and lean (if it must be so) so blended and running into each other, that both together make but one ambrosian result or common substance.

Behold him, while he is doing – it seemeth rather a refreshing warmth, than a scorching heat, that he is so passive to. How equally he twirleth round the string! – Now he is just done. To see the extreme sensibility of that tender age, he hath wept out his pretty eyes – radiant jellies – shooting stars. –

See him in the dish, his second cradle, how meek he lieth! – wouldst thou have had this innocent grow up to the grossness and indocility which too often accompany maturer swinehood? Ten to one he would have proved a glutton, a sloven, an obstinate, disagreeable animal – wallowing in all manner of filthy conversation – from these sins he is happily snatched away –

> Ere sin could blight, or sorrow fade,
> Death came with timely care –

His memory is odoriferous – no clown curseth, while his stomach

201

half rejecteth, the rank bacon – no coal-heaven bolteth him in reeking sausages – he hath a fair sepulchre in the grateful stomach of the judicious epicure – and for such a tomb might be content to die.

He is the best of Sapors. Pine-apple is great. She is indeed almost too transcendent – a delight, if not sinful, yet so like to sinning, that really a tender-conscienced person would do well to pause – too ravishing for mortal taste, she woundeth and excoriateth the lips that approach her – like lovers' kisses, she biteth – she is a pleasure bordering on pain from the fierceness and insanity of her relish – but she stoppeth at the palate – she meddleth not with the appetite – and the coarsest hunger might barter her consistently for a mutton chop.

Pig – let me speak his praise – is no less provocative of the appetite than he is satisfactory to the criticalness of the censorious palate. The strong man may batten on him, and the weakling refuseth not his mild juices.

Unlike to mankind's mixed characters, a bundle of virtues and vices inexplicably intertwisted, and not to be unravelled without hazard, he is good throughout. No part of him is better or worse than another. He helpeth, as far as his little means extend, all around. He is the least envious of banquets. He is all neighbours' fare.

I am one of those who freely and ungrudgingly impart a share of the good things of this life which fall to their lot (few as mine are in this kind) to a friend. I protest I take as great an interest in my friend's pleasures, his relishes, and proper satisfactions, as in mine own. 'Presents,' I often say, 'endear Absents.' Hares, pheasants, partridges, snipes, barn-door chickens (those 'tame villatic fowl'), capons, plovers, brawn, barrels of oysters, I dispense as freely as I receive them. I love to taste them, as it were, upon the tongue of my friend. But a stop must be put somewhere. One would not, like Leah, 'Give everything'. I make my stand upon pig. Methinks it is an ingratitude to the Giver of all good flavours to extra-domiciliate, or send out of the house slightingly (under pretext of friendship, or I know not what), a blessing so particularly adapted, predestined I may say, to my individual palate. – It argues an insensibility.

I remember a touch of conscience in this kind at school. My good old aunt, who never parted from me at the end of a holiday without stuffing a sweet-meat or some nice thing into my pocket, had dismissed me one evening with a smoking plum-cake fresh from the oven. In my way to school (it was over London Bridge) a grey-headed old beggar saluted me (I have no doubt, at this time of day, that he was a counterfeit). I had no pence to console him with, and in the vanity of self-denial and the very coxcombry of charity, schoolboy-like, I made him a present of – the whole cake! I walked on a little, buoyed up as one is on such occasions with a sweet soothing of self-satisfaction; but before I had got to the end of the bridge my better feelings returned, and I burst into tears, thinking how ungrateful I had been to my good aunt to go and give her good gift away to a stranger that I had never seen before and who might be a bad man for aught I knew; and then I thought of the pleasure my aunt would be taking in thinking that I – I myself, and not another – would eat her nice cake – and what should I say to her the next time I saw her – how naughty I was to part with her pretty present – and the odour of that spicy cake came back upon my recollection, and the pleasure and the curiosity I had taken in seeing her make it, and her joy when she sent it to the oven, and how disappointed she would feel that I had never had a bit of it in my mouth at last – and I blamed my impertinent spirit of almsgiving, and out-of-place hypocrisy of goodness; and above all I wished never to see the face again of that insidious, good-for-nothing, old, grey impostor.

Our ancestors were nice in their method of sacrificing these tender victims. We read of pigs whipt to death, with something of a shock, as we hear of any other obsolete custom. The age of discipline is gone by, or it would be curious to inquire (in a philosophical light merely) what effect this process might have towards intenerating and dulcifying a substance, naturally so mild and dulcet as the flesh of young pigs. It looks like refining a violet. Yet we should be cautious, while we condemn the inhumanity, how we censure the wisdom of the practice. It might impart a gusto.

I remember an hypothesis, argued upon by the young students when I was at St Omer's, and maintained with much learning and pleasantry on both sides, 'Whether, supposing that the flavour of a pig who obtained his death by whipping (*per flagellationem extreman*) superadded a pleasure upon the palate of a man more intense than any possible suffering we can conceive in the animal, is man justified in using that method of putting the animal to death?' I forget the decision.

His sauce should be considered. Decidedly a few bread crumbs done up with his liver and brains, and a dash of mild sage. But banish, dear Mrs Cook, I beseech you, the whole onion tribe. Barbecue your whole hog to your palate, steep them in shalots, stuff them out with plantations of the rank and guilty garlic; you cannot poison them, or make them stronger than they are – but consider, he is a weakling – a flower.

London Magazine, 1822

To Mr and Mrs Collier

Twelfth Day, '23.

The pig was above my feeble praise. It was a dear pigmy. There was some contention as to who should have the ears; but, in spite of his obstinacy (deaf as these little creatures are to advice,) I contrived to get at one of them.

It came in boots too, which I took as a favour. Generally these pretty toes, pretty toes! are missing; but I suppose he wore them to look taller.

He must have been the least of his race. His little foot would have gone into the silver slipper. I take him to have been a Chinese and a female.

If Evelyn could have seen him, he would never have farrowed two such prodigious volumes; seeing how much good can be contained in – how small a compass!

He crackled delicately.

I left a blank at the top of my letter, not being determined which to address it to: so farmer and farmer's wife will please to divide our thanks. May your granaries be full, and your rats empty, and your chickens plump, and your envious neighbours lean, and your labourers busy, and you as idle and as happy as the day is long!

How do you make your pigs so little:
They are vastly engaging at the age:
    I was so myself.
Now I am a disagreeable old hog,
A middle-aged gentleman-and-a-half,
My faculties (thank God!) are not much impaired.

I have my sight, hearing, taste, pretty perfect; and can read the Lord's Prayer in common type, by the help of a candle, without making many mistakes.

Believe me, that while my faculties last, I shall ever cherish a proper appreciation of your many kindnesses in this way, and that the last lingering relish of past favours upon my dying memory will be the smack of that little ear. It was the left ear, which is lucky. Many happy returns, not of the pig, but of the New Year, to both! Mary, for her share of the pig and the memoirs, desires to send the same. – Dr, Mr C. and Mrs C. –

Yours truly,

C. LAMB.

Thoughts on Presents of Game, &c.

'We love to have our friend in the country sitting thus at our table *by proxy*; to apprehend his presence (though a hundred miles may be between us) by a turkey, whose goodly aspect reflects to us his "plump corpusculum"; to taste him in grouse or woodcock; to feel him gliding down in the toast peculiar to the

205

latter; to concorporate him in a slice of Canterbury brawn. This is indeed to have him within ourselves; to know him intimately; such participation is, methinks, *unitive*, as the old theologians phrase it.' – *Last Essays of Elia*.

Elia presents his acknowledgements to his 'Correspondent Unknown' for a basket of prodigiously fine game. He takes for granted that so amiable a character must be a reader of the *Athenaeum*, else he had meditated a notice in *The Times*. Now if this friend had consulted the Delphic oracle for a present suited to the palate of Elia, he could not have hit upon a morsel so acceptable. The birds he is barely thankful for; pheasants are poor *fowls* disguised in fine feathers; but a hare, roasted hard and brown, with gravy and melted butter! Old Mr Chambers, the sensible clergyman in Warwickshire, whose son's acquaintance has made many hours happy in the life of Elia, used to allow a pound of Epping to every hare. Perhaps that was overdoing it. But, in spite of the note of Philomel, who, like some fine poets, that think no scorn to adopt plagiarisms from an humble brother, reiterates every spring her cuckoo cry of 'Jug, jug, jug', Elia pronounces that a hare, to be truly palated, must be roasted. Jugging sophisticates her. In *our* way it eats so 'crips', as Mrs Minikin says. Time was, when Elia was not arrived at his taste, that he preferred to all luxuries a roasted pig. But he disclaims all such green-sickness appetites in future, though he hath to acknowledge the receipt of many a delicacy in that kind from correspondents – good but mistaken men – in consequence of their erroneous supposition that he had carried up into mature life the prepossessions of childhood. From the worthy Vicar of Enfield he acknowledges a tithe contribution of extraordinary sapor. The ancients must have loved hares, else why adopt the word *lepores* (obviously from *lepus*) but for some subtle analogy between the delicate flavour of the latter and the finer relishes of wit in what we most poorly translate *pleasantries*? The fine madnesses of the poet are the very decoction of his diet. Thence is he hare-brained. Harum-scarum is a libellous, unfounded phrase, of modern usage. 'Tis true the hare is the most circumspect of animals, sleeping with her eye open. Her ears, ever erect, keep them in that

206

wholesome exercise which conduces them to form the very titbit of the admirers of this noble animal. Noble will I call her in spite of her detractors, who, from occasional demonstrations of the principle of self-preservation (common to all animals), infer in her a defect of heroism. Half a hundred horsemen, with thrice the number of dogs, scour the country in pursuit of puss across three counties; and because the well-flavoured beast, weighing the odds, is willing to evade the hue and cry (with her delicate ears shrinking perchance from discord), comes the grave naturalist, Linnaeus perchance, or Buffon, and gravely sets down the hare as a timid animal. Why, Achilles or Bully Dawson would have declined the preposterous combat.

In fact, how light of digestion we feel after a hare! How tender its processes after swallowing! What chyle it promotes! How ethereal! as if its living celerity were a type of its nimble coursing through the animal juices. The notice might be longer. It is intended less as a natural history of the hare than a cursory thanks to the country 'good unknown'. The hare has many friends, but none sincerer than

ELIA.
Athenaeum, 1833

Rejoicings upon the New Year's Coming of Age

The *Old Year* being dead, and the *New Year* coming of age, which he does, by Calendar Law, as soon as the breath is out of the old gentleman's body, nothing would serve the young spark but he must give a dinner upon the occasion, to which all the *Days* in the year were invited. The *Festivals*, whom he deputed as his stewards, were mightly taken with the notion. They had been engaged time out of mind, they said, in providing mirth and good cheer for mortals below; and it was time they should have a taste of their own bounty. It was stiffly debated among them whether the *Fasts* should be admitted. Some said the appearance of such lean, starved guests, with their mortified faces, would

207

pervert the ends of the meeting. But the objection was overruled by *Christmas Day*, who had a design upon *Ash Wednesday* (as you shall hear), and a mighty desire to see how the old *Domine* would behave himself in his cups. Only the *Vigils* were requested to come with their lanterns, to light the gentlefolks home at night.

All the *Days* came to their day. Covers were provided for three hundred and sixty-five guests at the principal table; with an occasional knife and fork at the side-board for the *Twenty-Ninth of February*.

I should have told you that cards of invitation had been issued. The carriers were the *Hours*; twelve little, merry, whirligig foot-pages, as you should desire to see, that went all round, and found out the persons invited well enough, with the exception of *Easter Day, Shrove Tuesday*, and a few such *Moveables*, who had lately shifted their quarters.

Well, they all met at last – foul *Days*, fine *Days*, all sorts of *Days*, and a rare din they made of it. There was nothing but, Hail! fellow *Day*, well met – brother *Day* – sister *Day* – only *Lady Day* kept a little on the aloof, and seemed somewhat scornful. Yet some said *Twelfth Day* cut her out and out, for she came in a tiffany suit, white and gold, like a queen on a frost-cake, all royal, glittering, and *Epiphanous*. The rest came, some in green, some in white – but old *Lent and his family* were not yet out of mourning. Rainy *Days* came in, dripping; and sunshiny *Days* helped them to change their stockings. *Wedding Day* was there in his marriage finery, a little the worse for wear. *Pay Day* came late, as he always does; and *Doomsday* sent word – he might be expected.

April Fool (as my young lord's jester) took upon himself to marshal the guests, and wild work he made with it. It would have posed old Erra Pater to have found out any given *Day* in the year to erect a scheme upon – good *Days*, bad *Days*, were so shuffled together, to the confounding of all sober horoscopy.

He had stuck the *Twenty-First of June* next to the *Twenty-Second of December*, and the former looked like a Maypole siding a marrow-bone. *Ash Wednesday* got wedged in (as was concerted) betwixt *Christmas* and *Lord Mayor's Days*. Lord! how he laid about him! Nothing but barons of beef and turkeys would go down with him – to the great greasing and detriment of his new sackcloth bib and tucker. And still *Christmas Day* was at his elbow, plying him with the wassail-bowl, till he roared, and hiccupp'd, and protested there was no faith in dried ling, but commended it to the devil for a sour, windy, acrimonious, censorious, hy-po-crit-crit-critical mess, and no dish for a gentleman. Then he dipt his fist into the middle of the great custard that stood before his *left-hand neighbour*, and daubed his hungry beard all over with it, till you would have taken him for the *Last Day in December*, it so hung in icicles.

At another part of the table, *Shrove Tuesday* was helping the *Second of September* to some cock broth, – which courtesy the latter returned with the delicate thigh of a hen pheasant – so that there was no love lost for that matter. The *Last of Lent* was spunging upon *Shrove-tide's* pancakes; which *April Fool* perceiving, told him that he did well, for pancakes were proper to a *good fry-day*.

In another part, a hubbub arose about the *Thirtieth of January*, who, it seems, being a sour, puritanic character, that thought nobody's meat good or sanctified enough for him, had smuggled into the room a calf's head, which he had cooked at home for that purpose, thinking to feast thereon incontinently; but as it lay in the dish, *March Manyweathers*, who is a very fine lady, and subject to the meagrims, screamed out there was a 'human head in the platter', and raved about Herodias' daughter to that degree, that the obnoxious viand was obliged to be removed; nor did she recover her stomach till she had gulped down a *Restorative*, confected of *Oak Apple*, which the merry *Twenty-Ninth of May* always carries about with him for that purpose.

The King's health being called for after this, a notable dispute arose between the *Twelfth of August* (a zealous old Whig gentlewoman) and the *Twenty-Third of April* (a new-fangled lady of the Tory stamp), as to which of them should have the honour to propose it. *August* grew hot upon the matter, affirming, time out of mind, the prescriptive right to have lain with her, till her rival had basely supplanted her; whom she represented as little better than a *kept* mistress, who went about in *fine clothes*, while she (the legitimate 'Birthday') had scarcely a rag, etc.

April Fool, being made mediator, confirmed the right, in the strongest form of words, to the appellant, but decided for peace'

sake, that the exercise of it should remain with the present pos-
sessor. At the same time, he slyly rounded the first lady in the
ear, that an action might lie against the Crown for *bi-geny*.

It beginning to grow a little duskish, *Candlemas* lustily bawled
out for lights, which was opposed by all the *Days*, who protested
against burning daylight. Then fair water was handed round in
silver ewers, and the *same lady* was observed to take an unusual
time in *Washing* herself.

May Day, with that sweetness which is peculiar to her, in a
neat speech proposing the health of the founder, crowned her
goblet (and by her example the rest of the company) with gar-
lands. This being done, the lordly *New Year*, from the upper end
of the table in a cordial but somewhat lofty tone, returned thanks.
He felt proud on an occasion of meeting so many of his worthy
father's late tenants, promised to improve their farms, and at the
same time to abate (if anything was found unreasonable) in their
rents.

At the mention of this, the four *Quarter Days* involuntarily
looked at each other, and smiled; *April Fool* whistled to an old
tune of 'New Brooms'; and a surly old rebel at the farther end of
the table (who was discovered to be no other than the *Fifth of
November*) muttered out, distinctly enough to be heard by the
whole company, words to this effect – that 'when the old one is
gone, he is a fool that looks for a better'. Which rudeness of his,
the guests resenting, unanimously voted his expulsion; and the
malcontent was thrust out neck and heels into the cellar, as the
properest place for such a *boutefeu* and firebrand as he had shown
himself to be.

Order being restored – the young lord (who, to say truth, had
been a little ruffled, and put beside his oratory) in as few and yet
as obliging words as possible, assured them of entire welcome;
and, with a graceful turn, singling out poor *Twenty-Ninth of
February*, that had sate all this while mumchance at the side-
board, begged to couple his health with that of the good company
before him – which he drank accordingly; observing that he had
not seen his honest face any time these four years – with a number
of endearing expressions besides. At the same time removing
the solitary *Day* from the forlorn seat which had been assigned

him, he stationed him at his own board, somewhere between the *Greek Calends* and *Latter Lammas*.

Ash Wednesday being now called upon for a song, with his eyes fast stuck in his head, and as well as the Canary he had swallowed would give him leave, struck up a Carol, which *Christmas Day* had taught him for the nonce; and was followed by the latter, who gave 'Miserere' in fine style, hitting off the mumping notes and lengthened drawl of *Old Mortification* with infinite humour. *April Fool* swore they had exchanged conditions; but *Good Friday* was observed to look extremely grave; and *Sunday* held her fan before her face that she might not be seen to smile.

Shrove-tide, Lord Mayor's Day, and *April Fool,* next joined in a glee –

Which is the properest day to drink?

in which all the *Days* chiming in, made a merry burden.

They next fell to quibbles and conundrums. The question being proposed, who had the greatest number of followers – the *Quarter Days* said, there could be no question as to that; for they had all the creditors in the world dogging their heels. But *April Fool* gave it in favour of the *Forty Days before Easter;* because the debtors in all cases outnumbered the creditors, and they kept *Lent* all the year.

All this while *Valentine's Day* kept courting pretty *May,* who sate next him, slipping amorous *billets-doux* under the table, till the *Dog Days* (who are naturally of a warm constitution) began to be jealous, and to bark and rage exceedingly. *April Fool,* who likes a bit of sport above measure, and had some pretensions to the lady besides, as being but a cousin once removed, – clapped and halloo'd them on; and as fast as their indignation cooled, those mad wags, the *Ember Days,* were at it with their bellows, to blow it into a flame; and all was in a ferment, till old Madam *Septuagesima* (who boasts herself the *Mother of the Days*) wisely diverted the conversation with a tedious tale of the lovers which she could reckon when she was young, and of one Master *Rogation Day* in particular, who was for ever putting the *question* to her; but she kept him at a distance, as the chronicle would tell – by which I apprehend she meant the Almanack. Then she rambled

211

on to the *Days that were gone*, the *good old Days*, and so to the *Days before the Flood* – which plainly showed her old head to be little better than crazed and doited.

Day being ended, the *Days* called for their cloaks and great-coats, and took their leave. *Lord Mayor's Day* went off in a Mist, as usual; *Shortest Day* in a deep black Fog, that wrapt the little gentleman all round like a hedge-hog. Two *Vigils* – a stout, sturdy patrole, called the *Eve of St Christopher* – seeing *Ash Wednesday* in a condition little better than he should be – e'en whipt him over his shoulders, pick-a-back fashion, and *Old Mortification* went floating home singing –

On the bat's back I do fly,

and a number of old snatches besides, between drunk and sober; but very few Aves or Penitentiaries (you may believe me) were among them. *Longest Day* set off westward in beautiful crimson and gold – the rest, some in one fashion, some in another; but *Valentine* and pretty *May* took their departure together in one of the prettiest silvery twilights a Lover's Day could wish to set in.

'Elia's Ghost'

First published *Morning Chronicle*, January 1823, and reprinted as an Elia essay in the *London Magazine* in the same month.

Dream-Children; A Reverie

Children love to listen to stories about their elders when *they* were children; to stretch their imagination to the conception of a traditionary great-uncle, or grandame, whom they never saw. It was in this spirit that my little ones crept about me the other evening to hear about their great-grandmother Field, who lived in a great house in Norfolk (a hundred times bigger than that in which they and papa lived) which had been the scene – so at least it was generally believed in that part of the country – of the tragic incidents which they had lately become familiar with from the ballad of the Children in the Wood. Certain it is that the whole story of the children and their cruel uncle was to be seen fairly carved out in wood upon the chimney-piece of the great hall, the whole story down to the Robin Redbreasts; till a foolish rich person pulled it down to set up a marble one of modern invention in its stead, with no story upon it. Here Alice put out one of her dear mother's looks, too tender to be called upbraiding. Then I went on to say, how religious and how good their great-grandmother Field was, how beloved and respected by every body, though she was not indeed the mistress of this great house, but had only the charge of it (and yet in some respects she might be said to be the mistress of it too) committed to her by the owner, who preferred living in a newer and more fashionable mansion which he had purchased somewhere in the adjoining county; but still she lived in it in a manner as if it had been her own, and kept up the dignity of the great house in a sort while she lived, which afterwards came to decay, and was nearly pulled down, and all its old ornaments stripped and carried away to the owner's other house, where they were set up, and looked as awkward as if some one were to carry away the old tombs they had seen lately at the Abbey, and stick them up in Lady C[lutterbuck]'s tawdry gilt drawing-room. Here John smiled, as much as to say, 'That would be foolish indeed.' And then I told how, when she came to die, her funeral was attended by a concourse of all the poor, and some of the gentry too, of the neighbourhood for many miles round, to show their respect for her memory, because she had been such a good and religious woman; so good indeed that she knew all the Psaltery by heart, ay, and a great part of the Testament besides. Here little Alice spread her hands. Then I told what a tall, upright, graceful person their great-grandmother Field once was; and how in her youth she was esteemed the best dancer – here Alice's little right foot played an involuntary movement, till, upon my looking grave, it desisted – the best dancer, I was saying, in the county, till a cruel disease called a cancer came and bowed her down with pain; but it could never bend her good spirits, or make them stoop, but they were still upright because she was so good and religious. Then I told how she was

213

used to sleep by herself in a lone chamber of the great lone house; and how she believed that an apparition of two infants was to be seen at midnight gliding up and down the great staircase near where she slept, but she said 'those innocents would do her no harm'; and how frightened I used to be, though in those days I had my maid to sleep with me, because I was never half so good or religious as she – and yet I never saw the infants. Here John expanded all his eyebrows and tried to look courageous. Then I told her how good she was to all her grandchildren, having us to the great-house in the holydays, where I in particular used to spend many hours by myself, in gazing upon the old busts of the twelve Cæsars that had been Emperors of Rome, till the old marble heads would seem to live again, or I to be turned into marble with them; how I never could be tired with roaming about that huge mansion, with its vast empty rooms, with their worn-out hangings, fluttering tapestry, and carved oaken panels, with the gilding almost rubbed out – sometimes in the spacious old-fashioned gardens, which I had almost to myself, unless when now and then a solitary gardening man would cross me – and how the nectarines and peaches hung upon the walls, without my ever offering to pluck them, because they were forbidden fruit, unless now and then, – and because I had more pleasure in strolling about among the old melancholy-looking yew-trees, or the firs, and picking up the red berries, and the fir-apples, which were good for nothing but to look at – or in lying about upon the fresh grass with all the fine garden smell around me – or basking in the orangery till I could almost fancy myself ripening too along with the oranges and the limes in that grateful warmth – or in watching the dace that darted to and fro in the fish-pond at the bottom of the garden, with here and there a great sulky pike hanging midway down the water in silent state, as if it mocked at their impertinent friskings, – I had more pleasure in these busy-idle diversions than in all the sweet flavours of peaches, nectarines, oranges, and such-like common baits of children. Here John slyly deposited back upon the plate a bunch of grapes, which, not unobserved by Alice, he had meditated dividing with her, and both seemed willing to relinquish them for the present as irrelevant. Then, in somewhat a more heightened tone, I told how, though their great-grandmother Field loved all her grandchildren, yet in an especial manner she might be said to love their uncle, John L[amb], because he was so handsome and spirited a youth and a king to the rest of us; and, instead of moping about in solitary corners, like some of us, he would mount the most mettlesome horse he could get, when but an imp no bigger than themselves, and make it carry him half over the county in a morning, and join the hunters when there were any out – and yet he loved the old great house and gardens too, but had too much spirit to be always pent up within their boundaries – and how their uncle grew up to a man's estate as brave as he was handsome, to the admiration of everybody, but of their great-grandmother Field most especially; and how he used to carry me upon his back when I was a lame-footed boy – for he was a good bit older than me – many a mile when I could not walk for pain; and how in after life he became lame-footed too, and I did not always (I fear) make allowances enough for him when he was impatient and in pain, nor remember sufficiently how considerate he had been to me when I was lame-footed; and how when he died, though he had not been dead an hour, it seemed as if he had died a great while ago, such a distance there is betwixt life; and how I bore his death as I thought pretty well at first, but afterwards it haunted and haunted me, and, though I did not cry or take it to heart as some do and as I think he would have done if I had died, yet I missed him all day long, and knew not till then how much I had loved him. I missed his kindness, and I missed his crossness, and wished him to be alive again to be quarrelling with him (for we quarrelled sometimes), rather than not have him again, and was as uneasy without him, as he, their poor uncle, must have been when the doctor took off his limb. Here the children fell a-crying, and asked if their little mourning which they had on was not for Uncle John, and they looked up, and prayed me not to go on about their uncle, but to tell them some stories about their pretty dead mother. Then I told how for seven long years, in hope sometimes, sometimes in despair, yet persisting ever, I courted the fair Alice W[interto]n; and, as much as children could understand, I explained to them what coyness, and difficulty, and denial, meant in maidens –

215

when suddenly turning to Alice, the soul of the first Alice looked out at her eyes with such a reality of re-presentment that I became in doubt which of them stood there before me, or whose that bright hair was; and, while I stood gazing, both the children gradually grew fainter to my view, receding and still receding, till nothing at last but two mournful features were seen in the uttermost distance, which, without speech, strangely impressed upon me the effects of speech: 'We are not of Alice, nor of thee, nor are we children at all. The children of Alice call Bartrum father. We are nothing; less than nothing, and dreams. We are only what might have been, and must wait upon the tedious shores of Lethe millions of ages before we have existence, and a name' – and, immediately awaking, I found myself quietly seated in my bachelor arm-chair, where I had fallen asleep, with the faithful Bridget unchanged by my side – but John L. (or James Elia) was gone for ever.

London Magazine, 1822

VI

CRITICAL AND ANTI-CRITICAL

There is a spirit in Mr Lamb's productions, which in itself is so *anti-critical*, and tends so much to reconcile us to all that is in the world, that the effect is almost neutralizing to everything but complacency and a queer admiration – his very criticisms chiefly tend to overthrow the critical spirit.

> Leigh Hunt (in a review of *Works of Charles Lamb*), *The Examiner*, 1819

My First Play

At the north end of Cross-court there yet stands a portal, of some architectural pretensions, though reduced to humble use, serving at present for an entrance to a printing-office. This old door-way, if you are young, reader, you may not know was the identical pit entrance to old Drury – Garrick's Drury – all of it that is left. I never pass it without shaking some forty years from off my shoulders, recurring to the evening when I passed through it to see *my first play*. The afternoon had been wet, and the condition of our going (the elder folks and myself) was, that the rain should cease. With what a beating heart did I watch from the window the puddles, from the stillness of which I was taught to prognosticate the desired cessation! I seem to remember the last spurt, and the glee with which I ran to announce it.

We went with orders, which my godfather [Francis] F[ielde] had sent us. He kept the oil shop (now Davies's) at the corner of Featherstone-building, in Holborn. F. was a tall grave person, lofty in speech, and had pretensions above his rank. He associated in those days with John Palmer, the comedian, whose gait and bearing he seemed to copy; if John (which is quite as likely) did not rather borrow somewhat of his manner from my godfather. He was also known to and visited by Sheridan. It was to his house in Holborn that young Brinsley brought his first wife on her elopement with him from a boarding-school at Bath – the beautiful Maria Linley. My parents were present (over a quadrille table) when he arrived in the evening with his harmonious charge. From either of these connections it may be inferred that my godfather could command an order for the then Drury-lane theatre at pleasure – and, indeed, a pretty liberal issue of those cheap billets in Brinsley's easy autograph I have heard him say was the sole remuneration which he had received for many years' nightly illumination of the orchestra and various avenues of that

219

theatre – and he was content it should be so. The honour of Sheridan's familiarity – or supposed familiarity – was better to my godfather than money.

F. was the most gentlemanly of oilmen; grandiloquent, yet courteous. His delivery of the commonest matters of fact was Ciceronian. He had two Latin words almost constantly in his mouth (how odd sounds Latin from an oilman's lips!), which my better knowledge since has enabled me to correct. In strict pronunciation they should have been sounded *vice versâ* – but in those young years they impressed me with more awe than they would now do, read aright from Seneca or Varro – in his own peculiar pronunciation, mono-syllabically elaborated, or Anglicised, into something like *verse verse*. By an imposing manner and the help of those distorted syllables he climbed (but that was little) to the highest parochial honours which St Andrew's has to bestow.

He is dead – and thus much I thought due to his memory, both for my first orders (little wondrous talismans! – slight keys, and insignificant to outward sight, but opening to me more than Arabian paradises!), and, moreover, that by his testamentary beneficence I came into possession of the only landed property which I could ever call my own – situate near the roadway village of pleasant Puckeridge, in Hertfordshire. When I journeyed down to take possession, and planted foot on my own ground, the stately habits of the donor descended upon me, and I strode (shall I confess the vanity?) with larger paces over my allotment of three-quarters of an acre with its commodious mansion in the midst, with the feeling of an English freeholder that all betwixt sky and centre was my own. The estate has passed into more prudent hands, and nothing but an agrarian can restore it.

In those days were pit orders. Beshrew the uncomfortable manager who abolished them! – with one of these we went. I remember the waiting at the door – not that which is left – but between that and an inner door in shelter (O when shall I be such an expectant again!) with the cry of nonpareils, an indispensable play-house accompaniment in those days. As near as I can recollect, the fashionable pronunciation of the theatrical fruiteresses then was, 'Chase some oranges, chase some nonpareils, chase a bill of the play'; – chase *pro* chuse. But when we got in, and I beheld the green curtain that veiled a heaven to my imagination, which was soon to be disclosed – the breathless anticipations I endured! I had seen something like it in the plate prefixed to *Troilus and Cressida,* in Rowe's Shakespeare – the tent scene with Diomede – and a sight of that plate can always bring back in a measure the feeling of that evening. – The boxes at that time, full of well-dressed women of quality, projected over the pit; and the pilasters reaching down were adorned with a glistering substance (I know not what) under glass (as it seemed), resembling – a homely fancy – but I judged it to be sugar-candy – yet to my raised imagination, divested of its homelier qualities, it appeared a glorified candy! – The orchestra lights at length rose, those 'fair Auroras'! Once the bell sounded. It was to ring out yet once again – and, incapable of the anticipation, I reposed my shut eyes in a sort of resignation upon the maternal lap. It rang the second time. The curtain drew up – I was not past six years old – and the play was *Artaxerxes*!

I had dabbled a little in the Universal History – the ancient part of it – and here was the court of Persia. It was being admitted to a sight of the past. I took no proper interest in the action going on, for I understood not its import – but I heard the word Darius, and I was in the midst of Daniel. All feeling was absorbed in vision. Gorgeous vests, gardens, palaces, princesses, passed before me. I knew not the players. I was in Persepolis for the time, and the burning idol of their devotion almost converted me into a worshipper. I was awe-struck, and believed those significations to be something more than elemental fires. It was all enchantment and a dream. No such pleasure has since visited me but in dreams. – Harlequin's invasion followed; where, I remember, the transformation of the magistrates into reverend beldams seemed to me a piece of grave historic justice, and the tailor carrying his own head to be as sober a verity as the legend of St Denys.

The next play to which I was taken was *The Lady of the Manor,* of which, with the exception of some scenery, very faint traces are left in my memory. It was followed by a pantomime, called *Lun's Ghost* – a satiric touch, I apprehend, upon Rich, not long since dead – but to my apprehension (too sincere for satire) Lun was as remote a piece of antiquity as Lud – the father of a line of Harlequins – transmitting his dagger of lath (the wooden sceptre) through countless ages. I saw the primeval Motley come from his silent tomb in a ghastly vest of white patchwork, like the apparition of a dead rainbow. So Harlequins (thought I) look when they are dead.

My third play followed in quick succession. It was *The Way of the World*. I think I must have sat at it as grave as a judge; for I remember the hysteric affectations of good Lady Wishfort affected me like some solemn tragic passion. *Robinson Crusoe* followed; in which Crusoe, man Friday, and the parrot, were as good and authentic as in the story. The clownery and pantaloonery of these pantomimes have clean passed out of my head. I believe, I no more laughed at them, than at the same age I should have been disposed to laugh at the grotesque Gothic heads (seeming to me then replete with devout meaning) that gape and grin in stone around the inside of the old Round Church (my church) of the Templars.

I saw these plays in the season 1781-2, when I was from six to seven years old. After the intervention of six or seven other years (for at school all play-going was inhibited) I again entered the doors of a theatre. That old *Artaxerxes* evening had never done ringing in my fancy. I expected the same feelings to come again with the same occasion. But we differ from ourselves less at sixty and sixteen than the latter does from six. In that interval what had I not lost? At the first period I knew nothing, understood nothing, discriminated nothing. I felt all, loved all, wondered all –

Was nourished, I could not tell how –

I had left the temple a devotee, and was returned a rationalist. The same things were there materially; but the emblem, the reference, was gone! The green curtain was no longer a veil, drawn between two worlds, the unfolding of which was to bring back past ages, to present a 'royal ghost' – but a certain quantity of green baize, which was to separate the audience for a given time from certain of their fellow-men who were to come forward and pretend those parts. The lights – the orchestra lights – came up a

222

clumsy machinery. The first ring, and the second ring, was now but a trick of the prompter's bell, which had been, like the note of the cuckoo, a phantom of a voice, no hand seen or guessed at which ministered to its warning. The actors were men and women painted. I thought the fault was in them; but it was in myself, and the alteration which those many centuries – of six short twelvemonths – had wrought in me. – Perhaps it was fortunate for me that the play of the evening was but an indifferent comedy, as it gave me time to crop some unreasonable expectations, which might have interfered with the genuine emotions with which I was soon after enabled to enter upon the first appearance to me of Mrs Siddons in Isabella. Comparison and retrospection soon yielded to the present attraction of the scene; and the theatre became to me, upon a new stock, the most delightful of recreations.

London Magazine, 1821

To William Wordsworth

December 11th, 1806.

Mary's love to all of you – I wouldn't let her write.

Dear Wordsworth, – Mr H. came out last night, and failed. John Bull must have solider fare than a *letter*. We are pretty stout about it; have had plenty of condoling friends; but, after all, we had rather it should have succeeded. You will see the prologue in most of the morning papers. It was received with such shouts as I never witnessed to a prologue. It was attempted to be encored. I low hard! – a thing I did merely as a task, because it was wanted, and set no great store by; and *Mr H.!!* The number of friends we had in the house – my brother and I being in public offices, &c. – was astonishing, but they yielded at length to a few hisses.

A hundred hisses! (Damn the word, I write it like kisses – how different!) – a hundred hisses outweigh a thousand claps. The former come more directly from the heart. Well 'tis withdrawn, and there is an end.

Better luck to us.

C. LAMB.

P.S. Pray, when any of you write to the Clarksons, give our kind loves, and say we shall not be able to come and see them at Christmas, as I shall have but a day or two, and tell them we bear our mortification pretty well.

On the Custom of Hissing at the Theatres

(With some account of a Club of Damned Authors)

Mr Reflector, – I am one of those persons whom the world has thought proper to designate by the title of Damned Authors. In that memorable season of dramatic failures, 1806-7, in which no fewer, I think, than two tragedies, four comedies, one opera, and three farces suffered at Drury Lane Theatre, I was found guilty of constructing an after-piece, and was *damned*.

Against the decision of the public in such instances there can be no appeal. The Clerk at Chatham might as well have protested against the decision of Cade and his followers, who were then *the public*. Like him, I was condemned because I could write.

Not but it did appear to some of us that the measures of the popular tribunal at that period savoured a little of harshness and of the *summum jus*. The public mouth was early in the season fleshed upon the 'Vindictive Man', and some pieces of that nature; and it retained, through the remainder of it, a relish of blood. As Dr Johnson would have said, 'Sir, there was a habit of sibilation in the house'.

Still less am I disposed to inquire into the reason of the comparative lenity, on the other hand, with which some pieces were treated, which to indifferent judges seemed at least as much deserving of condemnation as some of those which met with it.

I am willing to put a favourable construction upon the votes that were given against us. I believe that there was no bribery or designed partiality in the case: only 'our nonsense did not happen to suit their nonsense'; that was all.

But against the *manner* in which the public on these occasions think fit to deliver their disapprobation, I must and ever will protest.

Sir, imagine – but you have been present at the damning of a piece (those who never had that felicity, I beg them to imagine) – a vast theatre, like that which Drury Lane was before it was a heap of dust and ashes (I insult not over its fallen greatness, let it recover itself when it can for me; let it lift up its towering head once more, and take in poor authors to write for it; *hic caestus artemque repono*), – a theatre like that, filled with all sorts of disgusting sounds, shrieks, groans, hisses, but chiefly the last, like the noise of many waters, or that which Don Quixote heard from the fulling-mills, or that wilder combination of devilish sounds which St Anthony listened in to the wilderness.

O Mr Reflector! is it not a pity that the sweet human voice, which was given man to speak with, to sing with, to whisper tones of love in, to express compliance, to convey a favour or to grant a suit, – that voice which in a Siddons or a Braham rouses us, in a siren Catalani charms and captivates us, – that the musical, expressive human voice should be converted into a rival of the noises of silly geese and irrational venomous snakes?

I never shall forget the sounds on *my night*. I never before that time fully felt the reception which the Author of all ill, in the *Paradise Lost*, meets with from the critics in the *pit*, at the final close of his 'Tragedy upon the Human Race', – though that, alas! met with too much success: –

> – From innumerable tongues
> A dismal universal *hiss*, the sound
> Of public scorn. Dreadful was the din
> Of *hissing* through the hall, thick swarming now
> With complicated monsters, head and tail,
> Scorpion and asp, and Amphisbaena dire,
> Cerastes horned, Hydrus, and Elops drear,
> And Dipaas.

For *hall* substitute *theatre*, and you have the very image of what takes place at what is called the *damnation* of a piece, – and properly so called; for here you see its origin plainly, whence the custom was derived, and what the first piece was that so suffered. After this, none can doubt the propriety of the appellation.

But, sir, as to the justice of bestowing such appalling, heart-withering denunciations of the popular obloquy upon the venial mistake of a poor author, who thought to please us in the act of filling his pockets, – for the sum of his demerits amounts to no more than that, – it does, I own, seem to me a species of retributive justice, far too severe for the offence. A culprit in the pillory (bate the eggs) meets with no severer exprobation.

Indeed, I have often wondered that some modest critic has not proposed that there should be a wooden machine to that effect erected in some convenient part of the proscenium, which an unsuccessful author should be required to mount, and stand his hour, exposed to the apples and oranges of the pits. This *amende honorable* would well suit with the meanness of some authors, who, in their prologues, fairly prostrate their skulls to the audience, and seem to invite a pelting.

Or why should they not have their pens publicly broke over their heads, as the swords of recreant knights in old times were, and an oath administered to them that they should never write again?

Seriously, *Messieurs the Public*, this outrageous way which you have got of expressing your displeasure is too much for the occasion. When I was deafening under the effects of it, I could not help asking what crime of great moral turpitude I had committed: for every man about me seemed to feel the offence as personal to himself, as something which public interest and private feelings alike called upon him, in the strongest possible manner, to stigmatize with infamy.

The Romans, it is well known to you, Mr Reflector, took a gentler method of marking their disapprobation of an author's work. They were a humane and equitable nation. They left the *furca* and the *patibulum*, the axe and the rods, to great offenders; for these minor, and (if I may so term them) extra-moral offences, *the bent thumb* was considered as a sufficient sign of disapprobation,

226

– *vertere pollicem*; as *the pressed thumb, premere pollicem*, was a mark of approving.

And really there seems to have been a sort of fitness in this method, a correspondency of sign in the punishment to the offence. For as the action of writing is performed by bending the thumb forward, the retroversion or bending back of that joint did not inaptly point to the opposite of that action; implying that it was the will of the audience that the author should *write no more*: a much more significant as well as more humane way of expressing that desire than our custom of hissing, which is altogether sense-less and indefensible. Nor do we find that the Roman audiences deprived themselves, by this lenity, of any tittle of that supremacy which audiences in all ages have thought themselves bound to maintain over such as have been candidates for their applause. On the contrary, by this method they seem to have had the author, as we should express it, completely *under finger and thumb*.

The provocations to which a dramatic genius is exposed from the public are so much the more vexatious as they are removed from any possibility of retaliation, which sweetens most other injuries; for the public *never writes itself*. Not but something very like it took place at the time of the O[ld] P[rices] differences.* The placards which were nightly exhibited were, properly speaking, the composition of the public. The public wrote them, the public applauded them, and precious *morceaux* of wit and eloquence they were, – except some few, of a better quality, which it is well known were furnished by professed dramatic writers. After this specimen of what the public can do for itself, it should be a little slow in condemning what others do for it.

As the degrees of malignancy vary in people according as they have more or less of the Old Serpent (the father of hisses) in their composition, I have sometimes amused myself with analysing this many-headed hydra, which calls itself the public, into the component parts of which it is 'complicated, head and tail', and seeing how many varieties of the snake kind it can afford.

---

* Covent Garden Theatre was burnt down in 1808. On the opening of the new theatre in 1809, the audience rioted for 'Old Prices'.

First, there is the *Common English Snake*. This is that part of the auditory who are always the majority at damnations, but who, having no critical venom in themselves to sting them on, stay till they hear others hiss, and then join in for company.

The Blind Worm is a species very nearly allied to the foregoing. Some naturalists have doubted whether they are not the same.

The Rattlesnake. – These are your obstreperous talking critics, – the impertinent guides of the pit, – who will not give a plain man leave to enjoy an evening's entertainment, but, with their frothy jargon and incessant finding of faults, either drown his pleasure quite, or force him, in his own defence, to join in their clamorous censure. The hiss always originates with these. When this creature springs his *rattle*, you would think from the noise it makes there was something in it; but you have only to examine the instrument from which the noise proceeds, and you will find it typical of a critic's tongue, – a shallow membrane, empty, voluble, and seated in the most contemptible part of the creature's body.

The Whipsnake. – This is he that lashes the poor author the next day in the newspapers.

The Deaf Adder, or *Surda Echidna* of Linnaeus. – Under this head may be classed all that portion of the spectators (for audience they properly are not), who, not finding the first act of a piece answer to their preconceived notions of what a first act should be, like Obstinate in John Bunyan, positively thrust their fingers in their ears, that they may not hear a word of what is coming, though perhaps the very next act may be composed in a style as different as possible, and be written quite to their own tastes. These adders refuse to hear the voice of the charmer, because the tuning of his instrument gave them offence.

I should weary you and myself too, if I were to go through all the classes of the serpent kind. Two qualities are common to them all. They are creatures of remarkably cold digestions, and chiefly haunt *pits* and low grounds.

I proceed with more pleasure to give you an account of a club to which I have the honour to belong. There are fourteen of us, who are all authors that have been once in our lives what is called *damned*. We meet on the anniversary of our respective nights, and make ourselves merry at the expense of the public. The chief tenets which distinguish our society, and which every man among us is bound to hold for gospel, are –

That the public or mob, in all ages, have been a set of blind, deaf, obstinate, senseless, illiterate savages. That no man of genius, in his senses, would be ambitious of pleasing such a capricious, ungrateful rabble. That the only legitimate end of writing for them is to pick their pockets, and that failing, we are at full liberty to vilify and abuse them as much as ever we think fit.

That authors, by their affected pretences to humility, which they make use of as a cloak to insinuate their writings into the callous senses of the multitude, obtuse to everything but the grossest flattery, have by degress made that great beast their master, as we may act submission to children till we are obliged to practise it in earnest. That authors are and ought to be considered the masters and preceptors of the public, and not *vice versa*. That it was so in the days of Orpheus, Linus, and Musaeus, and would be so again if it were not that writers prove traitors to themselves. That, in particular, in the days of the first of those three great authors just mentioned, audiences appear to have been perfect models of what audiences should be; for though, along with the trees and the rocks and the wild creatures which he drew after him to listen to his strains, some serpents doubtless came to hear his music, it does not appear that any one among them ever lifted up a *dissentient voice*. They knew what was due to authors in those days. Now every stock and stone turns into a serpent and has a voice.

That the terms 'courteous reader' and 'candid auditors' as having given rise to a false notion in those to whom they were applied, as if they conferred upon them some right, *which they cannot have*, of exercising their judgements, ought to be utterly banished and exploded.

These are our distinguishing tenets. To keep up the memory of the cause in which we suffered, as the ancients sacrificed a goat, a supposed unhealthy animal, to Aesculapius on our feast nights we cut up a goose, an animal typical of the *popular voice*, to the deities of Candour and Patient Hearing. A zealous member of the society once proposed that we should revive the obsolete luxury of the viper-broth; but the stomachs of some of the company rising at the proposition, we lost the benefit of that highly salutary and *antidotal dish*.

The privilege of admission to our club is strictly limited to such as have been fairly *damned*. A piece that has met with ever so little applause, that has but languished its night or two and then gone out, will never entitle its author to a seat among us. An exception to our usual readiness in conferring this privilege is in the case of a writer who, having been once condemned, writes again, and becomes a candidate for a second martyrdom. Simple damnation we hold to be a merit; but to be twice damned we adjudge infamous. Such a one we utterly reject, and blackball without a hearing: –

'The common damned shun his society.'

Hoping that your publication of our regulations may be a means of inviting some more members into our society, I conclude this long letter. – I am, sir, yours,

SEMEL-DAMNATUS.
The Reflector, 1811

Stage Illusion

A play is said to be well or ill acted, in proportion to the scenical illusion produced. Whether such illusion can in any case be perfect, is not the question. The nearest approach to it, we are told, is when the actor appears wholly unconscious of the presence of spectators. In tragedy – in all which is to affect the feelings – this undivided attention to his stage business seems indispensable. Yet it is, in fact, dispensed with every day by our cleverest tragedians; and while these references to an audience, in the shape of rant or sentiment, are not too frequent or palpable, a sufficient quantity of illusion for the purposes of dramatic interest may be said to be produced in spite of them. But, tragedy apart, it may be inquired whether, in certain characters in comedy, especially those which are a little extravagant, or which involve some notion repugnant to the moral sense, it is not a proof of the highest skill in the comedian when, without absolutely appealing to an audience, he keeps up a tacit understanding with them; and makes them, unconsciously to themselves, a party in the scene. The utmost nicety is required in the mode of doing this; but we speak only of the great artists in the profession.

The most mortifying infirmity in human nature, to feel in ourselves, or to contemplate in another, is, perhaps, cowardice. To see a coward *done to the life* upon a stage would produce anything but mirth. Yet we most of us remember Jack Bannister's cowards. Could anything be more agreeable, more pleasant? We loved the rogues. How was this effected but by the exquisite art of the actor in a perpetual sub-insinuation to us, the spectators, even in the extremity of the shaking fit, that he was not half such a coward as we took him for? We saw all the common symptoms of the malady upon him; the quivering lip, the cowering knees, the teeth chattering; and could have sworn 'that man was frightened'. But we forgot all the while – or kept it almost a secret to ourselves – that he never once lost his self-possession; that he let out, by a thousand droll looks and gestures – meant at *us*, and not at all supposed to be visible to his fellows in the scene, that his confidence in his own resources had never once deserted him. Was this a genuine picture of a coward; or not rather a likeness, which the clever artist contrived to palm upon us instead of an original; while we secretly connived at the delusion for the purpose of greater pleasure, than a more genuine counterfeiting of the imbecility, helplessness and utter self-desertion, which we know to be concomitants of cowardice in real life, could have given us?

Why are misers so hateful in the world, and so endurable on the stage, but because the skilful actor, by a sort of subreference, rather than direct appeal to us, disarms the character of a great deal of its odiousness, by seeming to engage *our* compassion for the insecure tenure by which he holds his money-bags and parchments? By this subtle vent half of the hatefulness of the character – the self-closeness with which in real life it coils up from the sympathies of men – evaporates. The miser becomes sympathetic;

231

i.e., is no genuine miser. Here again a diverting likeness is substituted for a very disagreeable reality.

Spleen, irritability – the pitiable infirmities of old men, which produce only pain to behold in the realities, counterfeited upon a stage, divert not altogether for the comic appendages to them, but in part from an inner conviction that they are *being acted* before us; that a likeness only is going on, and not the thing itself. They please by being done under the life, or beside it; not *to the life*. When Gattie acts an old man, is he angry indeed? or only a pleasant counterfeit, just enough of a likeness to recognise, without pressing upon us the uneasy sense of a reality?

Comedians, paradoxical as it may seem, may be too natural. It was the case with a late actor. Nothing could be more earnest or true than the manner of Mr Emery; this told excellently in his Tyke, and characters of a tragic cast. But when he carried the same rigid exclusiveness of attention to the stage business, and wilful blindness and oblivion of everything before the curtain into his comedy, it produced a harsh and dissonant effect. He was out of keeping with the rest of the *dramatis personæ*. There was as little link between him and them, as betwixt himself and the audience. He was a third estate – dry, repulsive, and unsocial to all. Individually considered, his execution was masterly. But comedy is not this unbending thing; for this reason, that the same degree of credibility is not required of it as to serious scenes. The degrees of credibility demanded to the two things may be illustrated by the different sort of truth which we expect when a man tells us a mournful or a merry story. If we suspect the former of falsehood in any one tittle, we reject it altogether. Our tears refuse to flow at a suspected imposition. But the teller of a mirthful tale has latitude allowed him. We are content with less than absolute truth. 'Tis the same with dramatic illusion. We confess we love in comedy to see an audience naturalised behind the scenes – taken into the interest of the drama, welcomed as bystanders, however. There is something ungracious in a comic actor holding himself aloof from all participation or concern with those who are come to be diverted by him. Macbeth must see the dagger, and no ear but his own be told of it; but an old fool in farce may think he *sees something*, and by conscious words and looks express

232

it, as plainly as he can speak, to pit, box, and gallery. When an impertinent in tragedy, an Osric, for instance, breaks in upon the serious passions of the scene, we approve of the contempt with which he is treated. But when the pleasant impertinent of comedy, in a piece purely meant to give delight, and raise mirth out of whimsical perplexities, worries the studious man with taking up his leisure, or making his house his home, the same sort of contempt expressed (however *natural*) would destroy the balance of delight in the spectators. To make the intrusion comic, the actor who plays the annoyed man must a little desert nature; he must, in short, be thinking of the audience, and express only so much dissatisfaction and peevishness as is consistent with the pleasure of comedy. In other words, his perplexity must seem half put on. If he repel the intruder with the sober set face of a man in earnest, and more especially if he deliver his expostulations in a tone which in the world must necessarily provoke a duel, his real-life manner will destroy the whimsical and purely dramatic existence of the other character (which to render it comic demands an antagonist comicality on the part of the character opposed to it), and convert what was meant for mirth, rather than belief, into a downright piece of impertinence indeed, which would raise no diversion in us, but rather stir pain, to see inflicted in earnest upon any worthy person. A very judicious actor (in most of his parts) seems to have fallen into an error of this sort in his playing with Mr Wrench in the farce of *Free and Easy*.

Many instances would be tedious; these may suffice to show that comic acting at least does not always demand from the performer that strict abstraction from all reference to an audience which is exacted of it; but that in some cases a sort of compromise may take place, and all the purposes of dramatic delight be attained by a judicious understanding, not too openly announced, between the ladies and gentlemen – on both sides of the curtain.

ELIA.

London Magazine, 1825

On the Artificial Comedy of the Last Century

The artificial Comedy, or Comedy of Manners, is quite extinct on our stage. Congreve and Farquhar show their heads once in seven years only, to be exploded and put down instantly. The times cannot bear them. Is it for a few wild speeches, an occasional licence of dialogue? I think not altogether. The business of their dramatic characters will not stand the moral test. We screw everything up to that. Idle gallantry in a fiction, a dream, the passing pageant of an evening, startles us in the same way as the alarming indications of profligacy in a son or ward in real life should startle a parent or guardian. We have no such middle emotions as dramatic interests left. We see a stage libertine playing his loose pranks of two hours' duration, and of no after consequence, with the severe eyes which inspect real vices with their bearings upon two worlds. We are spectators to a plot or intrigue (not reducible in life to the point of strict morality), and take it all for truth. We substitute a real for a dramatic person, and judge him accordingly. We try him in our courts, from which there is no appeal to the *dramatis personæ*, his peers. We have been spoiled with – not sentimental comedy – but a tyrant far more pernicious to our pleasures which has succeeded to it, the exclusive and all-devouring drama of common life; where the moral point is every thing; where, instead of the fictitious half-believed personages of the stage (the phantoms of old comedy), we recognise ourselves, our brothers, aunts, kinsfolk, allies, patrons, enemies, – the same as in life, – with an interest in what is going on so hearty and substantial, that we cannot afford our moral judgment, in its deepest and most vital results, to compromise or slumber for a moment. What is *there* transacting, by no modification is made to affect us in any other manner than the same events or characters would do in our relationships of life. We carry our fireside concerns to the theatre with us. We do not go thither like our ancestors, to escape from the pressure of reality, so much as to confirm our experience of it; to make assurance double, and take a bond of fate. We must live our toilsome lives twice over, as it was the mournful privilege of Ulysses to descend twice to the shades.

All that neutral ground of character which stood between vice and virtue; or which in fact was indifferent to neither, where neither properly was called in question; that happy breathing-place from the burthen of a perpetual moral questioning – the sanctuary and quiet Alsatia of hunted casuistry – is broken up and disfranchised, as injurious to the interests of society. The privileges of the place are taken away by law. We dare not dally with images, or names, of wrong. We bark like foolish dogs at shadows. We dread infection from the scenic representation of disorder, and fear a painted pustule. In our anxiety that our morality should not take cold, we wrap it up in a great blanket surtout of precaution against the breeze and sunshine.

I confess for myself that (with no great delinquencies to answer for) I am glad for a season to take an airing beyond the diocese of the strict conscience, – not to live always in the precincts of the law-courts, – but now and then, for a dream-while or so, to imagine a world with no meddling restrictions – to get into recesses, whither the hunter cannot follow me –

> ——— Secret shades
> Of woody Ida's inmost grove,
> While yet there was no fear of Jove –

I come back to my cage and my restraint the fresher and more healthy for it. I wear my shackles more contentedly for having respired the breath of an imaginary freedom. I do not know how it is with others, but I feel the better always for the perusal of one of Congreve's – nay, why should I not add even of Wycherley's – comedies. I am the gayer at least for it; and I could never connect those sports of a witty fancy in any shape with any result to be drawn from them to imitation in real life. They are a world of themselves almost as much as fairy land. Take one of their characters, male or female (with few exceptions they are alike), and place it in a modern play, and my virtuous indignation shall rise against the profligate wretch as warmly as the Catos of the pit could desire; because in a modern play I am to judge of the right and the wrong. The standard of *police* is the measure of *political justice*. The atmosphere will blight it, it cannot live here. It has got into a moral world, where it has no business, from

235

which it must needs fall headlong; as dizzy, and incapable of making a stand, as a Swedenborgian bad spirit that has wandered unawares into the sphere of one of his Good Men, or Angels. But in its own world do we feel the creature is so very bad? The Fainalls and the Mirabels, the Dorimants and the Lady Touchwoods, in their own sphere do not offend my moral sense; in fact they do not appeal to it at all. They seem engaged in their proper element. They break through no laws, or conscientious restraints. They know of none. They have got out of Christendom into the land – what shall I call it? – of cuckoldry – the Utopia of gallantry, where pleasure is duty, and the manners perfect freedom. It is altogether a speculative scene of things, which has no reference whatever to the world that is. No good person can be justly offended as a spectator, because no good person suffers on the stage. Judged morally, every character in these plays – the few exceptions only are *mistakes* – is alike essentially vain and worthless. The great art of Congreve is especially shown in this, that he has entirely excluded from his scenes – some little generosities in the part of Angelica perhaps excepted, – not only anything like a faultless character, but any pretensions to goodness or good feelings whatsoever. Whether he did this designedly, or instinctively, the effect is as happy, as the design (if design) was bold. I used to wonder at the strange power which his *Way of the World* in particular possesses of interesting you all along in the pursuits of characters, for whom you absolutely care nothing – for you neither hate nor love his personages – and I think it is owing to this very indifference for any, that you endure the whole. He has spread a privation of moral light, I will call it, rather than by the ugly name of palpable darkness, over his creations; and his shadows flit before you without distinction or preference. Had he introduced a good character, a single gush of moral feeling, a revulsion of the judgment to actual life and actual duties, the impertinent Goshen would have only lighted to the discovery of deformities, which now are none, because we think them none.

Translated into real life, the characters of his, and his friend Wycherley's dramas, are profligates and strumpets, – the business of their brief existence, the undivided pursuit of lawless gallantry. No other spring of action, or possible motive of conduct, is recognised; principles which, universally acted upon, must reduce this frame of things to a chaos. But we do them wrong in so translating them. No such effects are produced in *their* world. When we are among them, we are amongst a chaotic people. We are not to judge them by our usages. No reverend institutions are insulted by their proceedings, – for they have none among them. No peace of families is violated, – for no family ties exist among them. No purity of the marriage bed is stained, – for none is supposed to have a being. No deep affections are disquieted, – no holy wedlock bands are snapped asunder, – for affection's depth and wedded faith are not of the growth of that soil. There is neither right nor wrong, – gratitude or its opposite, – claim or duty, – paternity or sonship. Of what consequence is it to Virtue, or how is she at all concerned about it, whether Sir Simon, or Dapperwit, steal away Miss Martha; or who is the father of Lord Froth's, or Sir Paul Pliant's children?

The whole is a passing pageant, where we should sit as unconcerned at the issues, for life or death, as at the battle of the frogs and mice. But, like Don Quixote, we take part against the puppets, and quite as impertinently. We dare not contemplate an Atlantis, a scheme, out of which our coxcombical moral sense is for a little transitory ease excluded. We have not the courage to imagine a state of things for which there is neither reward nor punishment. We cling to the painful necessities of shame and blame. We would indict our very dreams.

Amidst the mortifying circumstances attendant upon growing old, it is something to have seen *The School for Scandal* in its glory. This comedy grew out of Congreve and Wycherley, but gathered some allays of the sentimental comedy which followed theirs. It is impossible that it should be now *acted*, though it continues, at long intervals, to be announced in the bills. Its hero, when Palmer played it at least, was Joseph Surface. When I remember the gay boldness, the graceful solemn plausibility, the measured step, the insinuating voice – to express it in a word – the downright *acted* villainy of the part, so different from the pressure of conscious actual wickedness, – the hypocritical assumption of hypocrisy, – which made Jack so deservedly a favourite in that character,

I must needs conclude the present generation of play-goers more virtuous than myself, or more dense. I freely confess that he divided the palm with me with his better brother; that, in fact, I liked him quite as well. Not but there are passages, – like that, for instance, where Joseph is made to refuse a pittance to a poor relation, – incongruities which Sheridan was forced upon by the attempt to join the artificial with the sentimental comedy, either of which must destroy the other – but over these obstructions Jack's manner floated him so lightly, that a refusal from him no more shocked you than the easy compliance of Charles gave you in reality any pleasure; you got over the paltry question as quickly as you could, to get back into the regions of pure comedy, where no cold moral reigns. The highly artificial manner of Palmer in this character counteracted every disagreeable impression which you might have received from the contrast, supposing them real, between the two brothers. You did not believe in Joseph with the same faith with which you believed in Charles. The latter was a pleasant reality, the former a no less pleasant poetical foil to it. The comedy, I have said, is incongruous; a mixture of Congreve with sentimental incompatabilities: the gaiety upon the whole is buoyant, but it required the consummate art of Palmer to reconcile the discordant elements.

A player with Jack's talents, if we had one now, would not dare to do the part in the same manner. He would instinctively avoid every turn which might tend to unrealise, and so to make the character fascinating. He must take his cue from his spectators, who would expect a bad man and a good man as rigidly opposed to each other as the deathbeds of those geniuses are contrasted in the prints, which I am sorry to say have disappeared from the windows of my old friend Carrington Bowles, of St Paul's Church-yard memory – (an exhibition as venerable as the adjacent cathedral, and almost coeval) of the bad and good man at the hour of death; where the ghastly apprehensions of the former, – and truly the grim phantom with his reality of a toasting fork is not to be despised, – so finely contrast with the meek complacent kissing of the rod, taking it in like honey and butter, – with which the latter submits to the scythe of the gentle bleeder, Time, who wields his lancet with the apprehensive finger of a popular young ladies' surgeon. What flesh, like loving grass, would not covet to meet half-way the stoke of such a delicate mower? – John Palmer was twice an actor in this exquisite part. He was playing to you all the while that he was playing upon Sir Peter and his lady. You had the first intimation of a sentiment before it was on his lips. His altered voice was meant to you, and you were to suppose that his fictitious co-flutterers on the stage perceived nothing at all of it. What was it to you if that half reality, the husband, was over-reached by the puppetry, or the thin thing (Lady Teazle's reputation) was persuaded it was dying of a plethory? The fortunes of Othello and Desdemona were not concerned in it. Poor Jack has passed from the stage in good time, that he did not live to this our age of seriousness. The pleasant old Teazle *King*, too, is gone in good time. His manner would scarce have passed current in our day. We must love or hate – acquit or condemn – censure or pity – exert our detestable coxcombry of moral judgment upon every thing. Joseph Surface, to go down now, must be a downright revolting villain – no compromise – his first appearance must shock and give horror – his specious plausibilities, which the pleasurable faculties of our fathers' welcomed with such hearty greetings, knowing that no harm (dramatic harm even) could come, or was meant to come of them, must inspire a cold and killing aversion. Charles (the real canting person of the scene – for the hypocrisy of Joseph has its ulterior legitimate ends, but his brother's professions of a good heart centre in downright self-satisfaction) must be *loved*, and Joseph *hated*. To balance one disagreeable reality with another, Sir Peter Teazle must be no longer the comic idea of a fretful old bachelor bride-groom, whose teasings (while King acted it) were evidently as much played off at you, as they were meant to concern any body on the stage, – he must be a real person, capable in law of sustaining an injury – a person towards whom duties are to be acknowledged, the genuine crimcon antagonist of the villainous seducer Joseph. To realise him more, his sufferings under his unfortunate match must have the downright pungency of life – must (or should) make you not mirthful but uncomfortable, just as the same predicament would move you in a neighbour or old friend.

The delicious scenes which give the play its name and zest, must affect you in the same serious manner as if you heard the reputation of a dear female friend attacked in your real presence. Crabtree and Sir Benjamin – those poor snakes that live but in the sunshine of your mirth – must be ripened by this hot-bed process of realisation into asps or amphisbænas; and Mrs Candour – O! frightful! – become a hooded serpent. Oh who that remembers Parsons and Dodd – the wasp and butterfly of *The School for Scandal*, in those two characters; and charming natural Miss Pope, the perfect gentlewoman as distinguished from the fine lady of comedy, in this latter part – would forego the true scenic delight – the escape from life – the oblivion of consequences – the holiday barring out of the pedant Reflection – those Saturnalia of two or three brief hours, well won from the world – to sit instead at one of our modern plays – to have his coward conscience (that forsooth must not be left for a moment) stimulated with perpetual appeals – dulled rather, and blunted, as a faculty without repose must be – and his moral vanity pampered with images of notional justice, notional beneficence, lives saved without the spectator's risk, and fortunes given away that cost the author nothing?

No piece was, perhaps, ever so completely cast in all its parts as this *manager's comedy*. Miss Farren had succeeded to Mrs Abingdon in Lady Teazle; and Smith, the original Charles, had retired, when I first saw it. The rest of the characters, with very slight exceptions, remained. I remember it was then the fashion to cry down John Kemble, who took the part of Charles after Smith; but, I thought, very unjustly. Smith, I fancy, was more airy, and took the eye with a certain gaiety of person. He brought with him no sombre recollections of tragedy. He had not to expiate the fault of having pleased beforehand in lofty declamation. He had no sins of Hamlet or of Richard to atone for. His failure in these parts was a passport to success in one of so opposite a tendency. But, as far as I could judge, the weighty sense of Kemble made up for more personal incapacity that he had to answer for. His harshest tones in this part came steeped and dulcified in good humour. He made his defects a grace. His exact declamatory manner, as he managed it, only served to convey

240

the points of his dialogue with more precision. It seemed to head the shafts to carry them deeper. Not one of his sparkling sentences was lost. I remember minutely how he delivered each in succession, and cannot by any effort imagine how any of them could be altered for the better. No man could deliver brilliant dialogue – the dialogue of Congreve or of Wycherley – because none understood it – half so well as John Kemble. His Valentine, in *Love for Love*, was, to my recollection, faultless. He flagged sometimes in the intervals of tragic passion. He would slumber over the level parts of an heroic character. His Macbeth had been known to nod. But he always seemed to me to be particularly alive to pointed and witty dialogue. The relaxing levities of tragedy have not been touched by any since him – the playful court-bred spirit in which he condescended to the players in *Hamlet* – the sportive relief which he threw into the darker shades of Richard – disappeared with him. He had his sluggish moods, his torpors – but they were the halting-stones and resting-place of his tragedy – politic savings and fetches of the breath – husbandry of the lungs, where nature pointed him to be an economist – rather, I think, than errors of the judgment. They were, at worst, less painful than the eternal tormenting unappeasable vigilance, – the 'lidless dragon eyes', of present fashionable tragedy.

London Magazine, 1822

On the Tragedies of Shakespeare

(Considered with reference to their fitness for stage representation)

Taking a turn the other day in the Abbey, I was struck with the affected attitude of a figure, which I do not remember to have seen before, and which upon examination proved to be a whole-length of the celebrated Mr Garrick. Though I would not go so far with some good Catholics abroad as to shut players altogether out of consecrated ground, yet I own I was not a little scandalised at the introduction of theatrical airs and gestures into a place set apart to remind us of the saddest realities. Going nearer, I found inscribed under the harlequin figure the following lines: –

> To paint fair Nature, by Divine command,
> Her magic pencil in his glowing hand,
> A Shakespeare rose: then, to expand his fame
> Wide o'er this breathing world, a Garrick came.
> Though, like the bard himself, in night they lay,
> Immortal Garrick called them back to day:
> And till Eternity, with power sublime,
> Shall mark the mortal hour of hoary Time,
> Shakespeare and Garrick like twin-stars shall shine,
> And earth irradiate with a beam divine.

It would be an insult to my readers' understandings to attempt anything like a criticism on this farrago of false thoughts and nonsense. But the reflection it led me into was a kind of wonder how, from the days of the actor here celebrated to our own, it should have been the fashion to compliment every performer in his turn, that has had the luck to please the town in any of the great characters of Shakespeare, with a notion of possessing a *mind congenial with the poet's*; how people should come thus unaccountably to confound the power of originating poetical images and conceptions with the faculty of being able to read or recite the same when put into words;* or what connection that absolute mastery over the heart and soul of man, which a great dramatic poet possesses, has with those low tricks upon the eye and ear, which a player, by observing a few general effects, which some common passion, as grief, anger, &c., usually has upon the

---

* It is observable that we fall into this confusion only in *dramatic* recitations. We never dream that the gentleman who reads Lucretius in public with great applause is therefore a great poet and philosopher; nor do we find that Tom Davies, the bookseller, who is recorded to have recited the *Paradise Lost* better than any man in England in his day (though I cannot help thinking there must be some mistake in this tradition) was therefore, by his intimate friends, set upon a level with Milton.

gestures and exterior, can easily compass. To know the internal workings and movements of a great mind, of an Othello or a Hamlet, for instance, the *when* and the *why* and the *how far* they should be moved; to what pitch a passion is becoming; to give reins and to pull in the curb exactly at the moment when the drawing in or the slacking is most graceful; seems to demand a reach of intellect of a vastly different extent from that which is employed upon the bare imitation of the signs of these passions in the countenance or gesture, which signs are usually observed to be the most lively and emphatic in the weaker sort of minds, and which signs can, after all, but indicate some passion, as I said before, anger or grief, generally; but of the motives and grounds of the passion wherein it differs from the same passion in low and vulgar natures, of these the actor can give no more idea by his face or gesture than the eye (without a metaphor) can speak, or the muscles utter intelligible sounds. But such is the instantaneous nature of the impressions which we take in at the eye and ear at a playhouse, compared with the slow apprehension often-times of the understanding in reading, that we are apt not only to sink the play-writer in the consideration which we pay to the actor, but even to identify in our minds in a perverse manner the actor with the character which he represents. It is difficult for a frequent play-goer to disembarrass the idea of Hamlet from the person and voice of Mr K[emble]. We speak of Lady Macbeth, while we are in reality thinking of Mrs S[iddons]. Nor is this confusion incidental alone to unlettered persons, who, not possessing the advantage of reading, are necessarily dependent upon the stage-player for all the pleasure which they can receive from the drama, and to whom the very idea of *what an author is* cannot be made comprehensible without some pain and perplexity of mind: the error is one from which persons otherwise not meanly lettered find it almost impossible to extricate themselves.

Never let me be so ungrateful as to forget the very high degree of satisfaction which I received some years back from seeing for the first time a tragedy of Shakespeare performed in which these two great performers sustained the principal parts. It seemed to embody and realise conceptions which had hitherto assumed no distinct shape. But dearly do we pay all our life afterwards for

243

this juvenile pleasure, this sense of distinctness. When the novelty is past, we find to our cost that, instead of realising an idea, we have only materialised and brought down a fine vision to the standard of flesh and blood. We have let go a dream, in quest of an unattainable substance.

How cruelly this operates upon the mind, to have its free conceptions thus cramped and pressed down to the measure of a strait-lacing actuality, may be judged from that delightful sensation of freshness with which we turn to those plays of Shakespeare which have escaped being performed, and to those passages in the acting plays of the same writer which have happily been left out in performance. How far the very custom of hearing anything *spouted* withers and blows upon a fine passage, may be seen in those speeches from *Henry the Fifth,* &c., which are current in the mouths of schoolboys from their being found in 'Enfield Speakers', and such kind of books. I confess myself utterly unable to appreciate that celebrated soliloquy in *Hamlet* beginning 'To be or not to be', or to tell whether it be good, bad, or indifferent; it has been so handled and pawed about by declamatory boys and men, and torn so inhumanly from its living place, and principle of continuity in the play, till it is become to me, a perfect dead member.

It may seem a paradox, but I cannot help being of opinion that the plays of Shakespeare are less calculated for performance on a stage than those of almost any other dramatist whatever. Their distinguished excellence is a reason that they should be so. There is so much in them which comes not under the province of acting, with which eye, and tone, and gesture have nothing to do.

The glory of the scenic art is to personate passion and the turns of passion; and the more coarse and palpable the passion is, the more hold upon the eyes and ears of the spectators the performer obviously possesses. For this reason, scolding scenes, scenes where two persons talk themselves into a fit of fury, and then in a surprising manner talk themselves out of it again, have always been the most popular upon our stage. And the reason is plain, because the spectators are here most palpably appealed to, they are the proper judges in this war of words, they are the legitimate ring that should be formed round such 'intellectual prize-fighters'.

Talking is the direct object of the imitation here. But in the best dramas, and in Shakespeare above all, how obvious it is that the form of *speaking*, whether it be in soliloquy or dialogue, is only a medium, and often a highly artificial one, for putting the reader or spectator into possession of that knowledge of the inner structure and workings of mind in a character, which he could otherwise never have arrived at *in that form of composition* by any gift short of intuition. We do here as we do with novels written in the *epistolary form*. How many improprieties, perfect solecisms in letter-writing, do we put up with in *Clarissa* and other books, for the sake of the delight which that form upon the whole gives us.

But the practice of stage representation reduces everything to a controversy of elocution. Every character, from the boisterous blasphemings of Bajazet to the shrinking timidity of womanhood, must play the orator. The love dialogues of *Romeo and Juliet*, those silver-sweet sounds of lovers' tongues by night; the more intimate and sacred sweetness of nuptial colloquy between an Othello or a Posthumus with their married wives, all those delicacies which are so delightful in the reading, as when we read of those youthful dalliances in Paradise –

> As beseemed
> Fair couple linked in happy nuptial league
> Alone:

by the inherent fault of stage representation, how are these things sullied and turned from their very nature by being exposed to a large assembly; when such speeches as Imogen addresses to her lord come drawling out of the mouth of a hired actress, whose courtship, though nominally addressed to the personated Posthumus, is manifestly aimed at the spectators, who are to judge of her endearments and her returns of love.

The character of Hamlet is perhaps that by which, since the days of Betterton, a succession of popular performers have had the greatest ambition to distinguish themselves. The length of the part may be one of their reasons. But for the character itself, we find it in a play, and therefore we judge it a fit subject of dramatic representation. The play itself abounds in maxims and reflections beyond any other, and therefore we consider it a

245

proper vehicle for conveying moral instruction. But Hamlet himself – what does he suffer meanwhile by being dragged forth as a public schoolmaster to give lectures to the crowd! Why, nine parts in ten of what Hamlet does are transactions between himself and his moral sense, they are the effusions of his solitary musings, which he retires to holes and corners and the most sequestered parts of the palace to pour forth, or rather, they are the silent meditations with which his bosom is bursting, reduced to *words* for the sake of the reader, who must else remain ignorant of what is passing there. These profound sorrows, these light-and noise-abhorring ruminations, which the tongue scarce dares to utter to deaf walls and chambers, how can they be represented by a gesticulating actor, who comes and mouths them out before an audience, making four hundred people his confidants at once? I say not that it is the fault of the actor so to do; he must pronounce them *ore rotundo*, he must accompany them with his eye, he must insinuate them into his auditory by some trick of eye, tone, or gesture, or he fails. *He must be thinking all the while of his appearance because he knows that all the while the spectators are judging of it.* And this is the way to represent the shy, negligent, retiring Hamlet: –

It is true that there is no other mode of conveying a vast quantity of thought and feeling to a great portion of the audience, who otherwise would never learn it for themselves by reading, and the intellectual acquisition gained this way may, for aught I know, be inestimable; but I am not arguing that *Hamlet* should not be acted, but how much *Hamlet* is made another thing by being acted. I have heard much of the wonders which Garrick performed in this part; but as I never saw him, I must have leave to doubt whether the representation of such a character came within the province of his art. Those who tell me of him speak of his eye, of the magic of his eye, and of his commanding voice: physical properties, vastly desirable in an actor, and without which he can never insinuate meaning into an auditory, – but what have they to do with Hamlet? what have they to do with intellect? In fact, the things aimed at in theatrical representation are to arrest the spectator's eye upon the form and the gesture, and so to gain a more favourable hearing to what is spoken: it is not what the character is, but how he looks; not what he says, but how he speaks it. I see no reason to think that if the play of *Hamlet* were written over again by some such writer as Banks or Lillo, retaining the process of the story, but totally omitting all the poetry of it, all the divine features of Shakespeare, his stupendous intellect, and only taking care to give us enough of passionate dialogue, which Banks or Lillo were never at a loss to furnish; I see not how the effect could be much different upon an audience, nor how the actor has it in his power to represent Shakespeare to us differently from his representation of Banks or Lillo. Hamlet would still be a youthful, accomplished prince, and must be gracefully personated; he might be puzzled in his mind, wavering in his conduct, seemingly cruel to Ophelia, he might see a ghost, and start at it, and address it kindly when he found it to be his father; all this in the poorest and most homely language of the servilest creeper after nature that ever consulted the palate of an audience; without troubling Shakespeare for the matter: and I see not but there would be room for all the power which an actor has to display itself. All the passions and changes of passion might remain; for those are much less difficult to write or act than is thought; it is a trick easy to be attained; it is but rising or falling a note or two in the voice, a whisper with a significant foreboding look to announce its approach, and so contagious the counterfeit appearance of any emotion is, that let the words be what they will, the look and tone shall carry it off and make it pass for deep skill in the passions.

It is common for people to talk of Shakespeare's plays being *so natural* that everybody can understand him. They are natural indeed, they are grounded deep in nature, so deep that the depth of them lies out of the reach of most of us. You shall hear the same person say that *George Barnwell* is very natural, and *Othello* is very natural; that they are both very deep; and to them they are the same kind of thing. At the one they sit and shed tears because a good sort of young man is tempted by a naughty woman to commit *a trifling peccadillo*, the murder of an uncle or so,* that

---

* If this note could hope to meet the eye of any of the managers, I would entreat and beg of them, in the name of both the galleries, that this insult upon the

247

is all, and so comes to an untimely end, which is *so moving*; and at the other, because a blackamoor in a fit of jealousy kills his innocent white wife: and the odds are that ninety-nine out of a hundred would willingly behold the same catastrophe happen to both the heroes, and have thought the rope more due to Othello than to Barnwell. For of the texture of Othello's mind, the inward construction marvellously laid open, with all its strengths and weaknesses, its heroic confidences and its human misgivings, its agonies of hate springing from the depths of love, they see no more than the spectators at a cheaper rate, who pay their pennies apiece to look through the man's telescope in Leicester Fields see into the inward plot and topography of the moon. Some dim thing or other they see, they see an actor personating a passion, a grief or anger, for instance, and they recognise it as a copy of the usual external effects of such passion; or at least as being true to *that symbol of the emotion which passes current at the theatre for it*, for it is often no more than that: but of the grounds of the passion, its correspondence to a great and heroic nature, which is the only worthy object of tragedy, – that common auditors know anything of this, or can have any such notions dinned into them by the mere strength of an actor's lungs – that apprehension foreign to them should be thus infused into them by storm, I can neither believe, nor understand how it can be possible.

We talk of Shakespeare's admirable observation of life when we should feel that not from a petty inquisition into those cheap and everyday characters which surrounded him, as they surround us, but from his own mind, which was, to borrow a phrase of Ben Jonson's, the very 'sphere of humanity', he fetched those

---

morality of the common people of London should cease to be eternally repeated in the holiday weeks. Why are the 'Prentices of this famous and well-governed city, instead of an amusement, to be treated over and over again with the nauseous sermon of George Barnwell? Why *at the end of their vistas* are we to place the *gallows*? Were I an uncle, I should not much like a nephew of mine to have such an example placed before his eyes. It is really making uncle-murder too trivial to exhibit it as done upon such slight motives; – it is attributing too much to such characters as Millwood; it is putting things into the heads of good young men, which they would never otherwise have dreamed of. Uncles that think anything of their lives should fairly petition the Chamberlain against it.

images of virtue and of knowledge, of which every one of us recognising a part, think we comprehend in our natures the whole, and oftentimes mistake the powers which he positively creates in us, for nothing more than indigenous faculties of our own minds, which only waited the application of corresponding virtues in him to return a full and clear echo of the same.

To return to Hamlet. Among the distinguishing features of that wonderful character, one of the most interesting (yet painful) is that soreness of mind which makes him treat the intrusions of Polonius with harshness, and that asperity which he puts on in his interviews with Ophelia. These tokens of an unhinged mind (if they be not mixed in the latter case with a profound artifice of love, to alienate Ophelia by affected discourtesies, so to prepare her mind for the breaking off of that loving intercourse which can no longer find a place amidst business so serious as that which he has to do) are parts of his character, which to reconcile with our admiration of Hamlet, the most patient consideration of his situation is no more than necessary; they are what we *forgive afterwards*, and explain by the whole of his character, but *at the time* they are harsh and unpleasant. Yet such is the actor's necessity of giving strong blows to the audience, that I have never seen a player in this character who did not exaggerate and strain to the utmost these ambiguous features, – these temporary deformities in the character. They make him express a vulgar scorn at Polonius which utterly degrades his gentility, and which no explanation can render palatable; they make him show contempt, and curl up the nose at Ophelia's father, – contempt in its very grossest and most hateful form; but they get applause by it: it is natural, people say; that is, the words are scornful, and the actor expresses scorn, and that they can judge of; but why so much scorn, and of that sort, they never think of asking.

So to Ophelia. All the Hamlets that I have ever seen rant and rave at her as if she had committed some great crime, and the audience are highly pleased, because the words of the part are satirical, and they are enforced by the strongest expression of satirical indignation of which the face and voice are capable. But then, whether Hamlet is likely to have put on such brutal appearances to a lady whom he loved so dearly is never thought on.

The truth is, that in all such deep affections as had subsisted between Hamlet and Ophelia there is a stock of *supererogatory love* (if I may venture to use the expression), which in any great grief of heart, especially where that which preys upon the mind cannot be communicated, confers a kind of indulgence upon the grieved party to express itself, even to its heart's dearest object, in the language of a temporary alienation; but it is not alienation, it is a distraction purely, and so it always makes itself to be felt by that object: it is not anger, but grief assuming the appearance of anger, – love awkwardly counterfeiting hate, as sweet countenances when they try to frown: but such sternness and fierce disgust as Hamlet is made to show is no counterfeit, but the real face of absolute aversion, of irreconcilable alienation. It may be said he puts on the madman; but then he should only so far put on this counterfeit lunacy as his own real distraction will give him leave, that is, incompletely, imperfectly; not in that confirmed, practised way, like a master of his art, or, as Dame Quickly would say, 'like one of those harlotry players'.

I mean no disrespect to any actor, but the sort of pleasure which Shakespeare's plays give in the acting seems to me not at all to differ from that which the audience receive from those of other writers; and *they being in themselves essentially so different from all others*, I must conclude that there is something in the nature of acting which levels all distinctions. And, in fact, who does not speak indifferently of the 'Gamester' and of 'Macbeth' as fine stage performances, and praise the Mrs Beverley in the same way as the Lady Macbeth of Mrs Siddons? Belvidera, and Calista, and Isabella, and Euphrasia, are they less liked than Imogen, or than Juliet, or than Desdemona? Are they not spoken of and remembered in the same way? Is not the female performer as great (as they call it) in one as in the other? Did not Garrick shine, and was he not ambitious of shining in every drawling tragedy that his wretched day produced, the productions of the Hills and the Murphys and the Browns, and shall he have that honour to dwell in our minds for ever as an inseparable concomitant with Shakespeare? A kindred mind! O who can read that affecting sonnet of Shakespeare which alludes to his profession as a player:

O for my sake do you with Fortune chide,
The guilty goddess of my harmful deeds,
That did not better for my life provide
Than public means which public custom breeds –
Thence comes it that my name receives a brand;
And almost thence my nature is subdued
To what it works in, like the dyer's hand; –

Or that other confession –

Alas! 'tis true, I have gone here and there,
And made myself a motley to the view,
Gored mine own thoughts, sold cheap what is most dear; –

who can read these instances of jealous self-watchfulness in our
sweet Shakespeare and dream of any congeniality between him
and one that, by every tradition of him, appears to have been as
mere a player as ever existed; to have had his mind tainted with
the lowest player's vices, envy and jealousy, and miserable cravings after applause; one who in the exercise of his profession was
jealous even of the women performers that stood in his way; a
manager full of managerial tricks and stratagems and finesse:
that any resemblance should be dreamed of between him and
Shakespeare, – Shakespeare who, in the plenitude and consciousness of his own powers, could with that noble modesty which
we can neither imitate nor appreciate, express himself thus of
his own sense of his own defects: –

Wishing me like to one more rich in hope,
Featured like him, like him with friends possessed:
Desiring *this man's art and that man's scope.*

I am almost disposed to deny to Garrick the merit of being an
admirer of Shakespeare. A true lover of his excellences he certainly was not; for would any true lover of them have admitted
into his matchless scenes such ribald trash as Tate and Cibber,
and the rest of them, that

With their darkness durst affront his light,

have foisted into the acting plays of Shakespeare? I believe it

251

impossible that he could have had a proper reverence for Shakespeare, and have condescended to go through that interpolated scene in *Richard the Third*, in which Richard tries to break his wife's heart by telling her he loves another woman, and says, 'If she survives this she is immortal.' Yet I doubt not he delivered this vulgar stuff with as much anxiety of emphasis as any of the genuine parts; and for acting, it is as well calculated as any. But we have seen the part of Richard lately produce great fame to an actor in his manner of playing it, and it lets us into the secret of acting, and of popular judgements of Shakespeare derived from acting. Not one of the spectators who have witnessed Mr [G.F.] C[ooke]'s exertions in that part but has come away with a proper conviction that Richard is a very wicked man, and kills little children in their beds with something like the pleasure which the giants and ogres in children's books are represented to have taken in that practice; moreover, that he is very close and shrewd, and devilish cunning, for you could see that by his eye.

But is, in fact, this the impression we have in reading the Richard of Shakespeare? Do we feel anything like disgust, as we do at that butcher-like representation of him that passes for him on the stage? A horror at his crimes blends with the effect which we feel, but how is it qualified, how is it carried off, by the rich intellect which he displays, his resources, his wit, his buoyant spirits, his vast knowledge and insight into characters, the poetry of his part – not an atom of all which is made perceivable in Mr C.'s way of acting it. Nothing but his crimes, his actions, is visible; they are prominent and staring; the murderer stands out, but where is the lofty genius, the man of vast capacity, – the profound, the witty, accomplished Richard?

The truth is, the characters of Shakespeare are so much the objects of meditation rather than of interest or curiosity as to their actions, that while we are reading any of his great criminal characters, Macbeth, Richard, even Iago, we think not so much of the crimes which they commit as the ambition, the aspiring spirit, the intellectual activity which prompts them to overleap those moral fences. Barnwell is a wretched murderer; there is a certain fitness between his neck and the rope; he is the legitimate heir to the gallows; nobody who thinks at all can think of any alleviating circumstances in his case to make him a fit object of mercy. Or, to take an instance from the higher tragedy, what else but a mere assassin is Glenalvon? Do we think of anything but of the crime which he commits, and the rack which he deserves? That is all which we really think about him. Whereas, in corresponding characters in Shakespeare so little do the actions comparatively affect us, that while the impulses, the inner mind in all its perverted greatness, solely seems real and is exclusively attended to, the crime is comparatively nothing. But when we see these things represented, the acts which they do are comparatively everything, their impulses nothing. The state of sublime emotion into which we are elevated by those images of night and horror which Macbeth is made to utter, that solemn prelude with which he entertains the time till the bell shall strike which is to call him to murder Duncan, – when we no longer read it in a book, when we have given up that vantage-ground of abstraction which reading possesses over seeing, and come to see a man in his bodily shape before our eyes actually preparing to commit a murder, if the acting be true and impressive, as I have witnessed it in Mr [J.P.] K[emble]'s performance of that part, the painful anxiety about the act, the natural longing to prevent it while it yet seems unperpetrated, the too close pressing semblance of reality, give a pain and an uneasiness which totally destroy all the delight which the words in the book convey, where the deed doing never presses upon us with the painful sense of presence: it rather seems to belong to history, – to something past and inevitable, if it has anything to do with time at all. The sublime images, the poetry alone, is that which is present to our minds in the reading.

So to see Lear acted, to see an old man tottering about the stage with a walking-stick, turned out of doors by his daughters in a rainy night, has nothing in it but what is painful and disgusting. We want to take him into shelter and relieve him. That is all the feeling which the acting of Lear ever produced in me. But the Lear of Shakespeare cannot be acted. The contemptible machinery by which they mimic the storm which he goes out in, is not more inadequate to represent the horrors of the real elements than any actor can be to represent Lear: they might more easily propose to personate the Satan of Milton upon a stage, or one of

253

Michael Angelo's terrible figures. The greatness of Lear is not in corporal dimension, but in intellectual: the explosions of his passion are terrible as a volcano: they are storms turning up and disclosing to the bottom that sea his mind, with all its vast riches. It is his mind which is laid bare. The case of flesh and blood seems too insignificant to be thought on, even as he himself neglects it. On the stage we see nothing but corporal infirmities and weakness, the impotence of rage; while we read it, we see not Lear, but we are Lear – we are his mind, we are sustained by a grandeur which baffles the malice of daughters and storms; in the aberrations of his reason we discover a mighty irregular power of reasoning, immethodised from the ordinary purposes of life, but exerting its powers, as the wind blows where it listeth, at will upon the corruption and abuses of mankind.

What have looks, or tones, to do with that sublime identification, of his age with that of the *heavens themselves*, when in his reproaches to them for conniving at the injustice of his children, he reminds them that 'they themselves are old'? What gestures shall we appropriate to this? What has the voice or the eye to do with such things? But the play is beyond all art, as the tamperings with it show: it is too hard and stony; it must have love scenes, and a happy ending. It is not enough that Cordelia is a daughter, she must shine as a lover too. Tate has put his hook in the nostrils of this Leviathan, for Garrick and his followers, the showmen of scene, to draw the mighty beast about more easily. A happy ending! – as if the living martyrdom that Lear had gone through, the flaying of his feelings alive, did not make a fair dismissal from the stage of life the only decorous thing for him. If he is to live and be happy after, if he could sustain this world's burden after, why all this pudder and preparation – why torment us with this unnecessary sympathy? As if the childish pleasure of getting his gilt robes and sceptre again could tempt him to act over again his misused station – as if at his years, and with his experience anything was left but to die.

Lear is essentially impossible to be represented on a stage; but how many dramatic personages are there in Shakespeare which though more tractable and feasible (if I may so speak) than Lear, yet from some circumstance, some adjunct to their character, are improper to be shown to our bodily eye? *Othello*, for instance. Nothing can be more soothing, more flattering to the nobler parts of our natures, than to read of a young Venetian lady of the highest extraction, through the force of love and from a sense of merit in him whom she loved, laying aside every consideration of kindred, and country, and colour, and wedding with a *coal-black Moor* – (for such he is represented, in the imperfect state of knowledge respecting foreign countries in those days compared with our own, or in compliance with popular notions, though the Moors are now well enough known to be by many shades less unworthy of white woman's fancy) – it is the perfect triumph of virtue over accidents, of the imagination over the senses. She sees Othello's colour in his mind. But upon the stage, when the imagination is no longer the ruling faculty, but we are left to our poor unassisted senses, I appeal to every one that has seen *Othello* played whether he did not, on the contrary, sink Othello's mind in his colour; whether he did not find something extremely revolting in the courtship and wedded caresses of Othello and Desdemona; and whether the actual sight of the thing did not overweigh all that beautiful compromise which we make in reading; – and the reason it should do so is obvious, because there is just so much reality presented to our senses as to give a perception of disagreement, with not enough of belief in the internal motives – all that which is unseen – to overpower and reconcile the first and obvious prejudices.* What we see upon a stage is body and bodily action; what we are conscious of in reading is almost exclusively the mind and its movement: and this, I think, may sufficiently account for the very different sort of delight with

---

* The error of supposing that because Othello's colour does not offend us in the reading, it should also not offend us in the seeing, is just such a fallacy as supposing that an Adam and Eve in a picture shall affect us just as they do in the poem. But in the poem we for a while have paradisaical senses given us, which vanish when we see a man and his wife without clothes in the picture. The painters themselves feel this, as is apparent by the awkward shifts they have recourse to to make them look not quite naked, by a sort of prophetic anachronism antedating the invention of fig-leaves. So in the reading of the play, we see with Desdemona's eyes; in the seeing of it, we are forced to look with our own.

255

which the same play so often affects us in the reading and the seeing.

It requires little reflection to perceive that if those characters in Shakespeare which are within the precincts of nature have yet something in them which appeals too exclusively to the imagination to admit of their being made objects to the senses without suffering a change and a diminution, that still stronger the objection must lie against representing another line of characters, which Shakespeare has introduced to give a wildness and a supernatural elevation to his scenes, as if to remove them still farther from that assimilation to common life in which their excellence is vulgarly supposed to consist. When we read the incantations of those terrible beings the Witches in *Macbeth*, though some of the ingredients in their hellish composition savour of the grotesque, yet is the effect upon us other than the most serious and appalling that can be imagined? Do we not feel spell-bound as Macbeth was? Can any mirth accompany a sense of their presence? We might as well laugh under a consciousness of the principle of Evil himself being truly and really present with us. But attempt to bring these beings on to a stage, and you turn them instantly into so many old women, that men and children are to laugh at. Contrary to the old saying that 'seeing is believing', the sight actually destroys the faith; and the mirth in which we indulge at their expense when we see these creatures upon a stage, seems to be a sort of indemnification which we make to ourselves for the terror which they put us in when reading made them an object of belief – when we surrendered up our reason to the poet, as children to their nurses and their elders; and we laugh, at our fears, as children who thought they saw something in the dark, triumph when the bringing in of a candle discovers the vanity of their fears. For this exposure of supernatural agents upon a stage is truly bringing in a candle to expose their own delusiveness. It is the solitary taper and the book that generates a faith in these terrors: a ghost by chandelier light, and in good company, deceives no spectators, – a ghost that can be measured by the eye, and his human dimensions made out at leisure. The sight of a well-lighted house and a well-dressed audience shall arm the most nervous child against any apprehensions: as Tom

Brown says of the impenetrable skin of Achilles with his impenetrable armour over it, 'Bully Dawson would have fought the devil with such advantages.'

Much has been said, and deservedly, in reprobation of the vile mixture which Dryden has thrown into *The Tempest*: doubtless without some such vicious alloy, the impure ears of that age would never have sat out to hear so much innocence of love as is contained in the sweet courtship of Ferdinand and Miranda. But is *The Tempest* of Shakespeare at all a subject for stage representation? It is one thing to read of an enchanter, and to believe the wondrous tale while we are reading it; but to have a conjuror brought before us in his conjuring-gown, with his spirits about him, which none but himself and some hundred of favoured spectators before the curtain are supposed to see, involves such a quantity of the *hateful incredible*, that all our reverence for the author cannot hinder us from perceiving such gross attempts upon the senses to be in the highest degree childish and inefficient. Spirits and fairies cannot be represented, they cannot even be painted – they can only be believed. But the elaborate and anxious provision of scenery, which the luxury of the age demands, in these cases works a quite contrary effect to what is intended. That which in comedy or plays of familiar life adds so much to the life of the imitation, in plays which appeal to the higher faculties positively destroys the illusion which it is introduced to aid. A parlour or a drawing-room, a library opening into a garden, a garden with an alcove in it, a street or the piazza of Covent Garden, does well enough in a scene; we are content to give as much credit to it as it demands; or rather, we think little about it, – it is little more than reading at the top of a page, 'Scene, a garden'; we do not imagine ourselves there, but we readily admit the imitation of familiar objects. But to think by the help of painted trees and caverns, which we know to be painted, to transport our minds to Prospero and his island and his lonely cell;*

---

* It will be said these things are done in pictures. But pictures and scenes are very different things. Painting is a word of itself, but in scene-painting there is the attempt to deceive: and there is the discordancy, never to be got over, between painted scenes and real people.

or by the aid of a fiddle dexterously thrown in, in an interval of speaking, to make us believe that we hear those supernatural noises of which the isle was full: the Orrery Lecturer at the Haymarket might as well hope, by his musical glasses cleverly stationed out of sight behind his apparatus, to make us believe that we do indeed hear the crystal spheres ring out that chime, which, if it were to enwrap our fancy long, Milton thinks –

> Time would run back and fetch the age of gold,
> And speckled Vanity
> Would sicken soon and die,
> And leprous Sin would melt from earthly mould;
> Yea, Hell itself would pass away, ꞏ
> And leave its dolorous mansions to the peering day.

The garden of Eden, with our first parents in it, is not more impossible to be shown on a stage, than the Enchanted Isle, with its no less interesting and innocent first settlers.

The subject of scenery is closely connected with that of the dresses, which are so anxiously attended to on our stage. I remember the last time I saw Macbeth played, the discrepancy I felt at the changes of garment which he varied, the shiftings and reshiftings, like a Romish priest at mass. The luxury of stage improvements and the importunity of the public eye require this. The coronation robe of the Scottish monarch was fairly a counterpart to that which our King wears when he goes to the Parliament House, just so full and cumbersome, and set out with ermine and pearls. And if things must be represented, I see not what to find fault with in this. But in reading, what robe are we conscious of? Some dim images of royalty – a crown and sceptre – may float before our eyes; but who shall describe the fashion of it? Do we see in our mind's eye what Webb or any other robe-maker could pattern? This is the inevitable consequence of imitating everything to make all things natural. Whereas the reading of a tragedy is a fine abstraction. It presents to the fancy just so much of external appearances as to make us feel that we are among flesh and blood, while by far the greater and better part of our imagination is employed upon the thoughts and internal machinery of the character. But in acting, – scenery, dress, the most contemptible things, call upon us to judge of their naturalness.

Perhaps it would be no bad similitude, to liken the pleasure which we take in seeing one of these fine plays acted, compared with that quiet delight which we find in the reading of it, to the different feelings with which a reviewer, and a man that is not a reviewer, reads a fine poem. The accursed critical habit, the being called upon to judge and pronounce, must make it quite a different thing to the former. In seeing plays acted we are affected just as judges. When Hamlet compares the two pictures of Gertrude's first and second husband, who wants to see the pictures? But in the acting, a miniature must be lugged out, which we know not to be the picture, but only to show how finely a miniature may be represented. This showing of everything levels all things: it makes tricks, bows and curtseys of importance. Mrs Siddons never got more fame by anything than by the manner in which she dismisses the guests in the banquet scene in Macbeth: it is as much remembered as any of her thrilling tones or impressive looks. But does such a trifle as this enter into the imaginations of the readers of that wild and wonderful scene? Does not the mind dismiss the feasters as rapidly as it can? Does it care about the gracefulness of doing it? But by acting, and judging of acting, all these non-essentials are raised into an importance injurious to the main interest of the play.

I have confined my observations to the tragic parts of Shakespeare. It would be no very difficult task to extend the inquiry to his comedies, and to show why Falstaff, Shallow, Sir Hugh Evans, and the rest, are equally incompatible with stage representation. The length to which this essay has run will make it, I am afraid, sufficiently distasteful to the amateurs of the theatre, without going any deeper into the subject at present.

X [signature]
The Reflector, 1811

To Clara N[ovello]

The Gods have made me most unmusical,
With feelings that respond not to the call
Of stringéd harp or voice – obtuse and mute
To hautboy, sackbut, dulcimer, and flute;
King David's lyre, that made the madness flee
From Saul, had been but a jew's-harp to me:
Theorbos, violins, French horns, guitars,
Leave in my wounded ears inflicted scars;
I hate those trills, and shakes, and sounds that float
Upon the captive air; I know no note,
Nor ever shall, whatever folks may say,
Of the strange mysteries of *Sol* and *Fa*;
I sit at oratorios like a fish,
Incapable of sound, and only wish
The thing was over. Yet do I admire,
O tuneful daughter of a tuneful sire,
Thy painful labours in a science which
To your deserts I pray may make you rich
As much as you are loved, and add a grace
To the most musical Novello race.
Women lead men by the nose, some cynics say;
You draw them by the ear – a delicater way.

Athenæum, 1834

·A Chapter on Ears

I have no ear. –

Mistake me not, reader – nor imagine that I am by nature desti-
tute of those exterior twin appendages, hanging ornaments, and
(architecturally speaking) handsome volutes to the human capital. Better my mother had never borne me. – I am, I think, rather
delicately than copiously provided with those conduits; and I feel
no disposition to envy the mule for his plenty, or the mole for
her exactness, in those ingenious labyrinthine inlets – those indispensable side-intelligencers.

Neither have I incurred, or done anything to incur, with Defoe,
that hideous disfigurement, which constrained him to draw upon
assurance – to feel 'quite unabashed', and at ease upon that article. I was never, I thank my stars, in the pillory; nor, if I read
them aright, is it within the compass of my destiny, that I ever
should be.

When therefore I say that I have no ear, you will understand
me to mean – *for music*. To say that this heart never melted at the
concord of sweet sounds, would be a foul self-libel. *'Water parted
from the sea'* never fails to move it strangely. So does *'In infancy'*.
But they were used to be sung at her harpsichord (the old-fashioned
instrument in vogue in those days) by a gentlewoman – the
gentlest, sure, that ever merited the appellation – the sweetest –
why should I hesitate to name Mrs S[pinkes], once the blooming
Fanny Weatheral of the Temple – who had power to thrill the
soul of Elia, small imp as he was, even in his long coats; and to
make him glow, tremble, and blush with a passion that not faintly
indicated the dayspring of that absorbing sentiment which was
afterwards destined to overwhelm and subdue his nature quite
for Alice W[interto]n.

I even think that *sentimentally* I am disposed to harmony. But
organically I am incapable of a tune. I have been practising *God
save the King* all my life, whistling and humming of it over to
myself in solitary corners, and am not yet arrived, they tell me,
within many quavers of it. Yet hath the loyalty of Elia never been
impeached.

261

I am not without suspicion that I have an undeveloped faculty of music within me. For thrumming, in my wild way, on my friend A.'s piano, the other morning, while he was engaged in an adjoining parlour – on his return he was pleased to say, *'he thought it could not be the maid!'* On his first surprise at hearing the keys touched in somewhat an airy and masterful way, not dreaming of me, his suspicions had lighted on *Jenny*. But a grace, snatched from a superior refinement, soon convinced him that some being – technically perhaps deficient, but higher informed from a principle common to all the fine arts – had swayed the keys to a mood which Jenny with all her (less cultivated) enthusiasm could never have elicited from them. I mention this as a proof of my friend's penetration, and not with any view of disparaging Jenny.

Scientifically I could never be made to understand (yet have I taken some pains) what a note in music is; or how one note should differ from another. Much less in voices can I distinguish a soprano from a tenor. Only sometimes the thorough-bass I contrive to guess at, from its being supereminently harsh and disagreeable. I tremble, however, for my misapplication of the simplest terms of *that* which I disclaim. While I profess my ignorance, I scarce know what to *say* I am ignorant of. I hate, perhaps, by misnomers. *Sostenuto* and *adagio* stand in the like relation of obscurity to me; and *Sol, Fa, Mi, Re*, is as conjuring as *Baralipton*.

It is hard to stand alone in an age like this – (constituted to the quick and critical perception of all harmonious combinations, I verily believe, beyond all preceding ages, since Jubal stumbled upon the gamut), to remain, as it were, singly unimpressible to the magic influences of an art, which is said to have such an especial stroke at soothing, elevating, and refining the passions. – Yet, rather than break the candid current of my confessions, I must avow to you that I have received a great deal more pain than pleasure from this so cried-up faculty.

I am constitutionally susceptible of noises. A carpenter's hammer in a warm summer noon will fret me into more than midsummer madness. But those unconnected, unset, sounds are nothing to the measured malice of music. The ear is passive to those single strokes; willingly enduring stripes while it hath no task to con.

To music it cannot be passive. It will strive – mine at least will – spite of its inaptitude, to thrid the maze; like an unskilled eye painfully poring upon hieroglyphics. I have sat through an Italian Opera, till, for sheer pain and inexplicable anguish, I have rushed out into the noisiest places of the crowded streets, to solace myself with sounds which I was not obliged to follow, and get rid of the distracting torment of endless, fruitless, barren, attention! I take refuge in the unpretending assemblage of honest common-life sounds; – and the purgatory of the Enraged Musician becomes my paradise.

I have sat at an Oratorio (that profanation of the purposes of the cheerful playhouse) watching the faces of the auditory in the pit (what a contrast to Hogarth's Laughing Audience!) immoveable, or affecting some faint emotion – till (as some have said that our occupations in the next world will be but a shadow of what delighted us in this) I have imagined myself in some cold Theatre in Hades, where some of the *forms* of the earthly one should be kept up, with none of the *enjoyment*; or like that –

> ———Party in a parlour,
> All silent, and all DAMNED.

Above all, those insufferable concertos, and pieces of music, as they are called, do plague and embitter my apprehension. – Words are something; but to be exposed to an endless battery of mere sounds; to be long a dying, to lie stretched upon a rack of roses; to keep up languor by unintermitted effort; to pile honey upon sugar and sugar upon honey, to an interminable tedious sweetness; to fill up sound with feeling, and strain ideas to keep pace with it; to gaze on empty frames, and be forced to make the pictures for yourself; to read a book, *all stops*, and be obliged to supply the verbal matter; to invent extempore tragedies to answer to the vague gestures of an inexplicable rambling mime – these are the faint shadows of what I have undergone from a series of the ablest-executed pieces of this empty *instrumental music*.

I deny not that, in the opening of a concert, I have experienced something vastly lulling and agreeable: – afterwards followeth the languor and the oppression. Like that disappointing book in Patmos; or, like the comings on of melancholy, described by

263

Burton, doth music make her first insinuating approaches: – 'Most pleasant it is to such as are melancholy given, to walk alone in some solitary grove, betwixt wood and water, by some brook side, and to meditate upon some delightsome and pleasant subject, which shall affect him most, *amabilis insania*, and *mentis gratissimus error*. A most incomparable delight to build castles in the air, to go smiling to themselves, acting an infinite variety of parts, which they suppose, and strongly imagine, they act, or that they see done. – So delightsome these toys at first, they could spend whole days and nights without sleep, even whole years in such contemplations, and fantastical meditations, which are like so many dreams, and will hardly be drawn from them – winding and unwinding themselves as so many clocks, and still pleasing their humours, until at last the SCENE TURNS UPON A SUDDEN, and they being now habitated to such meditations and solitary places, can endure no company, can think of nothing but harsh and distasteful subjects. Fear, sorrow, suspicion, *subrusticus pudor*, discontent, cares, and weariness of life, surprise them on a sudden and they can think of nothing else: continually suspecting, no sooner are their eyes open, but this infernal plague of melancholy seizeth on them, and terrifies their souls, representing some dismal object to their minds; which now, by no means, no labour, no persuasions, they can avoid, they cannot be rid of, they cannot resist.'

Something like this 'SCENE TURNING' I have experienced at the evening parties, at the house of my good Catholic friend *Nov*——; who, by the aid of a capital organ, himself the most finished of players, converts his drawing-room into a chapel, his week days into Sundays, and these latter into minor heavens.*

When my friend commences upon one of those solemn anthems, which peradventure struck upon my heedless ear, rambling in the side aisles of the dime Abbey, some five-and-thirty years since, waking a new sense, and putting a soul of old religion into my young apprehension – (whether it be *that*,

---

* I have been there, and still would go;
  'Tis like a little heaven below. – DR WATTS.

in which the Psalmist, weary of the persecutions of bad men, wisheth to himself dove's wings – or *that other*, which, with a like measure of sobriety and pathos, inquireth by what means the young man shall best cleanse his mind) – a holy calm pervadeth me. – I am for the time

> ——rapt above earth,
> And possess joys not promised at my birth.

But when the master of the spell, not content to have laid a soul prostrate, goes on, in his power, to inflict more bliss than lies in her capacity to receive – impatient to overcome her 'earthly' with his 'heavenly', – still pouring in, for protracted hours, fresh waves and fresh from the sea of sound, or from that inexhausted *German* ocean, above which, in triumphant progress, dolphin-seated, ride those Arions *Haydn* and *Mozart*, with their attendant Tritons, *Bach*, *Beethoven*, and a countless tribe, whom to attempt to reckon up would but plunge me again in the deeps, – I stagger under the weight of harmony, reeling to and fro at my wit's end; – clouds, as of frankincense, oppress me – priests, altars, censers, dazzle before me – the genius of *his* religion hath me in her toils – a shadowy triple tiara invests the brow of my friend, late so naked, so ingenuous – he is Pope, – and by him sits, like as in the anomaly of dreams, a she-Pope too, – tri-coroneted like himself! – I am converted, and yet a Protestant; – at once *malleus hereticorum* and myself grand heresiarch: or three heresies centre in my person: – I am Marcion, Ebion, and Cerinthus – Gog and Magog, – what not? – till the coming in of the friendly supper-tray – dissipates the figment, and a draught of true Lutheran beer (in which chiefly my friend shows himself no bigot) at once reconciles me to the rationalities of a purer faith; and restores to me the genuine unterrifying aspects of my pleasant-countenanced host and hostess.

London Magazine, 1821

Free Thoughts on Several Eminent Composers

Some cry up Haydn, some Mozart,
Just as the whim bites; for my part,
I do not care a farthing candle
For either of them, or for Handel.
Cannot a man live free and easy
Without admiring Pergolese?
Or through the world with comfort go
That never heard of Doctor Blow?
So help me Heaven, I hardly have;
And yet I eat, and drink, and shave,
Like other people, if you watch it,
And know no more of stave or crotchet
Than did the primitive Peruvians;
Or those old ante-queer-diluvians
That lived in the unwashed world with Jubal,
Before that dirty blacksmith Tubal,
By stroke on anvil, or by summat,
Found out, to his great surprise, the gamut.

I care no more for Cimarosa
Than he did for Salvator Rosa,
Being no painter; and bad luck
Be mine, if I can bear that Gluck!
Old Tycho Brahe and modern Herschel
Had something in them; but who's Purcell?
The devil, with his foot so cloven,
For aught I care, may take Beethoven;
And, if the bargain does not suit,
I'll throw him Weber in to boot!
There's not the splitting of a splinter
To choose 'twixt him last named, and Winter.
Of Doctor Pepusch old Queen Dido
Knew just as much, God knows, as I do.
I would not go four miles to visit
Sebastian Bach (or Batch, which is it?)

No more I would for Bononcini.
As for Novello, or Rossini,
I shall not say a word to grieve 'em,
Because they're living; so I leave 'em.

London Magazine, 1835

Lamb obfuscated the origins of these verses –
probably deliberately. Almost certainly they
were written in 1830 and most probably for the
album of Vincent Novello in which there was
appended also the following verse:

The reason why my brother's so severe,
Vincentio, is – my brother has no *ear*:
And Caradori her mellifluous throat
Might stretch in vain to make him learn a note.
Of common tunes he knows not anything,
Nor 'Rule, Britannia!' from 'God save the King'.
He rail at Handel! He the gamut quiz!
I'd lay my life he knows not what it is.
His spite at music is a pretty whim –
He loves not it, because it loves not him.

written as if it was by Mary Lamb but more
likely by Charles himself. At about the same
time he insisted that he had written them in
response to a challenge from Ayrton. Apparently he was mighty pleased with this effort
because he also inscribed it into the albums of
several other friends.

Barrenness of the Imaginative Faculty in the Productions of Modern Art

Hogarth excepted, can we produce any one painter within the last fifty years, or since the humour of exhibiting began, that has treated a story *imaginatively*? By this we mean, upon whom his subject has so acted, that it has seemed to direct *him* – not to be arranged by him? Any upon whom its leading or collateral points have impressed themselves so tyrannically, that he dared not treat it otherwise, lest he should falsify a revelation? Any that has imparted to his compositions, not merely so much truth as is enough to convey a story with clearness, but that individualising property, which should keep the subject so treated distinct in feature from every other subject, however similar, and to common apprehensions almost identical; so that we might say, this and this part could have found an appropriate place in no other picture in the world but this? Is there anything in modern art – we will not demand that it should be equal – but in any way analogous to what Titian has effected, in that wonderful bringing together of two times in the 'Ariadne', in the National Gallery? Precipitous, with his reeling satyr rout about him, re-peopling and re-illuming suddenly the waste places, drunk with a new fury beyond the grape, Bacchus, born in fire, fire-like flings himself at the Cretan. This is the time present. With this telling of the story, an artist, and no ordinary one, might remain richly proud. Guido, in his harmonious version of it, saw no farther. But from the depths of the imaginative spirit Titian has recalled past time, and laid it contributory with the present to one simultaneous effect. With the desert all ringing with the mad cymbals of his followers, made lucid with the presence and new offers of a god, – as if unconscious of Bacchus, or but idly casting her eyes as upon some unconcerning pageant – her soul undistracted from Theseus – Ariadne is still pacing the solitary shore in as much heart-silence, and in almost the same local solitude, with which she awoke at daybreak to catch the forlorn last glances of the sail that bore away the Athenian.

Here are two points miraculously co-uniting; fierce society, with the feeling of solitude still absolute; noonday revelations, with the accidents of the dull gray dawn unquenched and lingering; the *present* Bacchus, with the *past* Ariadne: two stories, with double Time; separate, and harmonising. Had the artist made the woman one shade less indifferent to the God; still more, had she expressed a rapture at his advent, where would have been the story of the mighty desolation of the heart previous? merged in the insipid accident of a flattering offer met with a welcome acceptance. The broken heart for Theseus was not likely to be pieced up by a God.

We have before us a fine rough print, from a picture by Raphael in the Vatican. It is the Presentation of the new-born Eve to Adam by the Almighty. A fairer mother of mankind we might imagine, and a goodlier sire perhaps of men since born. But these are matters subordinate to the conception of the *situation*, displayed in this extraordinary production. A tolerable modern artist would have been satisfied with tempering certain raptures of connubial anticipation, with a suitable acknowledgment to the Giver of the blessing, in the countenance of the first bridegroom: something like the divided attention of the child (Adam was here a child-man) between the given toy, and the mother who had just blest it with the bauble. This is the obvious, the first-sight view, the superficial. An artist of a higher grade, considering the awful presence they were in, would have taken care to subtract something from the expression of the more human passion, and to heighten the more spiritual one. This would be as much as an exhibition-goer, from the opening of Somerset House to last year's show, has been encouraged to look for. It is obvious to hint at a lower expression yet, in a picture that, for respects of drawing and colouring, might be deemed not wholly inadmissible within these art-fostering walls, in which the raptures should be as ninety-nine, the gratitude as one, or perhaps zero! By neither the one passion nor the other has Raphael expounded the situation of Adam. Singly upon his brow sits the absorbing

269

sense of wonder at the created miracle. The *moment* is seized by
the intuitive artist, perhaps not self-conscious of his art, in which
neither of the conflicting emotions – a moment now abstracted!
– have had time to spring up, or to battle for indecorous mastery.
– We have seen a landscape of a justly-admired neoteric, in which
he aimed at delineating a fiction, one of the most severely beautiful in antiquity – the gardens of the Hesperides. To do Mr T[urner]
justice, he had painted a laudable orchard, with fitting seclusion,
and a veritable dragon (of which a Polypheme, by Poussin, is
somehow a fac-simile for the situation), looking over into the
world shut out backwards, so that none but a 'still-climbing Hercules' could hope to catch a peep at the admired Ternary of
Recluses. No conventual porter could keep his keys better than
this custos with the 'lidless eyes'. He not only sees that none *do*
intrude into that privacy, but, as clear as daylight, that none but
Hercules aut Diabolus by any manner of means *can*. So far all is
well. We have absolute solitude here or nowhere. *Ab extra*, the
damsels are snug enough. But here the artist's courage seems to
have failed him. He began to pity his pretty charge, and, to comfort the irksomeness, has peopled their solitude with a bevy of
fair attendants, maids of honour, or ladies of the bed-chamber,
according to the approved etiquette at a court of the nineteenth
century; giving to the whole scene the air of a *fête-champêtre*, if
we will but excuse the absence of the gentlemen. This is well,
and Watteauish. But what is become of the solitary mystery – the

> Daughters three,
> That sing around the golden tree?

This is not the way in which Poussin would have treated this
subject.

The paintings, or rather the stupendous architectural designs,
of a modern artist* have been urged as objections to the theory
of our motto. They are of a character, we confess, to stagger it.
His towered structures are of the highest order of the material
sublime. Whether they were dreams, or transcripts of some elder

---

* John Martin.

workmanship – Assyrian ruins old – restored by this mighty artist, they satisfy our most stretched and craving conceptions of the glories of the antique world. It is a pity that they were ever peopled. On that side, the imagination of the artist halts, and appears defective. Let us examine the point of the story in the 'Belshazzar's Feast'. We will introduce it by an apposite anecdote.

The court historians of the day record, that at the first dinner given by the late King (then Prince Regent) at the Pavilion, the following characteristic frolic was played off. The guests were select and admiring; the banquet profuse and admirable; the lights lustrous and oriental; the eye was perfectly dazzled with the display of plate, among which the great gold salt-cellar, brought from the regalia in the Tower for this especial purpose, itself a tower! stood conspicuous for its magnitude. And now the Rev. * * *, the then admired court Chaplain, was proceeding with the grace, when, at a signal given, the lights were suddenly overcast, and a huge transparency was discovered, in which glittered in gold letters –

'BRIGHTON – EARTHQUAKE – SWALLOW-UP-ALIVE!'

Imagine the confusion of the guests; the Georges and garters, jewels, bracelets, moulted upon the occasion! The fans dropped, and picked up the next morning by the sly court-pages! Mrs Fitz-what's-her-name* fainting, and the Countess of * * * holding the smelling-bottle, till the good-humoured Prince caused harmony to be restored, by calling in fresh candles, and declaring that the whole was nothing but a pantomime *hoax*, got up by the ingenious Mr Farley, of Covent Garden, from hints which his Royal Highness himself had furnished! Then imagine the infinite applause that followed, the mutual rallyings, the declarations that 'they were not much frightened', of the assembled galaxy.

The point of time in the picture exactly answers to the appearance of the transparency in the anecdote. The huddle, the flutter, the bustle, the escape, the alarm, and the mock alarm; the pretti-nesses heightened by consternation; the courtier's fear which

---

* Mrs Fitzherbert.

was flattery; and the lady's which was affection; all that we may conceive to have taken place in a mob of Brighton courtiers, sympathising with the well-acted surprise of their sovereign; all this, and no more, is exhibited by the well-dressed lords and ladies in the Hall of Belus. Just this sort of consternation we have seen among a flock of disquieted wild geese at the report only of a gun having gone off!

But is this vulgar fright, this mere animal anxiety for the preservation of their persons – such as we have witnessed at a theatre, when a slight alarm of fire has been given – an adequate exponent of a supernatural terror? the way in which the finger of God, writing judgments, would have been met with by the withered conscience? There is a human fear, and a divine fear. The one is disturbed, restless, and bent upon escape; the other is bowed down, effortless, passive. When the spirit appeared before Eliphaz in the visions of the night, and the hair of his flesh stood up, was it in the thoughts of the Temanite to ring the bell of his chamber, or to call up the servants? But let us see in the text what there is to justify all this huddle of vulgar consternation.

From the words of Daniel it appears that Belshazzar had made a great feast to a thousand of his lords, and drank wine before the thousand. The golden and silver vessels are gorgeously enumerated, with the princes, the king's concubines, and his wives. Then follows –

'In the same hour came forth fingers of a man's hand, and wrote over against the candlestick upon the plaster of the wall of the king's palace; and the *king* saw the part of the hand that wrote. Then the *king's* countenance was changed, and his thoughts troubled him, so that the joints of his loins were loosened, and his knees smote one against another.'

This is the plain text. By no hint can it be otherwise inferred, but that the appearance was solely confined to the fancy of Belshazzar, that his single brain was troubled. Not a word is spoken of its being seen by any else there present, not even by the queen herself, who merely undertakes for the interpretation of the phenomenon, as related to her, doubtless, by her husband. The lords are simply said to be astonished; *i.e.* at the trouble and the change of countenance in their sovereign. Even the prophet does not appear to have seen the scroll, which the king saw. He recalls it only, as Joseph did the Dream to the King of Egypt. 'Then was the part of the hand sent from him [the Lord], and this writing was written.' He speaks of the phantasm as past.

Then what becomes of this needless multiplication of the miracle? this message to a royal conscience, singly expressed – for it was said, 'Thy kingdom is divided', – simultaneously impressed upon the fancies of a thousand courtiers, who were implied in it neither directly nor grammatically?

But, admitting the artist's own version of the story, and that the sight was seen also by the thousand courtiers – let it have been visible to all Babylon – as the knees of Belshazzar were shaken, and his countenance troubled, even so would the knees of every man in Babylon, and their countenances, as of an individual man, have been troubled; bowed, bent down, so would they have remained, stupor-fixed, with no thought of struggling with that inevitable judgment.

Not all that is optically possible to be seen, is to be shown in every picture. The eye delightedly dwells upon the brilliant individualities in a 'Marriage at Cana', by Veronese, or Titian, to the very texture and colour of the wedding garments, the ring glittering upon the bride's finger, the metal and fashions of the winepot; for at such seasons there is leisure and luxury to be curious. But in a 'day of judgment', or in a 'day of lesser horrors, yet divine', as at the impious feast of Belshazzar, the eye should see, as the actual eye of an agent or patient in the immediate scene would see, only in masses and indistinction. Not only the female attire and jewelry exposed to the critical eye of the fashion, as minutely as the dresses in a Lady's Magazine, in the criticised picture – but perhaps the curiosities of anatomical science, and studied diversities of posture, in the falling angels and sinners of Michael Angelo, – have no business in their great subjects. There was no leisure for them.

By a wise falsification, the great masters of painting got at their true conclusions; by not showing the actual appearances, that is, all that was to be seen at any given moment by an indifferent eye, but only what the eye might be supposed to see in the doing or suffering of some portentous action. Suppose the moment of

273

the swallowing up of Pompeii. There they were to be seen – houses, columns, architectural proportions, differences of public and private buildings, men and women at their standing occupations, the diversified thousand postures, attitudes, dresses, in some confusion truly, but physically they were visible. But what eye saw them at that eclipsing moment, which reduces confusion to a kind of unity, and when the senses are upturned from their proprieties, when sight and hearing are a feeling only? A thousand years have passed, and we are at leisure to contemplate the weaver fixed standing at his shuttle, the baker at his oven, and to turn over with antiquarian coolness the pots and pans of Pompeii.

'Sun, stand thou still upon Gibeon, and thou, Moon, in the valley of Ajalon.' Who, in reading this magnificent Hebraism, in his conception, sees aught but the heroic son of Nun, with the out-stretched arm, and the greater and lesser light obsequious? Doubtless there were to be seen hill and dale, and chariots and horsemen, on open plain, or winding by secret defiles, and all the circumstances and stratagems of war. But whose eyes would have been conscious of this array at the interposition of the synchronic miracle? Yet in the picture of this subject by the artist of the 'Belshazzar's Feast' – no ignoble work, either – the marshalling and landscape of the war is everything, the miracle sinks into an anecdote of the day; and the eye may 'dart through rank and file traverse' for some minutes, before it shall discover, among his armed followers, *which is Joshua!* Not modern art alone, but ancient, where only it is to be found if anywhere, can be detected erring, from defect of this imaginative faculty. The world has nothing to show of the preternatural in painting, transcending the figure of Lazarus bursting his grave-clothes, in the great picture of Angerstein's. It seems a thing between two beings. A ghastly horror at itself struggles with newly-apprehending gratitude at second life bestowed. It cannot forget that it was a ghost. It has hardly felt that it is a body. It has to tell of the world of spirits. – Was it from a feeling, that the crowd of half-impassioned bystanders, and the still more irrelevant herd of passers-by at a distance, who have not heard, or but faintly have been told of the passing miracle, admirable as they are in design and hue – for it is a glorified work – do not respond adequately to the action

– that the single figure of the Lazarus has been attributed to Michael Angelo, and the mighty Sebastian unfairly robbed of the fame of the greater half of the interest? Now that there were not indifferent passers-by within actual scope of the eyes of those present at the miracle, to whom the sound of it had but faintly, or not at all, reached, it would be hardihood to deny; but would they see them? or can the mind in the conception of it admit of such unconcerning objects; can it think of them at all? or what associating league to the imagination can there be between the seers and the seers not, of a presential miracle?

Were an artist to paint upon demand a picture of a Dryad, we will ask whether, in the present low state of expectation, the patron would not, or ought not be fully satisfied with a beautiful naked figure recumbent under wide-stretched oaks? Dis-seat those woods, and place the same figure among fountains, and falls of pellucid water, and you have a – Naïad! Not so in a rough print we have seen after Julio Romano,* we think – for it is long since – *there*, by no process, with mere change of scene, could the figure have reciprocated characters. Long, grotesque, fantastic, yet with a grace of her own, beautiful in convolution and distortion, linked to her connatural tree, co-twisting with its limbs her own, till both seemed either – these, animated branches; those, disanimated members – yet the animal and vegetable lives sufficiently kept distinct – *his* Dryad lay – an approximation of two natures, which to conceive, it must be seen; analogous to, not the same with, the delicacies of Ovidian transformations.

To the lowest subjects, and, to a superficial comprehension the most barren, the Great Masters gave loftiness and fruitfulness. The large eye of genius saw in the meanness of present objects their capabilities of treatment from their relations to some grand Past or Future. How has Raphael – we must still linger about the Vatican – treated the humble craft of the ship-builder, in *his* 'Building of the Ark'? It is in that scriptural series, to which we have referred, and which, judging from some fine rough old graphic sketches of them which we possess, seem to be of a

---

* Giulio Pippi, 1492-1546, a pupil of Raphael.

higher and more poetic grade than even the Cartoons. The dim of sight are the timid and the shrinking. There is a cowardice in modern art. As the Frenchman, of whom Coleridge's friend made the prophetic guess at Rome, from the beard and horns of the Moses of Michael Angelo collected no inferences beyond that of a He Goat and a Cornuto; so from this subject, of mere mechanic promise, it would instinctively turn away, as from one incapable of investiture with any grandeur. The dock-yards at Woolwich would object derogatory associations. The depôt at Chatham would be the mote and the beam in its intellectual eye. But not to the nautical preparations in the ship-yards of Civita Vecchia did Raphael look for instructions, when he imagined the building of the Vessel that was to be conservatory of the wrecks of the species of drowned mankind. In the intensity of the action he keeps ever out of sight the meanness of the operation. There is the Patriarch, in calm forethought, and with holy prescience, giving directions. And there are his agents – the solitary but sufficient Three – hewing, sawing, every one with the might and earnestness of a Demiurgus; under some instinctive rather than technical guidance! giant-muscled; every one a Hercules; or liker to those Vulcanian Three, that in sounding caverns under Mongibello wrought in fire – Brontes, and black Steropes and Pyracmon. So work the workmen that should repair a world!

Artists again err in the confounding of *poetic* with *pictorial subjects*. In the latter, the exterior accidents are nearly everything, the unseen qualities as nothing. Othello's colour – the infirmities and corpulence of a Sir John Falstaff – do they haunt us perpetually in the reading? or are they obtruded upon our conceptions one time for ninety-nine that we are lost in admiration at the respective moral or intellectual attributes of the character? But in a picture Othello is *always* a Blackamoor; and the other only Plump Jack. Deeply corporealised, and enchained hopelessly in the grovelling fetters of externality, must be the mind, to which, in its better moments, the image of the high-souled, high-intelligenced Quixote – the errant Star of Knighthood, made more tender by eclipse – has never presented itself divested from the unhallowed accompaniment of a Sancho, or a rabblement at the heels of Rosinante. That man has read his book by halves; he has laughed, mistaking his author's purport, which was – tears. The artist that pictures Quixote (and it is in this degrading point that he is every season held up at our Exhibitions) in the shallow hope of exciting mirth, would have joined the rabble at the heels of his starved steed. We wish not to see *that* counterfeited, which we would not have wished to see in the reality. Conscious of the heroic inside of the noble Quixote, who, on hearing that his withered person was passing, would have stepped over his threshold to gaze upon his forlorn habiliments, and the 'strange bed-fellows which misery brings a man acquainted with'? Shade of Cervantes! who in thy Second Part could put into the mouth of thy Quixote those high aspirations of a super-chivalrous gallantry, where he replies to one of the shepherdesses, apprehensive that he would spoil their pretty net-works, and inviting him to be a guest with them, in accents like these: 'Truly, fairest Lady, Actæaon was not more astonished when he saw Diana bathing herself at the fountain, than I have been in beholding your beauty: I commend the manner of your pastime, and thank you for your kind offers; and, if I may serve you, so I may be sure you will be obeyed, you may command me: for my profession is this, To show myself thankful, and a doer of good to all sorts of people, especially of the rank that your person shows you to be; and if those nets, as they take up but a little piece of ground, should take up the whole world, I would seek out new worlds to pass through, rather than break them: and (he adds) that you may give credit to this my exaggeration, behold at least he that promiseth you this, is Don Quixote de la Mancha; if haply his name hath come to your hearing.' Illustrious Romancer! were the 'fine frenzies', which possessed the brain of thy own Quixote, a fit subject, as in this Second Part, to be exposed to the jeers of Duennas and Serving-men? to be monstered, and shown up at the heartless banquets of great men? Was that pitiable infirmity, which in thy First Part misleads him, *always from within*, into half-ludicrous, but more than half-compassionable and admirable errors, not infliction enough from heaven, that men by studied artifices must devise and practise upon the humour, to inflame where they should soothe it? Why, Goneril would have blushed to practise upon the abdicated king at this rate, and the she-wolf Regan not have endured to play the pranks upon his fled wits, which thou first made thy Quixote suffer in Duchesses' halls, and at the hands of that unworthy nobleman.*

In the First Adventures, even, it needed all the art of the most consummate artist in the Book way that the world hath yet seen, to keep up in the mind of the reader the heroic attributes of the character without relaxing; so as absolutely that they shall suffer no alloy from the debasing fellowship of the clown. If it ever obtrudes itself as a disharmony, are we inclined to laugh; or not, rather, to indulge a contrary emotion? – Cervantes, stung, perchance, by the relish with which *his* Reading Public had received the fooleries of the man, more to their palates than the generosities of the master, in the sequel let his pen run riot, lost the harmony and the balance, and sacrificed a great idea to the taste of his contemporaries. We know that in the present day the Knight has fewer admirers than the Squire. Anticipating, what did actually happen to him – as afterwards it did to his scarce inferior follower, the Author of *Guzman de Alfarache* – that some less knowing hand would prevent him by a spurious Second Part; and judging that it would be easier for his competitor to outbid him in the comicalities, than in the *romance*, of his work, he abandoned his Knight, and has fairly set up the Squire for his Hero. For what else has he unsealed the eyes of Sancho? and instead of that twilight state of semi-insanity – the madness at second-hand – the contagion, caught from a stronger mind infected – that war between native cunning, and hereditary deference, with which he has hitherto accompanied his master – two for a pair almost – does he substitute a downright Knave, with open eyes, for his own ends only following a confessed Madman; and offering at one time to lay, if not actually laying, hands upon him! From the moment that Sancho loses his reverence, Don Quixote is become – a treatable lunatic. Our artists handle him accordingly.

This essay was originally written for inclusion in the *Englishman's Magazine* in 1831. That paper closed down before the essay could appear and it was over a year before it appeared in print in Moxon's *Reflector* (December 1832). Next month, January 1833, it was printed in four weekly parts in the *Athenæum*.

---

* Yet from this Second Part, our cried-up pictures are mostly selected; the waiting-women with beards, etc.

ALLEN, Robert (1772-1803). Army surgeon and journalist. 'While we were wringing out coy sprightliness for the Post...Bob Allen, our quondam schoolfellow, was tapping his impracticable brains in a like service for the "oracle". Not that Robert troubled himself much about wit. If his paragraphs had a sprightly air about them it was sufficient.' Lamb, 'Newspapers Thirty-Five Years Ago'. *Englishman's Magazine*, 1831.

ASBURY, Jacob Vale. Doctor to the Lambs at Enfield.

AYRTON, William (1777-1858). Music critic. Director of King's Theatre, Haymarket. Introduced to the Lambs by the Burneys in 1803.

BANNISTER, John (1760-1836). Comedian. 'He gave you the idea of a good fellow, whom it would be most pleasant and profitable to live with; and this was his real character.' Leigh Hunt.

BARNES, Thomas (1786-1841). Editor of *The Times* from 1817 until his death, it was he who put thunder into the voice of 'The Thunderer'. He entered Christ's Hospital not long after Lamb had left and at school was Leigh Hunt's closest friend. Later he contributed articles to several of Leigh Hunt's journals.

'No man (had he cared for it) could have been more certain of attaining celebrity for wit and literature.' Leigh Hunt.

BARTON, Bernard (1784-1849). Quaker poet. He was for many years a regular contributor of devotional verse to the *London Magazine*. He met Lamb's father for the first time in 1822 at one of the *London's* dinners and soon became a close friend and a regular correspondent. In February 1823 Barton contributed to the *London Magazine* a sonnet 'To Elia'.

> From month to month has the exhauster's flow
> Of thy original mind, its wealth revealing,
> With quainter humour healing
> The World's rude wounds, revived Life's early glow.

BOYER, James (1736-1814). A product and later Under Grammar Master and Upper Grammar Master (Headmaster) of Christ's Hospital: an 'Educer of the intellect' (Coleridge). There must be more extensive and more colourful tributes to Boyer than to any other headmaster in the total history of English education. All three of his most eminent pupils – Lamb, Coleridge and Leigh Hunt – wrote about him, Lamb and Leigh Hunt several times, Coleridge in the passage in *Biographia Literaria* from which is taken the quotation reproduced in the introduction to the Section 'And in My Joyful Schooldays' (see page 21).

Lamb, Leigh Hunt and Coleridge also produced variants of a 'sore epitaph' for this outstanding representative of the 'grand old race of flogging schoolmasters' (Leigh Hunt). The best is by Coleridge: 'Poor J.B.! – may all his faults be forgiven; and may he be wafted to bliss by little cherub boys, all head and wings, with no bottoms to reproach his sublunary infirmities.'

BURNEY, James (1750-1821). Brother of FANNY BURNEY. Sailed round the world with Cook. Retired from the Navy as Admiral. His wife SARAH was possibly the model for Lamb's Mrs Battle. With their son MARTIN, a barrister, they met the Lambs in 1803 and thereafter remained close friends.

CANNING, George (1770-1829). A statesman of unusual ability and an eloquent orator, Canning held many Cabinet posts in Tory governments including Foreign Secretary and Prime Minister. He was the founder and a frequent contributor to the *Anti-Jacobin* and a deft writer of epigrammatic satirical verses directed against his political opponents.

In his *Autobiography* Leigh Hunt wrote of him with some leniency for 'the liberal meanness of his later days' but admits that earlier he had taken him 'for a great sort of impudent Eton boy'.

CARLYLE, Thomas (1795-1881). Historian, essayist and critic. He met Lamb in 1824 and thereafter called on him several times, presumably as an exercise in self-mortification for he was utterly out-of-sympathy with Lamb and, being himself devoid of humour, found nothing for pleasure and much for distaste in Elia.

In 1831, after visiting Lamb at Enfield, he wrote to his fellow-historian J.A. Froude: 'Not one of that class will tell you a straightforward story or even a credible one about any matter under the sun. All must be packed up into epigrammatic contrasts, startling exaggerations, claptraps that will get plaudits from the galleries.'

CARY, Henry (1772-1844). Best remembered as translator of Dante, he was a contributor to the *London Magazine* and Assistant Keeper of Printed Books at the British Museum. One of Lamb's most frequent correspondents and most regular visitors, he was described by Lamb as 'a dear fellow' though guilty of a vice, 'which in any less good than himself would be . . . past redemption. He has no relish for Parson Adams.'

CHAMBERS, Thomas. 'Old Mr Chambers, the sensible clergyman in Warwickshire'. His two sons, JOHN and CHARLES, were Lamb's schoolfellows and JOHN a colleague at the East India House.

CLARKSON, Thomas (1760-1841). A pioneer and leader of the anti-slavery movement.

COLERIDGE, Hartley (1796-1849). Poet and journalist. STC's eldest son.

COLERIDGE, Samuel Taylor (1772-1834). Poet, philosopher and critic. The most evident proof of Lamb's contention that a Christ's Hospital boy's friends at school are his friends through life.

'His mind was clothed with wings; and raised on them, he lifted philosophy to heaven.' (Hazlitt)

> 'He was a mystery poet and
> A subtle sould psychologist;
> All things he seemed to understand,
> Of old or new, on sea or land,
> Some his own soul, which was a mist.' (Lamb)

'An archangel a little damaged.' (Lamb)

DE QUINCEY, Thomas (1785-1859). A frequent contributor to the *London Magazine* which published his 'Confessions of an English Opium Eater' (1822). A friend and generally an admirer of Lamb, nevertheless he was disturbed by Lamb's frivolousness and, because he was himself incapable of light-heartedness, he set himself up more often than most of Lamb's friends as a butt for Lamb's teasing.

DYER, George (1755-1841). Educated at Christ's Hospital, Dyer was a poet 'of a sort'. A sound if pedestrian scholar, for almost a quarter-of-a-century he worked on Valpy's monumental edition of the classics. In 1814 he published his *History of the University of Cambridge*. Although Lamb often made fun of him, his affection and admiration for Dyer was intense. 'God never put a kinder heart into the flesh of man than George Dyer'.

The meeting with Dyer which Lamb describes in 'Oxford in the Vacation' (see page 170) actually took place not in the library of Oriel College, Oxford, but in the library of Dyer's own college, Emmanuel, Cambridge.

FAVELL, Robert (1775-1812). After Christ's Hospital he went up to Cambridge but left without a degree, according to Lamb, because he was ashamed of his father, a house-painter in the city. Poor W— in the essay 'Poor Relations'. He was invited – but refused – to join the Pantisocratic commune.

FENWICK, John (d.1820). Bigod in 'The Two Races of Men'. Editor of the *Albion* and the *Plough*. Author of a farce, *The Indian*.

FIELD, Barron (1786-1840). Essayist, dramatic critic. Judge of the Supreme Court of New South Wales and Chief Justice of Gibraltar. Introduced to Lamb in 1809 by his brother, a colleague in the East India House. It was to him that Elia addressed the essay 'Distant Correspondents'.

FIELDE, Francis (d.1809). Lamb's godfather. An oil-man in Holborn, it was he who gave to Charles and Mary the tickets which allowed them to frequent the Drury Lane Theatre even in their childhood. Lamb describes Fielde in 'My First Play' (see page 219). It was from his godfather by way of Fielde's widow that Lamb 'came into possession of the only landed property which I could ever call my own ['Button Snap'] near the road-way village of pleasant Puckeridge, in Hertfordshire'.

FITZHERBERT, Maria (1756-1837). Morganatic wife of the Prince Regent.

GIFFORD, William (1756-1826). In 1797 Gifford became Editor of the *Anti-Jacobin* and for twenty-four years from its inception in 1824 he edited John Murray's *Quarterly Review*. In politics High Tory and in literary taste reactionary, he expressed his opinions and designed his editorial policies with unusual bitterness, and he directed his hate with especial fury against all those writers – Lamb, Coleridge, Wordsworth, Leigh Hunt and Keats among them – whom he either knew or suspected of offence against both his political and literary principles.

'What he did at first out of a self-satisfied incompetence, he did at last out of an envious and angry one and he was, all the while, the humble servant of power, and never expressed one word of regret for his inhumanity.' (Leigh Hunt).

GODWIN, William (1756-1836). Philosopher, novelist and publisher of the Lambs' *Tales from Shakespear* and *Adventures of Ulysses*. Godwin was introduced to Lamb by Coleridge in 1800.

As a thinker Godwin exercised a considerable influence on many of his contemporaries. He was also in familial sense the nexus of a complex of relationships notable in literary history. His first wife, Mary Wollstonecraft (1759-97) wrote *The Rights of Women*. Their daughter Mary (1797-1851) was the author of *Frankenstein* and Shelley's second wife. Godwin's second wife, Mrs Clairmont, 'the Bitch', was the mother of Claire Clairmont who had an illegitimate daughter by Byron.

HAYDON, Benjamin Robert (1786-1846). Painter, famous for his historical canvases. His *Autobiography and Memoirs* includes many references to Lamb.

HAZLITT, William (1778-1830). Unsuccessful portrait painter and one of the greatest of all English critics and essayists. His 'Table Talk' appeared in the *London Magazine* at the same time as Lamb's Elia essays. He first met Lamb in 1799 and in 1804 painted his portrait.

> 'My friendship oft has made my heart to ache;
> Do be my Enemy for Friendship's sake.' (Blake)

> 'His manners are 99 in 100 singularly repulsive.' (Coleridge)

HESSEY, James (1781-1807). Partner in the publishing firm Taylor and Hessey which in 1821 took over the *London Magazine*. (See also JOHN TAYLOR.)

HESTER. Not more than a given name, yet Hester won lasting fame as the subject of Lamb's threnody, one of his finest poems and among the comparatively few of his works written before he emerged as an essayist which have stood the test of time. In 1808 Lamb wrote to Manning: 'I send you some verses I have made on the death of a young Quaker you may have heard me speak of as being in love with for some years while I lived at Pentonville, though I had never spoken to her in my life.'

HOOD, Thomas (1799-1845). Poet, critic and editor. Hood was sub-editor of the *London Magazine* when he first met Lamb and he was later his neighbour in Islington. It was while he was Editor of *The Gem* that he published in that magazine *Eugene Aram*. His literary reminiscences originally appeared scattered through the pages of *Hoods Own* and provide some of the most fascinating and perceptive information about Lamb.

HUNT, J.H. LEIGH (1784-1859). Critic, journalist, poet and editor. Son of a Philadelphia Tory lawyer, Leigh Hunt entered Christ's Hospital a few years after Lamb and Coleridge had left. Like Lamb he first made a reputation as a poet and, like Lamb, his fame as versifier is now held only by a few 'anthology pieces' ('Jenny Kissed Me' and 'Abou ben Adhem') but had there been no Lamb and no Hazlitt he might still be recognised as one of the finest of English essayists. A mentor of others greater than himself – Keats, Shelley, Byron (with whom later he quarrelled bitterly) and many another – he exercised a powerful influence on the literature of his time.

Founder-editor of many journals (*The Examiner, The Liberal, The Indicator, The Reflector* and others), most of them short-lived but some of them notably influential, Leigh Hunt was in his early days an ardent radical. In 1813 he was sent to prison for a libel against the Prince Regent, an offence no doubt compounded by the publication in his *Examiner* of Lamb's 'The Triumph of the Whale'. Later Leigh Hunt was himself libelled (without hope of legal redress) by Dickens' caricature of him as Skimpole in *Bleak House*.

Leigh Hunt's *Autobiography* (1859) is a prime source of information about London literary and artistic life in the first half of the nineteenth century. 'Wit, poet, prose-man, party-man, translator – H[unt], your best title yet is INDICATOR.' (Lamb)

HUTCHINSON, Sarah. Wordsworth's sister-in-law.

ISOLA, Emma (1809-1891). Daughter of Charles Isola, 'Esquire Bedell of the University of Cambridge'. When her father died she was adopted by the Lambs. 'A girl of gold' Lamb called her and both he and his sister gave to her upbringing and education much care and affection. Of the efforts to teach Emma Latin, Lamb wrote: ''Tis like feeding a child with chopped hay from a spoon. Sisyphus – his labours were as nothing to it. Actives and passives jostle in her nonsense till a deponent enter, like Chaos, more to embroil the fray.'

Emma married Edward Moxon (q.v.) in 1833. 'I will keep 30 July as long as my poor months last me, as a festival gloriously.' (Lamb)

KELLY, Fanny (1790-1882). Actress. She of 'the divine plain face', Fanny Kelly made her debut at Drury Lane in 1797. In 1819, when she was appearing in Bristol, Lamb wrote a letter, intended for publication, to his friend and school-fellow, John Gutch, the proprietor of *Felix Farley's Bristol Journal*, in which he compared her favourably with DOROTHEA JORDAN (1767-1830) – the mistress of the Duke of Clarence (Later William IV), an actress much admired by Lamb and much loved by the public both in London and the provinces. Of Fanny Kelly he wrote: '... [Hers] is the joy of a freed spirit escaping from care as a bird that has been limed; her smiles seemed saved out of the fire, relics which a good and innocent heart has snatched up as most portable.'

The Elia essay 'Barbara S' is based on the story of Fanny Kelly's childhood and, although Lamb himself implied that 'Dream Children' was inspired by an earlier love, Ann Simmons (the Ann of his sonnets), it seems likely that the wistfulness of that essay (written only eighteen months after she had rejected his suit) was fashioned by lingering thoughts of Fanny Kelly. Indeed, some eight years later, an American lady, observing the two of them at a large party, commented that he was '...evidently mentally acknowledging Miss Kelly to be the *rara avis* of his thoughts by the great attention he paid to every word she uttered.' Lamb's wish that their friendship might continue even after she had rejected his proposal was amply fulfilled. She was regular at his Thursday parties, was sometimes his partner on public occasions, visited the Lambs often and even after they moved to Enfield and after Charles's death continued to call on Mary – who in later years taught her Latin.

In her long life Fanny Kelly had many suitors. None expressed himself as beautifully as Lamb but one was more obstinate – for ten years he attended every performance she gave in London – he shot himself whilst she was on stage. Yet despite these offers and despite the protestation of previous commitment in her letter to Lamb (see page 124) Fanny Kelly died unmarried.

KEMBLE, Charles (1775-1854). Actor and theatre manager. Principal roles at Drury Lane included Hamlet (1803) and Romeo (1805). In 1822 he took over the management of Covent Garden. A member of one of the most talented families in the history of the London Theatre, his brothers, JOHN (q.v.) and STEPHEN and his daughter FANNY were all well-known in their time, his sister SARAH SIDDONS (q.v.), was one of the greatest tragediennes of all time. The whole family was close to Lamb, Charles and intimate friend.

KEMBLE, John (1757-1823). Actor and theatre manager. Between 1783 and 1802 he played more than 120 different roles at Drury Lane. Manager of Covent Garden at the time of the O[ld] P[rices] riots in 1800. (See also CHARLES KEMBLE and SARAH SIDDONS.)

KENNEY, James (1780-1849). Dramatist. His son CHARLES LAMB KENNEY was a librettist.

KEYMER, James. Stationer of Cheapside.

LAMB, John (1763-1821). Charles's brother. Like Charles he was educated at Christ's Hospital and, like Charles, on leaving school he entered the South-Sea House but, unlike Charles, he remained in the service of the Company for the rest of his life. In 1805 he became Accountant of the Company.

John had some pretensions to culture; he was undoubtedly knowledgeable about pictures and he published a few poems which demonstrate his technical capacity. But he lacked the sensibility so obvious in his brother and sister. Charles, who was for the most part blind to his brother's faults, even so hid from public attention John's failure to play any role in caring for Mary after the tragedy of their mother's death. His portrait of John (as James Elia) in the essay 'My Relations' is, as it were, without intention, stiff. '... the systematic opponent of innovations, and crier-down of every thing that has not stood the test of age and experiment...he is startled at the least approach to the romantic in others; and...commends *you* to the guidance of common sense on all occasions.' Most of Charles's friends disliked John and were disliked by him but on one occasion he won the commendation of Coleridge – and some dubious glory – by an uncommonsensical act. Incensed by what he took to be an impertinence from Hazlitt, he knocked him down.

LAMB, Mary (1764-1842). She wrote most of *Mrs Leicester's School* and all those parts of *Tales from Shakespear* which deal with the Comedies. Never in good health, the episode in 1796 was in its consequences the most tragic of her mental and physical inability; but Lamb never wavered in his care for his sister. Even so the debt was not one-sided. In 1805 he wrote: '...I am like a fool bereft of her co-operation. I dare not think lest I should think wrongly; so used am I to look up to her in any perplexity.' And in 1821 in the Elia essay 'Mackery End' he wrote of her (as Bridget Elia): '...[She] has been my house-keeper for many a long year. We house together...old bachelor and maid in a sort of double-singleness.'

In the same essay he offers Mary a public apology for forcing her to associate so often with 'free-thinkers – leaders and disciples of novel philosophers' and he pays tribute to her independence of mind: 'She neither wrangles with them nor accepts their opinions.' It was for this intellectual sturdiness as much as for her evident solicitude for her brother that, almost without exception, Lamb's friends – many of them 'free-thinkers and leaders of novel philoso-phies' – held Mary in affection and respect.

LE GRICE, Charles Valentine (1773-1858). After leaving Christ's Hospital he went up to Cambridge then took holy orders and became tutor to the son of a rich widow. He married the widow. He has his place in literary history not for his translation of Longus but because he was the source of several of the best anecdotes used by Lamb's early biographers.

LE GRICE, Samuel (1775-1802). Brother of Charles Valentine. After Christ's Hos-pital he joined the Army. He died in Jamaica of yellow fever. In the first edition of *Lord Byron and Some of his Contemporaries* (1828) Leigh Hunt asserted that Samuel Le Grice died 'a rake', but he apologised handsomely for this false statement in an appendix to the second edition.

LLOYD, Charles (1775-1839). In the last years of the eighteenth century almost without exception, whenever commentators wrote of the glorious innovations in English poetry, a fifth name, that of Charles Lloyd, was mentioned in tones that implied that its bearer was the peer of the four poets, Coleridge, Wordsworth, Southey and Lamb (all to this day honoured, if with some reser-vations, among the greats of English literature).

The poets themselves were as fervent as any in their praise of Lloyd's early works and even those who reviled the Romantic Movements, whose night-mares were filled with visions of its practitioners gleefully dancing round a guillotine in Hyde Park, paid to Lloyd the back-handed compliment of associating him in their diatribes as a target no less deserving of their hatred than the other four. Canning satirised him with Coleridge, Wordsworth, Southey and Lamb in the *Anti-Jacobin*. Gillray caricatured him in one of the most virulent of his many vicious cartoons, of course in company with Cole-ridge, Wordsworth, Southey and Lamb, and even as late as 1809, when Byron poured out in acid heroic couplets his contempt for most of his literary contem-poraries, he allowed to Lloyd a whisper of immortality by equating him yet again with Coleridge, Wordsworth, Southey and Lamb. But already a decade before Byron published 'English Bards and Scotch Reviewers' Lloyd had lost his foothold on the higher slopes of Parnassus and by then even his fellow-poets had made public their conviction that nothing that he had ever written justified his early fame.

285

In all the years that remained to him Lloyd achieved little and his tragedy was compounded because he lost not only the critical respect but also the friendship of Coleridge, Southey and Lamb. Generally the breach was caused by his flagrant indiscretions but Lamb, being more charitable than either Coleridge or Southey, took the blame to himself (see the fourth stanza of 'The Old Familiar Faces' p.93). Even so, though subsequently Lamb allowed Lloyd into the suburbs of his affection he never again returned him to the inner circle of his intimates. Lloyd died in a lunatic asylum in France.

MACKINTOSH, Sir James (1765-1832). Lawyer and writer on philosophical and political topics. He married Catherine, sister of Daniel Stuart, the Editor of the *Morning Post*, and it was through him that Coleridge, and later Lamb, became contributors to that paper. In his early writings he favoured the French Revolution but later repudiated his liberal views.

MANNING, Thomas (1772-1840). Mathematician, physician and orientalist. He first met Lamb in 1799 and thereafter was for several years one of his most frequent companions and, after Manning left for China in 1809, one of his most regular correspondents. He is said to have been one of the first Englishmen to enter Lhassa.

MARTIN, John (1789-1854). Painter of a series of lurid works of 'immeasurable spaces, innumerable multitudes, and gorgeous prodiges'. 'Belshazzar's Feast' was exhibited at the British Institution 1816.

MIDDLETON, Thomas Fanshawe (1769-1822). First Bishop of Calcutta. Another of Lamb's school contemporaries.

MONTAGU, Basil (1770-1851). Lawyer and essayist. He met Lamb in 1798 and, despite the fact that he was a notorious mischief-maker, remained his friend and the friend of many of Lamb's intimates for many years.

Montagu reprinted Lamb's 'Confessions of a Drunkard' in his *Some Enquiries into the effects of Fermented Liquors* (1814). The essay had appeared originally in 1812 in *The Philanthropist*. Later (in 1822), almost by chance and without substantial amendment, it became an Elia essay. Lamb was in France and had not left behind him his customary contribution to the *London Magazine*.

MOXON, Edward (1801-1858). Married Emma Isola (q.v.). When in 1830 with finances from Samuel Rogers (q.v.) he moved from Longman's to set up his own publishing house, the first book on his list was Lamb's *Album Verses*. Later he put out more books by Lamb, by Wordsworth, Southey, Landor, Tennyson and Browning.

Within a few weeks of Lamb's death Moxon wrote and printed privately a memoir unequivocally affectionate and admiring: '... No man was ever more sincerely regarded or will be longer remembered by his friends.'

MR NORRIS 'of Christ's Hospital'. Lamb writes warmly of the kindness shown to him by Mr and Mrs Norris 'of Christ's Hospital' at the time of the tragedy. Many efforts have been made to identify them but none is convincing. A Richard Norris was a surveyor at Christ's Hospital but he died in 1792 and so cannot be the one referred to. One scholar has been persuaded that the Mr Norris in question is his brother PHILIP, but there is no reference to a Philip Norris anywhere in the substantial Christ's Hospital archives.

NORTH, Christopher. See JOHN WILSON.

NOVELLO, Vincent (1781-1861). Organist, composer and music publisher. Father of Clara (1818-1908), in her time a noted singer, of Mary Victoria, who married Charles Cowdon Clarke, and of eight other children. The Novellos met the Lambs in 1816 and remained close friends ever after.

PALMER, John. Comedian 'In sock or buskin there was an air of swaggering gentility about Jack Palmer'. 'On Some of the Old Actors.'

PLUMER, William (1736-1822). MP for Hertfordshire and owner of Blakesware House. Plumer spent much time abroad and when in England generally lived at New Place (Gilston Park), his other Hertfordshire house, leaving Blakesware (Blakesmoor in the Elia essay) in the care of his housekeeper, Mary Field, Lamb's grandmother. When Plumer died he left Blakesware to his widow with the instructions that the house be pulled down. Demolition and the sale of the contents were completed in 1822, two years before the Elia essay was published in the *London Magazine*.

PORSON, Richard (1759-1808). Regius Professor of Greek at Cambridge and a most notable drinking man.

PROCTER, Bryan Waller (1787-1874). Poet. Wrote under the name of 'Barry Cornwall'.

ROBINSON, Henry Crabb (1775-1867). After some years in a London solicitor's office, he travelled widely on the Continent, studied at Jena University and met Goethe and Schiller. In 1807 he became Foreign Correspondent, one of the first of his kind, and was later Foreign Editor of *The Times* and its Special Correspondent during the Peninsular War. Later he became a barrister, and later still he was one of the founders of the Athenæum Club and of University College, London. A close friend and regular correspondent of Charles Lamb, his *Diary* is one of the most revealing sources of information about the Lambs and their circle.

ROGERS, Samuel (1763-1855). Millionaire, poet and wit. As poet now properly forgotten save for the fact that his magnificent edition of his *Poems* (published by Moxon in 1853) was illustrated by Turner and Stothard, in his long literary career he was much valued, sufficiently so to win him in 1850 an invitation to succeed Wordsworth as Poet Laureate. Rogers was ever ready to use his wealth for the benefit of his fellow-writers and was by them much loved – not only for his money but also for his liveliness as a companion.

SALT, Samuel (d.1792). A Director of the South-Sea Company and the East India Company and a Governor of Christ's Hospital, it was in his chambers in the Inner Temple that Charles Lamb was born and it was into his fine library of old books that Charles and Mary were 'tumbled early'. Their father served Salt as scrivener and as man-servant for almost fifty years and was for some time also First Waiter in the Inner Temple Hall. (John Sr. was himself a versifier.) Their mother acted as Salt's housekeeper. Salt treated all the Lambs as friends and recognised their devotion by generous benefactions in his Will and by his readiness to further the careers of the younger members of the family. It was through his influence that both Charles and his brother John (q.v.) were admitted to Christ's Hospital and through his influence that on leaving school both entered the South-Sea House.

SCOTT, John (1783-1821). Journalist. Born in Aberdeen and at school there had Byron as his school-fellow. He became Editor of *The Champion* and later of *The London Magazine*, and as such was responsible for the publication of Elia's essays. Died as a result of wounds received in a duel with Jonathan Christie.

SIDDONS, Sarah (1775-1831). Actress. Sister of John and Charles Kemble (q.v.), she made her debut in 1774 at Drury Lane as Portia in Garrick's production of *The Merchant of Venice*. After an unsuccessful first season she won and held fame, critical acclaim, wealth and social attention – but not personal popularity. Gainsborough and Reynolds ('The Tragic Muse') painted her portrait. 'She is out of the pale of all theories and annihilates all rules. Wherever she sits there is grace and grandeur, there is tragedy personified.' (Hazlitt)

SOUTHEY, Robert (1774-1843). A writer possessed of great versatility and abundant energy, in his lifetime (and for many years thereafter) his reputation was as high as that of any of his contemporaries. His prose-works are now generally forgotten and his poetry is now remembered for a few anthology pieces, even of them the best-known not for itself but for Lewis Carroll's parody ('You are old, Father William...').

Southey met Lamb in 1795 at about the same time that he met Coleridge (whose brother-in-law he became). He planned to emigrate to America with Coleridge and, (as he and Coleridge thought but Lamb did not) with Lamb also, there to establish 'peace on earth and Heaven to come' in a pantisocratic society 'on the banks of the Susquehanna'. In those early days of their acquaintance Lamb was much impressed by Southey's intellect but, though with one brief period of estrangement (see pp.139-52), and despite Southey's apostasising to the Tory cause, they remained friends and regular correspondents, Lamb never felt for Southey the affection which warmed so many of his friendships.

Southey was made Poet Laureate in 1818.

STUART, Daniel (1766-1846). Proprietor and editor of the *Morning Post* and of *The Courier*.

TALFOURD, Thomas Noon (1795-1854). Lawyer, MP, essayist, tragedian and biographer. Talfourd met Lamb in 1815 and ever after was one of his closest friends and most frequent correspondents. He was the executor of Lamb's Will and in 1837 and 1848 he published collections of Lamb's letters, both times with substantial biographies.

Himself an occasional contributor to the *London Magazine*, he also wrote four tragedies, but his contribution to literature and to its practitioners depends on much more than his care for Charles and Mary and his energy in sustaining Lamb's reputation, for with justice he can be described as the father of modern British copyright law. He began his vigorous campaign to secure the rights of authors in the mid-1830s and in 1837, as Whig Member for his home town, Reading, he introduced a Copyright Bill which failed to secure a majority. He was not in the House when the Copyright Act of 1842 was passed; the credit for that achievement must be given largely to Macauley whose two speeches on the subject were elegant and persuasive; but the Act as it was promulgated was to a large extent founded on Talfourd's drafting.

In 1849 Talfourd was made a judge and knighted.

TALMA, Francois Joseph (1763-1826). French tragedian.

TAYLOR, John (1788-1862). Partner in the publishing-house Taylor and Hessey, through its richest period proprietors of the *London Magazine*. It was Taylor much more than Hessey (q.v.) who made acceptance by the *London Magazine* something like admittance to a convivial club. Taylor and Hessey also distributed (and later published) Cary's translations of Dante, De Quincey's *Opium Eater* and the poems of John Clare, but the greatest glory of the firm is that it took on a virtually unknown poet, Keats, first with *Endymion* (1818) and that it made up for the mean advance (£20) by supporting him through all his difficulties.

THORNTON, Edward (1766-1822). At Christ's Hospital with Lamb, he was later Chargé d'Affairs in Washington and Minister Plenipotentiary in Stockholm. 'We have had an ambassador among us, but as he, I understand, is ashamed of us, we are hereby more ashamed of him, and accordingly omit him.' (Leigh Hunt)

WALES, William (?1734-98). Master of the Royal Mathematical School within Christ's Hospital. A Fellow of the Royal Society, Wales had been co-navigator with Captain Cook.

WHITE, James (1775-1820). Lamb's exact contemporary at Christ's Hospital, on leaving school he entered the Hospital's Counting House as Junior Clerk. Twenty-seven years later he resigned – still as Junior Clerk.

Despite this remarkable record of under-achievement White prospered, sufficiently so to allow him to put up, when Lamb's original bondsman died, the considerable sum demanded by the East India House as surety for one of its clerks. This he contrived by audacious moonlighting; through all the years when he was supposedly performing the humbler duties of the Counting House he was engineering the success of his own advertising agency. White used the duality of professions to add to the income of his friend. From time to time he employed Lamb as a copy-writer and particularly to compose what Lamb called 'lottery-puffs', advertising the public lotteries for which Christ's Hospital boys drew the winning ticket.

In the closing months of 1796 Lamb spent most of his evenings with White and then, as an exercise designed to remove from Lamb the trauma created by the tragic circumstances of his mother's death, together they worked on letters supposedly by Sir John Falstaff. When the *Falstaff Letters* were published the title-page gave all the credit to White but Lamb's hand is evident, and it is well-nigh certain that he wrote the 'Dedicacyon'. If this be so, it is the first of Lamb's prose-works to appear in print. However, it is not for the *Falstaff Letters* that White won literary glory but as the hero of the Elia essay 'The Praise of Chimney-Sweepers': 'My pleasant friend, Jim White, instituted an annual feast to chimney-sweepers at which it was his pleasure to officiate as host and waiter.'

Of all Lamb's many friends the staunchest, White's early death was to Lamb a vicious blow: 'He carried away half the fun of the world when he died – of my world at least.'

WILSON, John (1785-1854). 'Christopher North'. Professor of Moral Philosophy at Edinburgh. An ardent Tory, as one of the most active members of the staff of the then devoutly Tory *Blackwood's Magazine* he attacked 'the Cockney school', Lamb, Hazlitt, Keats and particularly Leigh Hunt. But Lamb he treated a trifle more gently than the others and in later life to a considerable extent he recanted his dismissive opinion of them all so that even Leigh Hunt could write (in his *Autobiography*): 'It would have been strange, indeed, when the heat of the battle was over, had not Christopher North stretched out his large and warm hand. . . .'

WORDSWORTH, Dorothy (1771-1855). Sister and constant companion of William Wordsworth (q.v.), her 'Journals' contain much on Lamb, Coleridge, Southey and others of her brother's friends and contemporaries.

WORDSWORTH, William (1770-1850). Coleridge introduced him to Lamb in 1797, soon after the publication of *Lyrical Ballads* and from then on he, his wife (Mary Hutchinson) and his sister Dorothy (q.v.) were close to the Lambs, though at times their intimacy was disturbed by what the Wordsworths took to be Lamb's frivolousness, by his distaste for all things pastoral and by his occasional criticism of William's poetry. Lamb did once describe Wordsworth as 'the greatest poet of these times' but immediately reduced the force of the encomium: 'Still he is not, nor yet is any man, an "Ancient Mariner"'.

Wordsworth succeeded Southey as Poet Laureate in 1843. Three lines by Wordsworth appear on the memorial to Lamb in Edmonton Church:

> . . . At the centre of his being lodged
> A soul by resignation sanctified. . .
> O, he was good, if e'er a good man lived.